EMPLOYMENT AND ECONOMIC PERFORMANCE

EMPLOYMENT AND ECONOMIC PERFORMANCE

Jobs, Inflation, and Growth

Edited by

JONATHAN MICHIE
and
JOHN GRIEVE SMITH

OXFORD UNIVERSITY PRESS
1997

Oxford University Press, Great Clarendon Street, Oxford OX2 6DP

Oxford New York
Athens Auckland Bangkok Bogota Bombay
Buenos Aires Calcutta Cape Town Dar es Salaam
Delhi Florence Hong Kong Istanbul Karachi
Kuala Lumpur Madras Madrid Melbourne
Mexico City Nairobi Paris Singapore
Taipei Tokyo Toronto
and associated companies in
Berlin Ibadan

Oxford is a trade mark of Oxford University Press

Published in the United States
by Oxford University Press Inc., New York

British Library Cataloguing in Publication Data
Data available

Library of Congress Cataloging in Publication Data
Data available
ISBN 0–19–829094–2
ISBN 0–19–829093–4 (Pbk)

Typeset by Hope Services (Abingdon) Ltd.
Printed in Great Britain
on acid-free paper by
Biddles Ltd., Guildford & King's Lynn

PREFACE AND ACKNOWLEDGEMENTS

All the following chapters were commissioned specifically for this book and draft versions were discussed at a working conference in May 1996 at Robinson College, Cambridge. We are grateful to the authors for travelling to Cambridge to participate in these discussions, and in particular to Bob Pollin and Betsy Zahrt for travelling from the USA.

We are grateful to Robinson College for hosting and helping to fund this event. We are also grateful to the contributors to our earlier books *Unemployment in Europe* (Academic Press, 1994), *Managing the Global Economy* (Oxford University Press, 1995) and *Creating Industrial Capacity: Towards Full Employment* (Oxford University Press, 1996) who kindly agreed that their royalty payments would go to the Robinson College Economic Research Fund which met the remainder of the expenses, and to the contributors to this book for similarly donating their royalties to help fund future such events. We are grateful for their participation to Kate Barker, Alex Bowen, David Dickinson, Laurence Harris, John Innes, Hidehiro Iwaki, Carol Jones, Seumas Milne, David Musson, Rory O'Donnell, Mića Panić, John Philpott, Shay Ramalingam, Andy Robinson, Bob Rowthorn, Malcolm Sawyer, Maura Sheehan, Giles Slinger, Stephen Smith, John Smithin, Chris Trinder, and John Wells.

Our thanks as editors go to all the authors for the speedy incorporation of points made in May 1996 on their draft chapters; David Blake, Larry Elliot, Jane Humphries, and Kit McMahon for chairing the sessions at the May conference; David Musson and Leonie Hayler of Oxford University Press for the speedy turn-round of the manuscript; Lesley Haird for typing and other help; and Brian Reddaway for contributing the Foreword. Our personal thanks for putting up with week-end editing go respectively to Carolyn, seven-year-old Alex, and one-year-old Duncan, and to Jean.

Jonathan Michie
John Grieve Smith

Robinson College, Cambridge
September 1996

CONTENTS

LIST OF FIGURES

LIST OF TABLES

LIST OF CONTRIBUTORS

SIMON DEAKIN	Lecturer in Law and Assistant Director, ESRC Centre for Business Research, Cambridge
JOHN EATWELL	President of Queens' College, Cambridge
KEITH EWING	Professor of Public Law, King's College, London
ANDREW GLYN	Fellow and Tutor in Economics, Corpus Christi College, Oxford
JOHN GRIEVE SMITH	Fellow of Robinson College, Cambridge
GEOFF HARCOURT	Reader, Faculty of Economics and Politics, Fellow of Jesus College, Cambridge and Professor Emeritus, University of Adelaide
BRIAN HENRY	Professor of Economics, London Business School
MICHAEL KITSON	Fellow of St Catharine's College and Lecturer in Economics, Newnham College, Cambridge
KEVIN LEE	Professor of Economics, University of Leicester
JONATHAN MICHIE	Judge Institute of Management Studies and Fellow of Robinson College, Cambridge
ROBERT POLLIN	Professor of Economics, University of California-Riverside and Research Associate, Economic Policy Institute, Washington, DC
BRIAN REDDAWAY	Professor Emeritus, Faculty of Economics and Politics, Cambridge
PETER ROBINSON	Research Officer, Centre for Economic Performance, LSE
AJIT SINGH	Professor, Faculty of Economics and Politics and Fellow of Queens' College, Cambridge
HOLLY SUTHERLAND	Director, Micro Simulation Unit, Department of Applied Economics, Cambridge
ROGER TARLING	Cambridge Policy Consultants
FRANK WILKINSON	Senior Research Officer, Department of Applied Economics, Cambridge
ELIZABETH ZAHRT	Doctoral Candidate, Department of Economics, University of California-Riverside

FOREWORD

Brian Reddaway

The main driving force which led to the production of this book was the feeling, held by a number of people, that 'full employment' had been wrongly down-graded by many governments as an objective of policy; and that in most countries unemployment (including disguised unemployment) had been most undesirably high in the last twenty years or so.

As always, the authors have had to recognize the many complexities which affect economic performance and policy-making. In any country, the community has other objectives besides full employment, and policies which might help to raise the level of employment have to be scrutinized for possible adverse effects on other objectives, e.g. the growth of the real national income, or greater equality of incomes or opportunities, greater freedom for people to make their own decisions, the achievement of a satisfactory balance of payments, etc. Moreover different people—and different political parties—attach different weights to these various objectives. There cannot be any single set of policies and institutions which is clearly 'ideal' from all points of view—quite apart from the differing views which people have about how the economy would respond to various policy combinations.

Nevertheless, it is clearly true that 'full employment' has nothing like the same importance in governments' objectives as it had (for example) in the all-important discussions which took place around the end of World War II, and which are conveniently labelled 'Bretton Woods'. Of course, 'full employment' was not taken as implying literally 'no involuntary unemployment': labour is not a homogeneous commodity, and markets are not perfect, so that even during the war there was some unemployment, even though labour shortages were so acute that direction of labour was used to favour production which was considered essential to the war effort.[1] But the broad idea was clear, and—more important—unemployment in many countries was, with negligible exceptions, held below the yardsticks commonly used to define 'full employment' for a quarter of a century. Moreover most governments openly proclaimed that it was *their* responsibility to produce conditions in which this would happen.

The demotion of full employment as a policy objective owes a good deal to the 'Counter-revolution' in economic thinking against Keynesian ideas, together with doubts about whether governments could in practice

---

[1] The UK Government's famous White Paper avoided the phrase 'full employment', and referred to a 'high and stable level of employment'.

implement the complex set of policies which seemed in theory to promise a good compromise between the various objectives. In particular, there was the view that attempts to reduce unemployment through an increase in aggregate demand (whether induced by monetary action or fiscal action, or by a combination of the two) could only mean that demand would increase *in money terms*, and that the consequences of this might well be a rise in *prices*, rather than in output and employment.

This is not the place to get involved in theoretical arguments, but two points do need to be stressed. First, the theorists usually make strong assumptions (often only implicitly, by saying *'ceteris paribus'*, with no explanation of what this means); these assumptions may well not hold in a great many cases, so that the theory is inapplicable. And secondly, measures to expand aggregate demand do not have to be taken 'on their own': one cannot over-emphasize the need for governments to consider *packages* of measures, which may well be far more effective than one might expect from considering each measure separately (*'ceteris paribus'*) and adding up the effects.

A simple example may help to clarify this point. Two of the chapters consider the question of pay policy. In the absence of any such policy, the expansion of demand may lead to an undesirable rise in money wages, and hence prices; a government which had strong views about inflation might call off the expansion of demand before it had significantly increased employment. But a combination of demand expansion with an effective pay policy might well produce a reduction in unemployment to more acceptable levels.[2]

Another complexity which is handled in this book is the problem of *disguised* unemployment, which arises when people are unable to find 'proper' jobs, but seek to generate some income for themselves by such activities as 'selling matches in the Strand' (to take the classic illustration given by Joan Robinson). In the recession of the 1990s disguised unemployment seems to have been of considerable quantitative importance, and once again the most effective way of reducing it is by combining expansion of aggregate demand with suitable supply-side measures.[3]

INFLATION

The demotion of full employment as an objective owes a good deal to the importance given by governments to eliminating inflation, or at least re-

[2] I have similarly set out (in 'Newsletter No. 93' of the Royal Economic Society for April 1996) the case for combining measures to expand aggregate demand with 'supply-side' measures to render the long-term unemployed more acceptable to employers who wish to increase their labour-force.

[3] This provides another illustration of the illegitimacy of theoretical analyses which assume homogenous labour (and goods) and perfect markets.

ducing it to negligible levels (e.g. under 2.5 per cent). A great many points ought to be made on that, but space permits only two examples.

First, it is often argued (or implied) that good growth of real national income cannot be achieved unless inflation is kept at a very low level. On this I can only say that I have seen no empirical analyses which convincingly support this assertion; in particular I would refer the reader to the article by W. Stanners in the *Cambridge Journal of Economics* for March 1993, entitled 'Is Low Inflation an Important Condition for High Growth?'.[4]

Secondly, it is at least implied by some writers and speakers that inflation has evil consequences in the social field (e.g. by producing serious inequities in the distribution of income and wealth) which are more serious than the effects of unemployment.

On this I would refer the reader to my chapter about inflation in the book, edited by G. C. Harcourt and P. A. Riach, entitled 'A "Second Edition" of *The General Theory*' (which will have been published before this book appears). In particular, I would like to stress the numerous changes in British practices which have been progressively introduced since the end of World War II to eliminate (or at least mitigate) the inequities which inflation used to bring in years when it happened.[5] Thus many long-term contracts (e.g. pensions) are now 'index-linked', and investors who wish to be protected against 'the ravages of inflation' can buy index-linked bonds or I-L national savings certificates; in addition, the Rooker–Wise amendment to the Finance Bill provides that the amount of income which is exempt from income-tax shall be raised each year with inflation, unless Parliament decides otherwise in a particular year.

CONCLUSION

At the risk of being accused of needless repetition, I would like to conclude this foreword with two rather dogmatic statements:

1. Governments should state explicitly that one of their main objectives is to secure and maintain something like 'full employment' (for which they might if they liked add a definition). The same applies to relevant international institutions (e.g. the International Monetary Fund).

---

[4] This is not, of course, to deny that really high (and escalating) inflation may be bad for growth—though some Latin American countries have achieved reasonable growth, in spite of persistent high inflation.

[5] The main reason why reforms of these kinds were not introduced before World War II seems to be that before World War II prices did not rise every year, but frequently fell. Inflation was essentially 'unforeseen', and the case for (e.g.) index linking and against 'fixed salary scales' was not obvious, in view of the administrative work which the change would involve.

2. Since governments have other objectives besides full employment, they should attempt the difficult task of implementing a *package* of measures which would produce an acceptable set of results on all their objectives—with a high weight being given to full employment.

INTRODUCTION

Jonathan Michie

With the end of the long post-war boom in the early 1970s, the world economy has experienced varying degrees of relatively large-scale unemployment. From an assumption that the 'unemployment problem' had been solved, and that a state of full employment could be maintained through demand management techniques, we now live in an entirely different world. Any suggestion of a return to full employment is immediately met with questions of whether such a thing is really possible, whether it would not lead to inflation or to excessive trade union power, or in the case of individual economies, to unsustainable balance of payment deficits. It is asked whether the economic policies required for a return to full employment would be affordable, or would they not inevitably lead to yawning fiscal deficits, which in turn would in the end require a U-turn in policy with unemployment reappearing.

The problems of large-scale unemployment in Europe, of the lack of the sort of international institutions which helped underpin the post-war era of full employment, and of the current lack of sufficient economic capacity to allow economies to operate at much higher levels of employment than they already are, have been analysed in our three previous books (*Unemployment in Europe*, Academic Press, 1994; *Managing the Global Economy*, Oxford University Press, 1995; and *Creating Industrial Capacity: Towards full employment*, Oxford University Press, 1996). The present volume considers in detail what would be involved in a move to much lower levels of unemployment.

GLOBAL LESSONS AND PROSPECTS

The approach of the book is necessarily international as the issues being analysed are international in character and of global significance. Some of the individual chapters are explicitly international, such as Ajit Singh's analysis of the North–South divide and how the pressures of a fully employed economy manifest themselves in a global context as well as within individual countries. However, an early decision was taken in planning the book *not* to attempt a tour of the world, with one chapter on Britain, one on Germany and so on; rather the authors reflect on the global evidence and lessons.

Ajit Singh argues that the present euphoria in international economic circles concerning liberalization and globalization is unwarranted by evidence,
and is in policy terms dangerously misleading. The leading industrial countries have been effectively operating under a liberalized global regime since
about 1980, but the economic record of these countries in the post-1980
period is not inspiring. Ajit Singh suggests that this poor performance is not
due to exogenous factors, but is directly linked to the intrinsic features of
the current liberal economic order which regards the market as supreme.
Further, he argues that the present policy regime will not be able to achieve
the substantial rise in economic growth required to create sufficient remunerative employment to meet people's needs. Such failure will jeopardize the
continuation of the liberal regime. The paradox is that while faster growth
may not follow from liberalization and globalization it is nevertheless
required to sustain the liberal economic order. The chapter outlines an alternative strategy of achieving a sustained trend increase in the growth of real
world demand and output. Instead of market supremacy, this strategy is
based on co-operative economic arrangements between, as well as within,
nation states. The strategy is shown to be both feasible and also the first-
best solution to the employment question. The analysis of the chapter indicates that the current freedom of the unruly financial markets will need to
be curbed in order to sustain the liberal trading order.

While the global economy has suffered high unemployment in recent
years, the American economy has been seen as something of an exception,
having created several million net new jobs. But as Robert Pollin and
Elizabeth Zahrt report, this has to be seen in the context of the material
well-being of the majority of people in the USA having been stagnating or
even declining for roughly a quarter-century, with the USA having become
an increasingly difficult place to find a secure job and to earn a living wage.
At the same time, income and wealth have soared for the richest 1 per cent
of households, with inequality having risen sharply. Pollin and Zahrt argue
that no matter how the specific issues of global competition or technological change are dealt with, the worsening conditions for the majority will
continue unless the problems of output growth and distribution are successfully addressed. Considering the viability of an expansionary programme in today's environment, Pollin and Zahrt look back at the last time
the USA economy operated under tight labour-market conditions, namely
as a result of the domestic economic experience during the Vietnam War
years, to consider both the benefits of a stronger labour market and the
problems associated with inflation. They then consider whether the positive
results due to the Vietnam experience could be achieved once again.

In Chapter 3 John Eatwell points to two issues having dominated the
employment experience of the major industrial countries over the past
twenty years: first, the common rise in unemployment throughout the lead-

ing industrialized countries and secondly, the diversity in the scale and content of that rise as between the countries of the European Union on the one hand, and Japan and the USA on the other. It is this second issue—the diverse aspects of the problem—which Eatwell focuses on in this volume, the first issue of the common experience having been analysed in Eatwell (1995) where he argues that the most important determinant of the common experience of growing unemployment has been the slow-down in the growth of aggregate demand in the 1980s throughout the major industrialized countries. In Chapter 3 of this book, Eatwell argues that the differential experience of the major industrialized countries is attributable to the interaction between changes in the growth of effective demand and national labour market structures. These different labour-market policies determine whether there is any employment in excess of that which might be expected from the growth in effective demand. Such additional employment is likely to be greater wherever unemployment benefits are either low or of short duration, or where low-productivity employment is subsidized or protected. The activities undertaken by the additionally employed will be characterized by significantly lower productivity than is typical of the advanced sector of the economy. This additional employment is thus 'disguised unemployment' in the sense that a higher level of effective demand would result in workers being reallocated to jobs with much higher productivity per person employed. Eatwell both analyses the origins and structure of disguised unemployment, and provides an illustrative estimate of the magnitude of disguised unemployment in different countries from 1979 to 1990.

UNEMPLOYMENT AND INEQUALITY

In Chapter 4, Roger Tarling and Frank Wilkinson argue that low wages and poor working conditions offer a means by which firms can compensate for their own weaknesses and shortcomings. The growing availability of undervalued labour allows firms to compensate for organizational and managerial inadequacies, delay the scrapping of obsolete capital equipment, and engage in destructive price competition. The absence of wage discipline means that technologically and managerially backward firms can survive, and this helps prevent more progressive firms from expanding their share of the market. The overall effect is a lower average level of productivity and a slower rate of introduction and diffusion of new techniques and products. More generally, the growing availability of undervalued labour and high unemployment create the environment in which entrepreneurship takes the form of cutting pay, worsening the conditions of employment and the exploitation of low-paid labour. This can be expected to crowd out the 'high road' to competitiveness requiring product and process innovation and a highly skilled, well motivated and co-operative work-force. Competition based on the development of new products has the effect of continuously shifting product-market boundaries. If firms fail to respond, they are trapped in declining market niches. Although they may remain viable by cutting labour costs and capturing a larger share of a reduced demand, this can only be a short-term expedient. The long term depends on product-based competition rather than price competition, and this requires an emphasis on research and development, product design and quality. Wage cutting is thus a trap from which it may be hard to escape. Tarling and Wilkinson discuss a number of other such traps and set out an alternative policy agenda to overcome these traps. But as they warn, the single great-est obstacle to adopting policies to reverse economic and social decline is the current conventional economic wisdom.

Brian Henry and Kevin Lee in Chapter 5 consider whether there is evi-dence that the behavioural relationships which determine wage and employ-ment levels have altered due to recent reforms and, in providing answers to this question, pay close attention to the interplay between wage setting, unemployment levels, and wage dispersion. Their empirical work favours what might be described as the pessimistic school in the debate over whether or not the UK has experienced an improvement in its supply-side institu-tions during the last ten to fifteen years. They suggest instead that recent labour-market behaviour can more readily be interpreted as an (unchanged) response to unprecedentedly high unemployment rates experienced over a protracted period.

In Chapter 6 Deakin and Ewing examine the type of labour-law institu-tions which would be required in Britain to underpin an economic strategy aimed at containing inflation and enhancing competitiveness, without hav-ing to resort to unemployment as an instrument of labour discipline. The chapter argues that the basic elements of such a labour-law system would need to be: legal guarantees of work-force representation at the level of the firm; the putting in place of associational institutions at sector level, designed to promote framework agreements on such issues as working time and the division between family and professional responsibilities, as envis-aged by EU law and practice; the setting of a statutory floor to pay and conditions, through a minimum wage and, in due course, through sectoral bargaining; and the enactment of a comprehensive labour code designed to ensure respect for the basic rights at work of the individual. The chapter argues that the conflict between employment rights and the modernization of the economy has been vastly overstated, and that labour law would be strengthened, not weakened, by a more explicit linkage between social and economic policy. Aside from the strong moral case for the enactment of legal protections in the labour field, a strong economic case exists for hav-ing a body of law which would be aimed at promoting co-operation between management and labour and enhancing competitiveness by placing incentives on both firms and individuals to invest in improvements in labour quality.

PAY AND EMPLOYMENT STRATEGIES

In Chapter 7 Peter Robinson argues that estimates of a 'Natural Rate' or 'Non-Accelerating Inflation Rate of Unemployment' vary so widely between economists, and all too often seem just to follow with a lag the actual rate of unemployment, that it would be dangerous to base monetary policy decisions on any one estimate of such a rate. Instead a moderate and balanced expansion of aggregate demand and output would allow for a continuous slow reduction in unemployment, which for those economists who believe in a 'Natural' or 'Non-Accelerating Inflation' Rate of Unemployment would in any case represent a move towards their various different claims as to what this single rate actually is.

Geoff Harcourt in Chapter 8 sets out a policy agenda for sustained full employment. He starts from Salter (1960) whose work suggests that the most favourable conditions for achieving high rates of economic growth is that expanding industries should do so quickly and declining industries likewise, with labour being transferred from the declining to the expanding. For this to occur, the last thing one wants is a flexible labour market with money wages reflecting the respective levels and rates of change of productivity in their particular industries. This just allows declining industries to linger on, paying low wages to keep going. What is needed is rather a flexible *economy* which enables an easy transfer of resources from declining, high-cost, and high-price industries to expanding, low-cost, and low-price ones. And this requires a high rate of investment to allow the structure of production to change quickly and, given the structure of demand, increase the output and productivity of those industries where technical advances are most rapid.

The question we face today, John Grieve Smith argues in Chapter 9, is not a technical one about detailed ways of changing the economy, but a fundamental social and political choice of whether to accept high unemployment as a 'price well worth paying' for regulating inflation, or whether rather to replace such brute force methods for tackling inflation with instead an approach based on consent. Both unions and employers have a great deal to gain from a successful pay agreement which would allow more expansionary policies to be pursued. Such an approach would involve government, employers, and trade unions participating in a national forum to discuss, and so far as possible agree, government proposals for a strategy for restoring full employment. This would provide a setting for discussion not only of pay but also of the key supply-side problems of the economy to be overcome, the most important and difficult of which is in particular the need to persuade firms to base their decisions about investment in new capacity on the assumption of a trend in demand and output consistent with a reduction in unemployment, rather than a continuation of existing conditions. There may also be potential shortages of certain skills, remedying which (in so far as they can be identified) should be top priority in any education and training programme. Other key topics to be covered in a 'Strategy for Full Employment' would be public expenditure programmes, public revenue and the PSBR, and the outlook for the balance of payments. The challenge to any government which is serious about reducing unemployment is to bring the trade unions and employers together in this sort of constructive partnership.

POLICIES FOR FULL EMPLOYMENT

In Chapter 10 Andrew Glyn discusses how an expansionary programme aimed at reducing unemployment might be financed. There are limits on increased borrowing due to the subsequent burden of debt repayment. And there is uncertainty as to how strongly the private sector would respond to any public-investment-led programme, and hence how much additional tax revenue would be generated from this source, particularly given the weak response of UK manufacturing to the expanded demand and rising profitability in the 1980s (Glyn 1992). So it may be that a higher share of taxation will be inevitable if public services are to be improved, the trend towards greater inequality stemmed, and high employment levels restored. However, this needs to be seen in the light of the relatively low tax burden in the UK at present. The shocking increase in poverty and the perceived shortfall in public-service provision in the UK can only be tackled through a significant increase in government expenditure. Restoration of greater progressivity in the tax system could mean that in the first instance much of the extra revenue could come from the best-off 10 per cent. But in the longer run, extra tax would have to come from middle incomes. The political difficulties of gaining support for such increases in taxation may be daunting but have to be overcome by vigorous campaigning about the benefits which the spending from the higher taxation would bring.

The issue of how costly the economic policies required to expand employment would be are set in Chapter 11 within the context of the more general fiscal impact which a fall in unemployment would have. Using a sophisticated analysis of 7,000 representative households, Michael Kitson, Jonathan Michie, and Holly Sutherland simulate not just the direct fiscal effects from changed levels of unemployment pay and taxation receipts but also the likely indirect effects, through changes in income support, housing benefit, and the like. They also show the changed taxation picture if the reduction in unemployment either caused or at least was accompanied by a change in the dispersion of incomes at the lower end of the scale. This detailed simulation work was commissioned from Holly Sutherland's Microsimulation Unit in Cambridge's Department of Applied Economics. It suggests that a public-sector-led expansion designed to create one million new jobs is entirely realistic, economically, politically, and electorally. The gains in improved education, health services, housing, and the like would be tangible and generally appreciated. The savings from reduced unemployment would make the net cost quite modest. And certainly a price well worth paying.

CONCLUSION

Unemployment is both an immense social evil and a colossal economic waste. There is strong evidence that rising unemployment increases ill-health (Burchell 1992) and rising crime, especially domestic burglary (Dickinson 1995; Wells 1995). It is unjust *and* inefficient. Unemployment has been a major cause of the alarming growth of inequality and poverty in Britain (and indeed in many other countries); in Britain, while the richest tenth of households have become 60 per cent better off since 1979, the poorest tenth are 20 per cent worse off. Wage inequality is greater than at any time since records began in 1886. Such inequality and poverty have detrimental effects on the balance of payments constraint, with a transfer of resources to the better-off who spend a greater proportion of their incomes on imported goods (see Borooah 1988); on the real economy as consumer spending is depressed and the pressure on firms to upgrade their production processes is weakened (Michie and Wilkinson 1993); and on the government's own fiscal deficit (the Public Sector Borrowing Requirement or PSBR) (Michie and Wilkinson 1994). Rising poverty means that the cost to the state of benefits and income support increases. A growing share of the income of the working poor is met not by their employers but by the taxpayers. This not only increases both the spread and the grip of the poverty trap (whereby any increase in pay by employers is matched by an equivalent loss of benefits from government), it also increases the burden on public expenditure. And if total government spending is constrained—for example by the Maastricht requirement that fiscal deficits be less than 3 per cent of GNP—then this burden has to be met by public-spending cuts imposed elsewhere, cuts which may well exacerbate unemployment.

In the face of these deeply entrenched problems, many doubt the ability of governments to generate jobs and tackle inequality. We take a more optimistic view. Governments can create jobs; moreover these can be high-quality jobs that not only meet social need but also contribute to national economic prosperity. It is the alternative—of continued high unemployment and increased economic and social inequality—that cannot be afforded and is ultimately unsustainable.

REFERENCES

Borooah, V. (1988), 'Income Distribution, Consumption Patterns and Economic Outcomes in the United Kingdom', *Contributions to Political Economy*, 7: 49–63.
Burchell, B. (1992), 'Changes in the Labour Market and the Psychological Health of the Nation', in J. Michie (ed.), *The Economic Legacy: 1979–1992* (London: Academic Press).
Dickinson, D. (1995), 'Crime and Unemployment', *New Economy*, 2: 115–20.
Eatwell, J. (1995), 'The International Origins of Unemployment', in J. Michie and J. Grieve Smith (eds.), *Managing the Global Economy* (Oxford: Oxford University Press).
Glyn, A. (1992), 'The "Productivity Miracle", Profits and Investment', in J. Michie (ed.), *The Economic Legacy: 1979–1992* (London: Academic Press).
Michie, J. and Wilkinson, F. (1993), *Unemployment and Workers' Rights* (London: Institute of Employment Rights).
—— —— (1994), 'The Growth of Unemployment in the 1980s', ch. 1 of J. Michie and J. Grieve Smith (eds.), *Unemployment in Europe* (London: Academic Press).
Salter, W. E. G. (1960), *Productivity and Technical Change* (Cambridge: Cambridge University Press).
Wells, J. (1995), 'Crime and Unemployment', *Employment Policy Institute Economic Report*, 9/1 (February) (London: Employment Policy Institute).

Part I

Global Lessons and Prospects

1. Liberalization and Globalization: An Unhealthy Euphoria

Ajit Singh

INTRODUCTION

As we approach the new millennium, there is a remarkable consensus in international economic circles that liberalization and globalization are not only the order of the day but also the wave of the future; that these derive from inexorable technological forces connected with the information and communication technology revolution presently sweeping the globe. More importantly, it is further asserted that liberalization and globalization will promote faster economic growth, both in rich and poor countries. Thus the World Bank (1995) argues that: 'the increasing integration of developing countries into the global economy represents a major—perhaps the most important—opportunity for raising the welfare of both developing and industrial countries over the long term. But countries will need to rise to the challenge.'[1]

The consensus about the virtues of liberalization and globalization not only encompasses, as one would expect, the City, Wall Street, and pro-market institutions such as the IMF and the World Bank,[2] but surprisingly also includes international organizations like the ILO and the UNCTAD.[3] The latter two institutions have traditionally been less beholden to the free market and far more concerned with social and developmental issues. Nevertheless, following the new wisdom, developing countries are today being told by all leading multilateral agencies that it is necessary for them to integrate as quickly as possible with the global economy to benefit from the emerging new world economic order. Thus the ILO (1996):

Adherence to these [new] rules [of liberalization and globalization] will place heavier burdens on domestic policy but the benefits in terms of higher growth will also be greater. There will be stronger pressure to maintain sound macroeconomics policies, to eschew market distortions, and to improve allocative efficiency. In many cases this will imply economic reforms such as trade and financial liberalization, the removal of price controls and other forms of deregulation. These reforms will be beneficial for growth since they will create incentives for resources to be allocated to

---

[1] See Qureshi (1996), 31.   [2] World Bank (1995); IMF (1995).
[3] ILO (1996); UNCTAD (1996).

activities with higher productivity and more in line with a country's comparative advantage. This higher growth will in turn favour employment creation. In addition employment creation will also be enhanced by the removal of distortions such as the under pricing of capital and overvalued exchange rates which increase the capital-intensity of production and hence reduce employment.

Countries are being advised that if they do not follow this prescription, they risk being 'marginalized' in the way African countries have been in the last two decades. It is further suggested that the development debate is over and that what developing countries require in addition to integrating with the global economy is to reduce the role of the state and to enhance that of the market. Free and flexible internal and external markets for goods and services and capital are thought to be the best vehicles for achieving an efficient allocation of resources, promoting competitiveness and technical progress, and hence economic growth. The role of the state in this analysis is confined to providing a stable macroeconomic environment and creating conditions for private enterprise and competitive markets to operate effectively.[4]

Orthodox academic economists are not to be left behind the international agencies in their espousal of the merits of liberalization and globalization. In a long recent paper, Sachs and Warner (1996) point to the overwhelming trend among developing countries, particularly since the demise of the Soviet Union in 1989, to seek close integration with the world economy. This is reflected in their view in the fact that 120 countries have already joined the new World Trading Organisation and others like China are queuing up to do so. Similarly, the two authors note that the IMF 'now boasts nearly universal membership, with member countries pledged to the basic principles of currency convertibility'. Their analysis shows that developing countries with more open economies perform considerably better than those with less open economies. Moreover, they suggest that open trade leads to convergent rates of economic growth and that open economies successfully avoid balance of payments crisis. In the light of what they regard as such obvious and evident virtues of openness, Sachs and Warner are puzzled why developing countries for so long in the post-war period generally maintained illiberal and dirigiste economic regimes.

This chapter will argue that these propositions of multilateral agencies as well as orthodox academic economists concerning liberalization and globalization are seriously flawed, both analytically and empirically and that the euphoria about these phenomena is misplaced. It will be suggested that there is considerable evidence that the liberal economy has not delivered, and that unless the current strategy is fundamentally altered the prospects

----

[4] See World Bank (1991). For a critical analysis of the World Bank theses see for example Singh (1994, 1995a) and Fishlow (1994).

for the world economy, for the people in the North as well as the South, are bleak. The chapter will propose that it is not that liberalization and globalization promote economic growth, but that rather faster growth of production and employment are essential for sustaining the new liberal economic order. It will also be argued that the development debate is far from over and that there still exist valid alternative strategies for developing countries to follow. In addition, it will be suggested that liberalization and globalization have made the task of achieving fast long-term economic growth in developing as well as advanced countries more, rather than less difficult.

In establishing these conclusions, the chapter will devote most attention to the experience of the advanced countries. This is because leading industrial countries have operated under a regime of more or less free trade and capital markets for the last fifteen years. The economic evolution of these countries over this period therefore provides an excellent vantage point for at least a first assessment of the virtues ascribed to liberalization and globalization by the prevailing conventional wisdom.

LIBERALIZATION AND GLOBALIZATION AND THE ADVANCED ECONOMIES

In common usage, liberalization and globalization are used to connote a variety of different phenomena.[5] However, in the context of this chapter, these terms will be considered in a narrow economic sense. Liberalization will be taken to mean the free movement of goods and services as well as investment and capital flows between countries. Globalization will refer not only to the integration and unification of the product and capital markets, but it will also include the cross-national production activities of multinationals.

Liberalization and globalization have occurred at varying speeds and to different degrees in countries and regions throughout the post-war period. However, the important point is that these are invariably cumulative processes that have advanced the furthest in leading industrial countries. These countries for all practical purposes have been operating under a regime of more or less free trade in manufactures and free capital movements since about 1980. By the mid-1970s, as a consequence of the various rounds of tariff reductions, the average tariff for industrial goods was only

---

[5] The concept of globalization in particular often involves non-economic notions, such as that of globalization of culture, education, science, technology, tastes, etc. Here, however, these processes are discussed in their narrow economic sense. To sharpen the debate, the terms liberalization and globalization have been defined in exactly the same way as the World Bank does. In particular, free movement of labour across national boundaries has not been included in this definition. See, however, further discussion below on this point.

a little over 6 per cent among these countries.[6] The process of liberalization of capital movements started with the collapse of the Bretton Woods regime and the introduction of flexible exchange rates in the early 1970s. It gained momentum from the concurrent deregulation of domestic financial markets in these countries. By 1980, leading industrial countries had abolished all exchange controls and there was a more or less free movement of capital between them. A global market for foreign exchange came to be established in the mid-1970s; it is still the biggest and is regarded by some as the most complete global market.[7]

Although liberalization has not encompassed free international movement of labour, it is significant that there has been considerable deregulation of the domestic labour markets in many industrial countries in the 1980s. This has involved reductions in welfare entitlements, diminution of trade union rights, de-indexation of wages, etc. Again, the speed and degree of labour-market deregulation has varied between industrial countries. In Western Europe, the process seems to have advanced furthest in the United Kingdom.[8]

In view of the fact that leading advanced countries have effectively been operating under a liberal and integrated economic regime for the last ten to fifteen years, their experience provides important evidence for assessing the a priori expectations of orthodox economists concerning the effects of liberalization and globalization. However, as outlined below, the economic record of these countries in the relevant period has unfortunately been far from comforting. In short, it would appear that the liberal economy has so far failed to deliver in important dimensions.

Tables 1.1 and 1.2 provide information on the growth of output and productivity in leading industrial countries as well as for the European Union and the OECD as a whole, for various periods between 1960 and 1993. Four sub-periods are identified. The first, 1960–73 is a segment of the post-World War II Golden Age economic boom which lasted for nearly a quarter of a century until the first oil-price rise in 1973. The significant point here is that during this period the economies of industrial countries, compared with today, were extensively regulated both externally and internally. Not only were they subject to international capital controls under the Bretton Woods regime, they also had a plethora of controls, regulations, and other restrictive practices in the domestic product, capital, and labour markets. The second period in Tables 1.1 and 1.2, 1973–9, is the time span between the two oil shocks, sometimes called the 'inter-shock' period. In retrospect, these five years are best viewed as an interregnum during which industrial countries attempted to deal with the post-1973 economic crisis by basically following the broadly Keynesian policies of the Golden Age. These policies were

---

[6] See Nayaar (1995).   [7] See further *The Economist* (1995).
[8] Glyn *et al.* (1990); UN (1994).

Table 1.1. Real Gross Domestic Product in industrial countries, 1960–1993 (average annual % changes)

	1960–73	1973–9	1979–89	1989–93
United States	3.9	2.5	2.5	1.7
Japan	9.6	3.6	4.0	2.5
Germany	4.3	2.4	1.8	2.9
United Kingdom	3.1	1.5	2.4	0.0
TOTAL OF G7 COUNTRIES	4.8	2.7	2.7	1.6
TOTAL EU15	4.7	2.5	2.2	1.2
TOTAL OECD	4.9	2.8	2.6	1.7

Source: OECD (1995), *Historical Statistics* (Paris).

Table 1.2. Real Gross Domestic Product per capita in industrial countries, 1960–1993 (average annual % changes)

	1960–73	1973–9	1979–89	1989–93
United States	2.6	1.4	1.5	0.8
Japan	8.3	2.5	3.4	2.2
Germany	3.7	2.5	1.7	2.1
United Kingdom	2.6	1.5	2.2	−0.3
TOTAL OF G7 COUNTRIES	3.7	2.0	2.0	1.0
TOTAL EU15	4.0	2.2	2.0	0.8
TOTAL OECD	3.7	1.8	1.8	0.9

Source: OECD (1995), *Historical Statistics* (Paris).

finally abandoned in 1979 and the industrial countries, at greater or less speed, have been implementing the present liberal economic regime both externally and internally. Apart from external liberalization in terms of trade and capital movements, domestically this regime is characterized by privatization, deregulation, and the supremacy of market forces.

The two tables show that the long-term trend rate of growth of output and productivity in industrial countries since 1980 has been approximately half that achieved by these countries during the illiberal and regulated 1960s. It is significant that the deterioration in long-term economic growth has been across the board rather than just confined to a few countries. Of the twenty-two OECD countries, twenty-one of them have recorded a lower growth rate both in the 1980s and in the 1990s, compared with 1960–73. Further, most analysts agree that the long-term growth performance of industrial countries is unlikely to be better in the 1990s than in the 1980s; indeed, all present indications are it is likely to be worse.[9]

The 1980s and 1990s have not only been marked by slower economic growth, but also much more unstable growth. Apart from growth, other important economic variables—nominal as well as real exchange rates, short- as well as long-term nominal and real interest rates—have also been subject to far greater fluctuations in the recent period than in the 1960s.[10]

The most conspicuous failure of the liberal economy in the last decade or so has been with respect to employment. After enjoying more or less full employment during the 1950s and 1960s, leading European countries have been faced with the spectre of mass unemployment in the 1980s and 1990s. As Table 1.3 indicates, the average rate of unemployment in the European Union countries has increased from a little over 3 per cent in the 1960s to over 10 per cent in 1993. In the OECD as a whole, there were 8 million people unemployed in 1970; in 1994 there are 35 million. If unemployment in the form of involuntary part-time work, short-time working, and discouragement of job-seekers in looking for new employment are included, these could add another 40 to 50 per cent to these unemployment figures. (OECD 1994).

Table 1.3. Standardized unemployment rate, 1964–1993 (average annual % changes)

	1964–73	1974–9	1980–9	1990–3
United States	4.5	6.7	7.2	6.5
Japan	1.2	1.9	2.5	2.2
Germany	1.1	3.2	5.9	4.9
United Kingdom	3.0	5.0	10.0	9.1
TOTAL OF G7 COUNTRIES	3.1	5.0	6.8	6.4
TOTAL EU15	2.7	4.7	9.3	9.2
TOTAL OECD	3.0	4.9	7.3	7.0

Source: OECD (1995), *Historical Statistics* (Paris).

The US record with respect to employment is apparently better than that of the European Union countries. However, these relatively low US unemployment figures must be seen in the context of the fact that real wages in the USA have not increased over the last two decades, and indeed for unskilled workers real wages have fallen over this period. One reason for the lower unemployment in the USA is that compared with Western Europe, it has relatively little public provision to assist the unemployed. The

[9] See Economic Commission for Europe (1996).   [10] See further Felix (1995).

result is that the latter are obliged to work however unremunerative the job may be. In other words, in the absence of an adequately developed welfare state, a number of American workers are employed in low-productivity jobs of the kind which Joan Robinson described in the 1930s as 'disguised unemployment'.[11]

There is, however, a silver lining in the economic record of the recent period. The rate of inflation in industrial countries is now as low as it was in the 1950s and 1960s. Inflation had accelerated in the 1970s in many countries in the wake of the economic crisis triggered[12] by the first oil shock. The economic policies of the 1980s and 1990s can be credited with containing price increases and bringing inflation down to its Golden Age levels.

ALTERNATIVE HYPOTHESES ABOUT THE POOR ECONOMIC PERFORMANCE SINCE 1980

The generally poor economic record of industrial countries under liberalization and globalization over the last ten to fifteen years,[13] especially when it is compared with their performance in the illiberal Golden Age, raises two important analytical questions:

1. Could the observed deterioration be due to exogenous factors rather than any intrinsic features of the liberal and global regime itself?
2. If the poor economic performance has not been caused by exogenous factors, then the question arises, why has the liberal economy failed to deliver despite predictions to the contrary of the orthodox economic models?

Both of these are critical questions and will be taken up in turn in this and the following sections.

The Role of Technology

On the question of exogeneity, one major argument concerns the role of technology. It is argued that the poor economic performance in the recent period is not due to the economic regime, but rather brought about by exogenous changes in technology. The pace of technological progress, it is suggested, has been so fast that it has resulted in jobless growth. However,

---

[11] On which, see Eatwell (this volume).

[12] There is no suggestion here that the oil shock 'caused' the crisis. See further discussion below.

[13] It may be argued that the market supremacist liberal economy was not properly operational until the mid-1980s and therefore the relevant period for assessing performance of such a regime should be 1985–95. However, economic performance over the last ten years in industrial countries has been no better than over the last fifteen years.

evidence for industrial countries provides no support for this contention at all. Although the average rate of economic growth was halved in the recent period compared with the Golden Age, productivity growth in this period has fallen even more sharply. As a consequence, the employment elasticity of growth has risen, not fallen, i.e. a 1 per cent increase in GDP growth leads to a greater increase in employment now than during the 1960s (Boltho and Glyn 1995). Thus the reason for much higher unemployment in the post-1980 period is not 'jobless growth', but rather a much slower rate of economic growth than before. Similarly, since average productivity growth has fallen, rather than risen, the pace of achieved technical progress has been slower rather than faster than before.

There is however, an important paradox with respect to technological developments in the recent period. Leading students of the subject such as Professor Freeman (1989) suggest that the rapid advances in information and communication technology in fact constitute a new technological paradigm. This is because these innovations have not only led to the intro-duction of new products but more importantly they also have the potential of reducing the costs of production and raising productivity in most exist-ing industries. Freeman therefore regards these technological changes as constituting a far reaching technical revolution. In terms of its overall potential economic impact, he views this information and technology revo-lution to be on a par with the previous three major technical revolutions which have occurred over the last two centuries. The latter are identified as being based: firstly, on a cluster of textile innovations (approximately 1770–1830); secondly on railways (approximately 1840–90); and thirdly, on electricity, the internal combustion engine, and the chemical industry (approximately 1890–1930).

Thus, on the supply side, the new information technology does provide an enormous potential for increasing production and productivity. However, this potential is not being realized due to the slow rate of growth of real demand and output over the last fifteen years. Freeman *et al.* (1995) shows that those countries in East Asia which have grown very fast in the recent period are the only ones which have been able to use the new tech-nology at all effectively.

The Post-1980 Period in Long-Term Historical Perspective

There is, however, another important line of argument in defence of the eco-nomic record of the post-1980 liberal economy. Here the contention is that although the post-1980 period does not compare favourably with the Golden Age, it is very much in line with the long-term historical record of industrial countries in the pre-Golden Age period. Thus it is suggested that it is not the recent period which has unusually poor performance, but rather, it is the Golden Age which had an exceptionally strong record. The latter it was argued was made possible by the exceptional circumstances of the period, for example, the post-war reconstruction boom and the 'catch-up' effort by European countries to reach the USA levels of productivity. These are clearly important arguments which require fuller examination.

It is indeed true that in statistical terms the Golden Age is an aberration and the post-1980 period is not. During the Golden Age the economies of industrial countries expanded at a rate of approximately 5 per cent per annum which is twice their trend rate of long-term economic growth in previous phases of economic development since 1820 (Maddison 1982). Thus after 1980, these countries appear to have reverted to their normal long-run growth trajectory.

However, a close analysis of the period shows that the Golden Age was not simply a chance product of a favourable combination of circumstances, nor that industrial countries were just plain lucky. This dynamic period was the outcome of a fundamental change in economic strategy, indeed a new model of economic development which leading West European countries adopted in the quarter century following the end of World War II. This model differed radically from that followed by these nations either during the interwar period or that which has been implemented since 1980. The Golden Age model of social market economy emphasized co-operation—both at the international level between nation states and at the national level between workers, employers, and governments. This new co-operative model arose partly out of the harsh experience of the Great Depression. It also owed a great deal to the particular historical conjuncture which prevailed at the end of World War II in Europe which involved a contention between the liberal economic order represented by the USA and the state-controlled planned economy represented by the Soviet Union.[14]

During the Golden Age, the governments committed themselves to full employment as a key economic objective. Employers agreed that the fruits of economic development should be fairly shared between workers and capital by allowing wages to increase in line with productivity and by their willingness to pay their share of the costs of the welfare state. In turn the workers' organizations practised moderation in wage demands. Similarly, at the international level, the world economy worked with orderly trading and monetary arrangements under the hegemonic leadership of the United States.[15] The implementation of this social consensus involved institutional innovations at both the national and international levels.

The co-operative social and economic environment of the Golden Age, in a regulated national and international economy, provided the necessary long-term stability and certainty required for high rates of private

[14] See further Singh (1995b).
[15] For a full discussion of these issue see Glyn et al. (1990); Kindleberger (1992).

investment which in turn made possible high rates of productivity growth. Real wages rose in step with productivity and the share of profits in national income remained more or less stable during this period. As long as the system was working it had a strong positive feed-back mechanism, generating high rates of growth of production, consumption, and employment.

However, following Glyn *et al.* (1990), Singh (1995*b*) suggests that this was an unstable equilibrium. Relatively small exogenous shocks, or changes in endogenous variables outside their normal range, could push industrial economies off their high-growth path. In this analysis, the Golden Age would have come to an end through its own internal logic, even if there had been no exogenous shocks such as the oil-price increases. The efficiency of the central institutions of the economic regime gradually eroded the longer the system was in operation. Internally, the long period of full employment increased the power of workers and their successful wage demands undermined the social compromise with employers. Similarly, international co-ordination became much more difficult with the relative economic decline over time of the United States, whose currency was the linchpin of the whole system. The continuation of the Golden Age would have required institutional renewal to address these difficulties. However, after the second oil shock of the late 1970s, instead of seeking such renewal of the Golden Age model, the governments of industrial countries led by the United States and the UK turned decisively towards the alternative model of market supremacy and of external and internal liberalization and globalization.

To sum up, the high-growth path of the Golden Age was based on a unique model of economic development. Post-World War II reconstruction as well as the 'catch-up' of the European countries with the US were important stimuli for economic growth. However, without the social market economy and the social consensus that it embodied, such stimuli may not have translated into greater rates of investment and faster overall economic growth. As Matthews and Bowen (1988) point out the European levels of productivity relative to those of the USA were as low in 1913 as they were in 1950. Yet there was no 'catch-up' in the interwar period. Similarly post-war reconstruction at the end of World War I did not lead to twenty-five years of sustained economic growth and full employment as happened in the Golden Age. As Abramovitz (1986) rightly notes it is not enough for there to be differences in productivity levels between countries for the 'catch-up' to occur; what is also required is what he calls 'social capabilities'. Construed broadly, the institutional arrangements of the Golden Age provided such capabilities for the 'catch-up' to take place.

Finally, turning to the post-1980 period, it is not a valid argument to suggest that because economic growth during these years has broadly been in line with the long-term historical record of industrial countries bar the Golden Age, it is therefore satisfactory. The important point here is that the level and the growth of economic activity achieved in the 1980s and the 1990s has not been sufficient to meet the needs of the people. The mass unemployment and stagnant or slow-growing real wages (despite the supply-side potentialities of the new technological revolution), constitute eloquent evidence of economic failure.

WHY HASN'T THE LIBERAL ECONOMY DELIVERED?

If the poor economic performance of industrial countries cannot be ascribed to exogenous factors, we then turn to the second main question posed above: why has the liberal economy failed to deliver despite predictions to the contrary of orthodox economic models and much prevailing conventional wisdom? Why are the expectations of such wisdom not borne out by events? Are there perhaps negative aspects of the liberal integrated economic regime which do not receive adequate attention in conventional thinking?

Trade Openness

Orthodox analysis ascribes many virtues to a liberal trading order and free capital movements. As Chakravarty and Singh (1988) note, the case for trade openness is in principle very robust. Apart from the usual comparative static advantages of trade emphasized in textbooks, openness can be a source of great advantage for an economy for any of the following reasons:

1. it may enable a country to concentrate its relatively specialized resources in areas of production where the world demand is highly income and price elastic;
2. it may lead to diffusion of knowledge which can lead to considerable upgrading of the quality of local factors of production;
3. it may lead to sufficient competitive pressure to eliminate certain forces of what Leibenstein has described as X-inefficiency;
4. trade may lead to changes in the distribution of income which can lead to a greater share of accumulation in national output;
5. trade may accelerate a Schumpeterian process of creative destruction and thereby lead to faster economic growth.

However, in order for these benefits to be realized, certain conditions need to be met which are ignored in conventional models. The most important of these are the role of the government and the question of co-ordination failures with respect to the integrated international economy. The first is particularly important for developing countries. The second concerns both developed and developing countries and is also connected with the issue of financial openness.

It will be appreciated that some of the potential dynamic positive advantages of free trade outlined above can also easily go in the opposite direction. Thus a redistribution of income towards profits instead of leading to a higher rate of investment, may simply increase capitalist consumption or lead to capital flight. With incomplete and imperfect markets in developing countries, the role of the government in monitoring and co-ordinating activities of entrepreneurs becomes critical in order to avoid negative outcomes and to increase the likelihood of positive benefits. This is especially so in relation to the question of 'learning' from trade. Economic analysis as well as the experience of highly successful East Asian countries like Japan and Korea suggest that trade openness works positively if the phenomenon of 'learning' from contacts with the rest of the world are suitably institutionalized, through adaptations on the policy side involving appropriate government interventions which make the domestic economy more responsive to change. Indeed, Freeman (1989) notes that, following the example of nineteenth-century Germany, governments in Japan and Korea have long established national systems of technological development which enables them to reap maximum benefits from such learning from the outside world, whether done through trade or through other interactions.

However, even if there were appropriate government policies at the national level, the benefits of trade liberalization may not materialize because of co-ordination failures at the international level, leading to low-level equilibrium of world demand, output, and employment. Based on the experience of the 1930s, Keynes was particularly worried about this problem in relation to the post-war world. He noted that

the problem of maintaining equilibrium in the balance of payments between countries has never been solved . . . the failure to solve the problem has been a major cause of impoverishment and social discontent and even of wars and revolutions . . . to suppose that there exists some smoothly functioning automatic mechanism of adjustment which preserves equilibrium if only we trust to matters of *laissez faire* is a doctrinaire delusion which disregards the lessons of historical experience without having behind it the support of sound theory. (Moggridge 1980)

During the Golden Age, the problem of the balance-of-payments surpluses and deficits between nation states was indeed resolved at high rates of growth of world demand, output, and employment. This was made possible by international co-ordination, achieved through the post-war Bretton Woods system and also importantly through the activities of the USA government as the hegemon in that system. The Bretton Woods agreements as these finally emerged—rather than as Keynes or even White had originally envisaged them to be—did still have a deflationary bias. However, because of the activities of the USA government, this bias did not turn out to be a problem during the Golden Age. The USA provided adequate liquidity to the international economy to permit high rates of growth of world demand

and output. This was done in the early post-war years through the Marshall Plan and subsequently through American military expenditures and foreign investment abroad. The latter policies, however, contributed to the persistent US balance-of-payments deficits in the 1960s which ultimately led to the demise of the Bretton Woods system in 1971 with the ending of the gold convertibility by the USA government.

Financial Openness

In the post-1980 period, with financial liberalization, the problem of international co-ordination failures in the sense outlined above has become very serious. There is much less economic co-operation between leading industrial countries today (the USA, West Germany, and Japan) than was the case when the USA was the single hegemonic power and was thereby able to foist its own design on everyone else. In the absence of adequate international co-operation, the financial markets have come to dominate. This is not to suggest that there is no intergovernment co-operation at all in the field of money and finance. There is still the IMF, but its role has long been restricted to monitoring and disciplining the Third World. Leading industrial countries, which have effectively been outside the IMF disciplines, only occasionally and episodically co-operate on an *ad hoc* basis as for example, the Plaza Agreement in September 1985. In general, however, as Panić (1995) notes the degree of international co-operation during the last ten to fifteen years has been limited to the minimum level necessary to stop the repetition of the mutually destructive acts of the 1930s, such as the competitive currency devaluations.

The increasingly globalized financial markets have in general worked in a 'deflationary' way, penalizing governments which follow expansionary policies. In the formation of average market opinion, far more weight is given to the perceived dangers of inflation rather than to the need to obtain full utilization of resources. Eatwell (1995) outlines the process by which such market psychology becomes predominant.[16]

However, the markets have sometimes also been expansionary. The most conspicuous example of this is the huge portfolio financial flows which went to Latin America in the 1990s. Spurred by the euphoria about emerging markets as well as by other factors, Latin American countries received enormous inflows of funds between 1990 and 1994, largely from USA institutional investors.[17] These funds relaxed the foreign-exchange constraint and

---

[16] This is of course the Keynesian view of price formation on the foreign-exchange markets. For a discussion of the rational expectations perspective, see Dam (1982). For a critical analysis of the rational expectations view, see Felix (1995).

[17] International equity flows to Latin America rose from $0.43b. in 1987 and $0.72b. in 1988 to nearly $7b. in 1989, to almost $10b. in 1990, and $20b. in 1993 (El-Erain and Kumar 1995, table 3).

enabled many Latin American countries to resume the process of real economic growth after the 'lost decade' of the 1980s. However as Rodrick
(1994) and Krugman (1995) point out there was a herd instinct in these
portfolio flows to Latin America. The market was not rewarding virtue, fru-
gality, and restraint, but in many countries subsidizing consumption at the
expense of investment. Despite clear evidence that countries like Mexico
were running huge current-account deficits and using the new inflows of foreign capital largely for current consumption, such flows continued. The
bubble finally burst in December 1994 when these flows to Mexico suddenly
stopped. This resulted not only in a serious crisis in that country but also,
through the Tequila effect, in other emerging markets as well. Consequently
in 1995, real GDP is estimated to have fallen by nearly 10 per cent in
Mexico and 7 per cent in Argentina. Thus, even when the financial markets
have been expansionary, their bandwagon and herd characteristics generate
considerable instability for the real economy.

Apart from these international co-ordination failures arising from the
operation of liberalized global financial markets which may lead to deflation, low rates of growth of demand and/or instability, there are also other
channels through which such markets may produce negative outcomes.
These channels also tend to be ignored or not given adequate weight by conventional wisdom and orthodox economists. Specifically, unfettered capital
movements provide enormous scope for destabilizing speculation which in
turn leads to high volatility of both monetary and real variables.

The sheer size of transactions on the global foreign-exchange markets
today is gigantic. The average daily volume of trade in the global foreign-
exchange market has risen from a mere US$15b. in 1973, to US$60b. in
1983, to US$900b. in 1992. To put the 1992 figure in perspective, the aver-
age value of GDP per day in that year was US$64b.; the corresponding
value of world exports was only US$10b., and that of global foreign-
exchange transactions was US$900b. By 1995, the volume of average daily
global exchange transactions had reached US$1,300b. (*The Economist*
1995). Most of these transactions were very short term—nearly half of them
involved round trips of two days and more than 80 per cent round trips of
seven days or less (BIS 1993; Felix 1995).

These enormous foreign exchange dealings are largely driven by short-
term differences in interest and exchange rates rather than by fundamentals.
Such market behaviour has in part been responsible for the prolonged over-
valuation or undervaluation of key currencies (for example, the US dollar
in the 1980s) which in turn contributes to the volatility of other financial
variables. Fluctuations of financial variables can affect real variables such
as investment, both directly and indirectly. Investment is discouraged
directly by the rising cost of capital which is in part caused by volatility in
financial variables. In addition, the overall uncertainty which now increas-

ingly characterizes the economic environment as well as the greater fluctuations in the components of final demand[18] also have a negative effect on
the corporate inducement to invest. Despite the rise in profits in the 1980s
and booming stock markets, the trend rate of growth of investment in
industrial countries since 1980 has been about half of what it was in the
Golden Age. The fluctuations in interest and foreign exchange rates are by
themselves likely to have been significant in this outcome.

To sum up, financial liberalization can in principle increase economic
welfare by a more efficient allocation of scarce capital resources. Further,
in addition to its potential merits noted earlier, trade openness, under certain conditions, can also promote convergence in the sense of factor-price
equalization. Financial openness can reinforce that process and lead to
quicker convergence. However, economic analysis and experience indicate
that such benefits of openness can only be realized provided there are no
co-ordination failures in the domestic as well as international markets. As
Stiglitz (1994) has noted, unregulated financial markets are particularly
prone to problems of co-ordination failure. These have played a significant
part in contributing to the poor economic performance of industrial
countries in the post-1980 period. These countries have been harmed by liberalized global financial markets in a number of interrelated ways. First, in
the absence of adequate international co-operation between governments,
the problem of maintaining balance-of-payments equilibrium between countries has only been resolved at low rates of growth of world demand.
Secondly, individual countries have been obliged by financial markets to follow generally restrictive policies. These by themselves would discourage
investment. Thirdly, however, the much greater volatility of key financial
and economic variables under liberalized global markets would reinforce
that trend. This would result in lower rates of growth of output and employment.

MISPLACED EUPHORIA AND THE SUSTAINABILITY OF LIBERALIZATION AND GLOBALIZATION

This chapter has shown that the economic performance of industrial countries with respect to growth of output, employment, and productivity under

[18] UNCTAD (1995) notes that financial deregulation has made aggregate demand more
unstable by increasing the volatility of consumption expenditures, exports, and imports. Easier
access to credit has enabled consumers to spend more freely, but their accumulated debt has
made their current expenditure more vulnerable to changes in interest rates. The increase in
the coefficient of variation in the volume growth of private consumption in five major OECD
countries from 1961–73 to 1982–94 ranged from 78 per cent to 167 per cent. Export and import
volatilities have also increased due to sharp changes in competitiveness brought about by
exchange-rate fluctuations and to swings in economic activity.

a liberalized global regime in the recent period has been poor. It has further been argued above that these failings can be linked directly to the intrinsic features of the new order—the co-ordination failures caused by diminished international co-operation and the consequent dominant role of the financial markets. The important question is what are the future prospects of industrial economies under liberalization and globalization. What is the likelihood that there will be a marked improvement in economic performance in the foreseeable future?

The most pressing economic problem confronting industrial countries today is to create sufficient jobs with rising real wages for all those who seek them. Past statistical relationships and economic analysis suggest that this would only be possible if there is a large and sustained trend increase in the rate of growth of output and productivity in these economies.[19] It was noted earlier that the necessary expansion of output and productivity are certainly feasible on the supply side. The main constraint is on the demand side: how to bring about a sustained rise in the rate of growth of real aggregate demand without risking unacceptable inflation.

As mentioned before, most observers do not expect any increase in the long-term growth rate of west European economies in the foreseeable future.[20] An important reason for this is that under the post-1980 economic order of market supremacy, the main policy programme, favoured by leading industrial-country governments and multilateral institutions alike, to improve economic performance and particularly to reduce unemployment is that of labour-market flexibility. Some supply-side measures are also advocated, but the main thrust is on improving the functioning of the labour markets.

The intellectual basis of this approach is rooted in the concept of NAIRU. The main cause of unemployment or inadequate employment opportunities in terms of this theory lies in rigidities in the labour market and the provisions of the welfare state which make it unattractive for people to seek work. Hence the remedy of increasing market flexibility through means such as deregulation, reduction of trade-union power, and a pruning of the welfare state.

Several economists have, however, observed that the NAIRU analysis is incompatible with some of the most important stylized facts about both the labour-market characteristics and outcomes in industrial countries during this century. To illustrate, consider the following. In the highly regulated Golden Age, when labour markets were characterized by far greater rigidities than they have been in the 1980s and 1990s, leading European countries enjoyed more or less full employment with moderate inflation for more than two decades. By contrast, in the recent period these countries have been

---

[19] See further Boltho and Glyn (1995); Singh (1995b); ILO (1996).
[20] ECE (1996); Dreze and Malinvaund (1993); Singh and Zammit (1995).

afflicted with mass unemployment. These are quite the reverse of the outcomes which the NAIRU theory would predict for the two periods. Similarly, Matthews and Bowen (1988) observe that real-product wages rose more slowly and there was greater labour-market flexibility in the 1930s in the UK as compared with the Golden Age, and yet the former period witnessed mass unemployment and the latter full employment.

However, one of the main arguments put forward by the proponents of NAIRU is that in the recent period, the USA record of unemployment is much better than that of Western Europe. This in turn is ascribed to the greater labour-market flexibility and hence the lower NAIRU in the USA compared with Western Europe. It will be recalled from the earlier discussion that although the US labour-market performance has been superior to that of Europe in terms of employment in the recent period, real wages and productivity have grown much more slowly in the USA compared with Western Europe. The more important point in this context, however, is that the Western European labour markets have been more rigid than those in the USA not only in the 1980s and 1990s, but also in the Golden Age. However, in the Golden Age, European countries had a much better employment record than the USA.

These facts concerning inter-temporal variations in unemployment rates and real wages in industrial countries are much more easily explained by variations in the rate of growth of real demand than by the NAIRU approach. The main reason for full employment with rising real wages in the Golden Age was that real demand in industrial countries was increasing at a rate of nearly 5 per cent per annum, almost twice the trend rate of growth in the 1980s and 1990s. At an intellectual level, the main weakness of the NAIRU approach is that it is rooted in microeconomics and is based on a partial equilibrium approach. It assumes that other things being equal, faced with a cut in wages as a consequence of competition among the unemployed, a profit-maximizing firm will increase employment and output. An alternative view, conceptualized by Keynes, is that the firm will expand its output only if it can be sure that it will be able to sell it. In other words, employment will expand only if there is an increase in real demand and output, and not just because there is a cut in wages. A reduction in wages in a closed economy could, in principle, reduce real-aggregate demand through its adverse effects on business expectations and investment; hence the overall consequence may be a fall rather than a rise in employment.[21]

In more practical terms, in the present circumstances of many industrial countries, without a significant increase in aggregate demand, greater labour-market flexibility is likely to lead to greater competition among job seekers and hence reduce the price of labour; this will often result in disguised

---

[21] See also Michie and Wilkinson (1995) on this point.

unemployment rather than an increase in well-paid employment. More importantly, in open economies, at the international level, the labour-market flexibility hypothesis also suffers from the fallacy of composition. Any single country, by cutting wages may be able to improve its international competitiveness and thereby achieve a real increase in demand for its products. But if all countries try to improve their competitive position by reducing wages the net result may be the competitive devaluations of the kind which occurred in the 1930s and hence even greater instability for the international economy. Such a strategy will also lead to a competitive erosion of labour standards and would be socially divisive. It will pit First-World workers against each other as well as against Third-World workers.

To sum up, under the market supremacy model of the 1980s and 1990s, liberalization and globalization in industrial countries have not resulted in increased long-term economic growth nor are these likely to do so in the foreseeable future under the present policy regime. In these circumstances, the question arises why are all the multilateral international organizations extolling the virtues of liberalization and globalization and telling developing countries that if they were to integrate fully with the world economy they would be rewarded with faster economic growth.

There are two plausible hypotheses. The first is that this is a misplaced euphoria, a false appreciation of economic reality, a herd stampede of the kind which led to huge capital flows to Latin America in the 1990s referred to earlier. Such irrational behaviour by the institutions of the economic establishment is perhaps best explained in terms of the sociology of the formation of conventional wisdom as Krugman (1995) has suggested. In the analogous case of the mistaken euphoria concerning the benefits of the 'Washington Consensus', he observed as follows:

. . . the endless round of meetings, speeches, . . . occupy much of the time of the economic opinion leaders. Such interlocking social groupings tend at any given time to converge on a conventional wisdom, about economics among many other things. People believe certain stories because everybody important tells them, and people tell these stories because everyone important believes them. Indeed, when a conventional wisdom is at its fullest strength, one's agreement with that conventional wisdom becomes almost a litmus test of one's suitability to be taken seriously. (Krugman 1995)

The second hypothesis would, however, ascribe a greater rationality to the stance of the multilateral institutions. Many of these organizations suggest that whatever the record of industrial countries under liberalization and globalization, *developing* countries which have implemented this regime— particularly those in East Asia—have done outstandingly well. If this argument were true, it would be a perfectly legitimate defence for the policies recommended by the multilateral institutions and one would not need to resort to a Krugman-type analysis of conventional wisdom.

Regrettably, as a host of independent scholars have observed, this thesis, relating the success of East Asian countries to liberalization and globalization, is not valid.[22] Very briefly,[23] countries like Japan and South Korea, during their periods of fast economic growth did not have a 'close', but what Chakarvarty and Singh (1988) have called a 'strategic' integration with the world economy, i.e. they were only integrated up to the point that it was useful for them to do so. Thus, both Japan between 1950 and 1973 (Japan's high-growth period) and Korea in the 1970s and 1980s were definitely export-oriented economies. However, the important point is that although they were open to exports, they were not open to imports. As late as 1978, manufacturing imports as a proportion of GDP in Japan was only about 2 per cent compared with corresponding figures in the teens for comparable European countries. Similarly, Korean companies, by the end of this century are likely to become the third largest car producers in the world after Japan and the USA. Yet in 1994, South Korea imported only 4,000 cars.

Again, contrary to the wisdom of liberalization and globalization, Japan and Korea actively discouraged foreign direct investment. The two countries were certainly fully open to foreign technology, but not in the form of foreign direct investment. In the same way, contrary to the nostrums of the Bretton Woods institutions, these countries adopted a vigorous industrial policy rather than letting unfettered market forces dictate the priorities and content of economic development. As Wade (1990) has argued, the states in these countries 'governed the markets' so as to bring about structural change in line with the governments' strategic priorities and thereby achieve fast economic growth.

So we are still left with Krugman's theory of the euphoria of the multilateral institutions concerning liberalization and globalization. This euphoria is, however, not only misplaced, but is also misleading and potentially dangerous. This is because the future of the present liberal international economic regime itself depends on its ability to meet people's legitimate needs for remunerative jobs and productive work. As Sir John Hicks observed with respect to the 1930s:

The main thing which caused so much liberal opinion in England to lose faith in Free Trade was the helplessness of the older liberalism in the face of massive unemployment, and the possibility of using import restriction as an element in an active programme fighting unemployment. One is, of course, obliged to associate this line of thought with the names of Keynes. It was this, almost alone, which lead Keynes to abandon his early belief in Free Trade.[24]

[22] The World Bank thesis on this subject is contained in World Bank (1993). For a critical analysis of these theses, see among others, Amsden (1994); Lall (1994); Kwon (1994); Rodrik (1994, 1996); Singh (1994, 1995c, 1996a).
[23] For a fuller discussion see the review article by Singh (1995c).
[24] Hicks (1959), quoted in Bhagwati (1994), 233. On this point see also Fischer (1995).

To sum up, the above analysis suggests that the belief that liberalization and globalization will lead to faster economic growth is not justified by available evidence. However, what is indeed true is that faster long-term growth of output and employment is required to sustain the liberal and global economic regime. Not only the history of the 1930s, but also of the post-World War II period suggests that if the problem of mass unemployment and/or low real wages in industrial countries is not solved, it is likely to lead to a negative sum *ad hoc* protectionism in these countries, particularly against Third-World products.[25] That would be a negation of the globalized liberal economy.

RESTORATION OF FULL EMPLOYMENT IN INDUSTRIAL COUNTRIES: AN ALTERNATIVE POLICY PROGRAMME

It has been argued above that the main constraint on improved economic performance in industrial countries lies in the rate of growth of real aggregate demand, not on the supply side. To that extent, the present mass unemployment would appear to be a self-inflicted injury. It is a problem created by humans and their organizations through the lack of adequate international co-operation and the workings of the essentially unregulated financial markets. If there were a sustained rise in the rate of growth of real demand to anywhere near the Golden Age levels, this would not only lead to full employment but by harnessing the potentialities of the new information and communication technologies revolution, it will also promote productivity growth in a virtuous circle of cumulative causation in accordance with Verdoon's Law.

The salient question is whether a faster growth of real demand, output, and productivity is feasible in the world economy today under any reasonable set of policies. Or, is it simply the case that there is no viable alternative to liberalization and globalization as the Bretton Woods Institutions insist. It was suggested in Singh (1995*b*) that there does exist an alternative policy programme, but this would involve a decisive move away from the present market-supremacist model towards one based on social consensus between, as well as within, countries. However, in order to obtain a trend increase in the rate of growth of real demand (rather than simply money demand) in the OECD countries, new institutions and institutional mechanisms would be necessary both at the national and international levels. These are required to achieve international macroeconomic policy co-ordination and to maintain wage-price restraint during the growth process.

[25] For a fuller discussion see Singh (1994*b*).

This alternative strategy of demand growth and its institutional requirements has been set out in detail in Singh (1995*b*). Here it will be useful to
note the following points which are salient to this programme.

First, it is not a reversion to Bretton Woods or to the other specific institutional arrangements of the Golden Age. The discussion above showed
that the Bretton Woods regime relied heavily for its success on the paramount hegemonic role of the United States. Such hegemony no longer
exists, although the USA is of course still a very big player. International
co-operation among leading countries is therefore far more difficult today
than it was in the Golden Age, but it is no less essential if the world is to
achieve a sustained trend increase in the rate of growth of real aggregate
demand. In an interdependent global economy closely linked by financial
markets, any large uncoordinated economic expansion even by one of the
big players is likely to be thwarted by current account disequilibria and
financial instability. Similarly, with respect to domestic regulation, more
robust pay co-ordinating institutions than those which existed in the Golden
Age will be required to ensure continuing wage stability with sustained full
employment.

Secondly, unlike the labour-market flexibility approach, the demand-
growth strategy is a positive-sum game which benefits the rich as well as the
poor countries. Thus, full employment in OECD countries and faster economic growth will help developing countries in several ways. Specifically,
poor countries will gain from an acceleration in OECD growth through
much the same channels by which they were disadvantaged by slower economic growth in industrial countries after the Golden Age. Thus, faster
OECD growth will have a positive effect on the demand for products of
poor countries as well as on the terms of trade. It may also result in greater
capital flows—both private and public from the rich to the poor countries.
Other things being equal, all this should lead to faster growth of output and
employment in developing economies.

Thirdly, a sustained increase in economic growth and job creation will
also be able to contribute towards addressing some of the other
unfavourable labour-market developments in industrial countries in the
recent period. It has been suggested for example that the concentration of
unemployment among the unskilled workers in these countries is partly due
to a displacement effect. As a result of weak demand for labour only the
skilled workers get hired, even when the firms may not need such skills.
Similarly, a slack labour market has a disproportionately negative effect on
the bargaining power and wages of unskilled workers relative to that of
skilled workers. Thus, other things being equal, a weak demand for labour
over a long period also contributes to the observed increase in inequality
between skilled and unskilled workers which has surfaced in the last two
decades. A sustained increase in the long-term rate of economic growth and

a tight labour market will therefore help not only towards eliminating mass unemployment but will also help reverse these other negative labour-market characteristics of the post-1980 period.

CONCLUSION

There exists today a palpable euphoria in international economic circles and among multilateral institutions concerning the benefits of liberalization and globalization. This chapter has argued that the euphoria is unwarranted by evidence, and at a policy level it is dangerously misleading.

Most attention has been given here to leading industrial countries because these economies have effectively operated under a regime of more or less free trade in manufactures and free-capital movements for the last ten to fifteen years. The experience of these countries therefore provides a useful test case for assessing the benefits of liberalization and globalization.

The chapter shows that the economic record of industrial countries in the post-1980 period is far from inspiring. It is argued here that this poor performance has not been caused by exogenous factors, but is directly linked to the intrinsic features of the new market-supremacist liberal economic order. Moreover, it is suggested that the situation is unlikely to improve greatly under the current policy regime with its emphasis on labour-market flexibility and supply-side measures. There is little likelihood that such policies will be able to achieve the trend increase in economic growth required to create sufficient numbers of good jobs to meet the needs of the people. This will jeopardize the sustainability of the liberal regime. The paradox is that faster growth may not follow from liberalization and globalization but it is nevertheless required to sustain the liberal economic order.

The last part of this chapter outlines an alternative strategy based on achieving a sustained trend increase in the rate of growth of real demand. This is not only capable of leading to full employment with rising real wages in industrial countries but it will also benefit the developing world. This is clearly the first-best solution to the employment question. It is what I have called elsewhere the 'high road'[26] and since it is feasible this is what international organizations should strive for rather than the 'low road' represented by the labour-market flexibility approach (which is not only inadequate but is also divisive). The consolidation and survival of the liberal international economic order depends on whether or not nations and peoples are willing to take the 'high road' and bring about the institutional changes which are necessary for its achievement. The analysis of the chapter indicates that the freedom of the unruly financial markets will need to be curbed in order to sustain the liberal trading order.

[26] Singh (1996b).

REFERENCES

Abramovitz, M. (1986), 'Catching Up, Forging Ahead, and Falling Behind', *Journal of Economic History*, 46/2: 385–406.

Amsden, A. (1994), 'Why Isn't the Whole World Experimenting with the East Asian Model to Develop? Review of the East Miracle', *World Development*, 22/4: 627–33.

Boltho, A. and Glyn, A. (1995), 'Can Macroeconomic Policies Raise Employment?', *International Labour Review*, 134/4–5: 451–70.

Chakravarty, S. and Singh, A. (1988), 'The Desirable forms of Economic Openness in the South', mimeo (Helsinki: WIDER).

Dam, K. W. (1982), *The Rules of the Game* (Chicago: University of Chicago Press)

Dreze, J. H. and Malinvaund, E. (1993), *Growth and Employment: The Scope of a European Initiative*, mimeo, July (Louvain-la-Neuve and Paris).

Eatwell, J. (1995), 'The International Origins of Unemployment', in J. Michie and J. Grieve Smith (eds.), *Managing the Global Economy* (Oxford: Oxford University Press).

Economic Commission for Europe (1996), *Economic Survey 1995–96*.

The Economist (1995), 'Who's in the Driving Seat? A Survey of the World Economy', 7 Oct.

El-Erain, M. A. and Kumar, M. S. (1995), 'Emerging Equity Markets in Middle Eastern Countries', paper delivered at World Bank Conference on Stock Markets, Corporate Finance and Economic Growth, 16 and 17 February.

Felix, D. (1995), 'Financial Globalization Versus Free Trade: The Case for the Tobin Tax, UNCTAD Discussion Paper, No. 108 (Geneva).

Fischer, S. (1995), 'Comment on Sachs, J. D. and Warner, A., *Economic Reform and the Process of Global Integration*', Brookings Paper on Economic Activity, No. 1, 100–5.

Fishlow, A. (1994), 'Economic Development in the 1990s', *World Development*, 22/12: 1825–32.

Freeman, C. (1989), 'New Technology and Catching Up', *European Journal of Development Research*, 1/1: 85–99.

Glyn, A., Hughes, A., Lipietz, A., and Singh, A. (1990), 'The Rise and Fall of the Golden Age', in S. Marglin and J. Schor (eds.), *The Golden Age of Capitalism: Reinterpreting the Postwar Experience* (Oxford: Clarendon Press), 39–125.

Howes, C. and Singh, A. (1995), 'Long-term Trends in the World Economy: The Gender Dimension', *World Development*, 23/11: 1895–911.

International Labour Office (1996), *Employment Policies in a Global Context*, Report V (Geneva).

IMF (1995), *World Economic Outlook*, ch. 4 (Washington, DC).

Kindelberger, C. A. (1992), 'Why did the Golden Age last so long?' in F. Cairncross and A. Cairncross (eds.), *The Legacy of the Golden Age: The 1960s and Their Economic Consequences* (London: Routledge).

Krugman, P. (1995), 'Dutch Tulips and Emerging Markets', *Foreign Affairs*, 74/4: 28–44.

Kwon, J. (1994), 'The East Asia Challenge to Neoclassical Orthodoxy', *World Development*, 22/4: 635–44.

Lall, S. (1994), 'The East Asian Miracle: Does the Bell Toll for Industrial Strategy?', *World Development*, 22/4: 645–54.

Maddison, A. (1982), *Phases of Capitalist Development* (Oxford: Oxford University Press).

Matthews, R. C. O. and Bowen, A. (1988), 'Keynesian and Other Explanations of Post-war Macroeconomic Trends', in W. Eltis and P. Sinclair (eds.), *Keynes and General Policy: The Relevance of the General Theory after Fifty Years* (London: Macmillan).

Michie, J. and Wilkinson, F. (1995), 'Wages, Government Policy and Unemployment', *Review of Political Economy*, 7/2 (Apr.): 133–49.

Moggridge, D. (1980), *The Collected Writings of John Maynard Keynes*, xxv (Cambridge: Cambridge University Press).

Nayaar, D. (1995), 'Globalisation: The Past in Our Present', Presidential address given to the 78th Annual Conference of the Indian Economic Association (Chandigarh), 28–30.

OECD (1994), *Jobs Study* (Paris: OECD).

—— (1995), *Historical Statistics* (Paris: OECD).

Panić, M. (1995), 'The Bretton Woods System: Concept and Practice', in J. Michie and J. Grieve Smith (eds.), *Managing the Global Economy* (Oxford: Oxford University Press).

Qureshi, Z. (1996), 'Globalization: New Opportunities, Tough Challenges', *Finance and Development* (March) (Washington, DC: IMF).

Rodrik, D. (1994), 'The Rush to Free Trade in the Developing World: Why so Late? Why Now? Will it Last?', in S. Haggard and S. B. Webb (eds.), *Voting for Reform: The Politics of Adjustment in New Democracies* (New York: Oxford University Press).

—— (1996), 'Understanding Economic Policy Reform', *Journal of Economic Literature*, 34/1: 9–41.

Singh, A. (1994*a*), 'Openness and the Market Friendly Approach to Development: Learning the Right Lessons from Development Experience', *World Development*, 22/12: 1811–24.

—— (1994*b*), 'Industrial Policy in Europe and Industrial Development in the Third World', in P. Bianchi, K. Cowling, and R. Sugden (eds.), *Europe's Economic Challenge: Analyses of Industrial Strategy and Agenda for the 1990s* (London: Routledge).

—— (1995*a*), 'Competitive Markets and Economic Development: A Commentary on World Bank Analyses', *International Papers in Political Economy*, 2/1.

—— (1995*b*), 'Institutional Requirements for Full Employment in Advanced Economies', *International Labour Review*, 134/4–5: 471–96.

—— (1995*c*), 'The Causes of Fast Economic Growth in East Asia', *UNCTAD Review*, 91–128.

—— (1996*a*), *Savings, Investment and the Corporation in the East Asian Miracle*, Study No. 9 (Geneva: UNCTAD).

—— (1996*b*), 'Expanding Employment in the Global Economy: The High Road or the Low Road?', in P. Arestis, G. Palma, and M. Sawyer (eds.), *Capital Controversy, Post Keynesian Economics and the History of Economic Theory: Essays in Honour of Dr. G. C. Harcourt* (London: Routledge).

—— and Zammit, A. (1995), 'Employment and Unemployment, North and South', in J. Michie and J. Grieve Smith (eds.) *Managing the Global Economy* (Oxford: Oxford University Press), 93–110.

Stiglitz, J. E. (1994), 'The Role of the State in Financial Markets', *Proceedings of the World Bank Annual Conference on Development Economics, 1993* (Washington, DC: World Bank).

United Nations (1994), *World Economic and Social Survey* (New York).

UNCTAD (1995), *Trade and Development Report* (Geneva).

—— (1996), *Report on Least Developed Countries* (Geneva).

Wade, R. (1990), *Governing the Market* (Princeton: Princeton University Press).

World Bank (1991), *World Development Report* (Washington, DC).

—— (1993), *East Asian Miracle* (Washington, DC).

—— (1995), *Global Economic Prospects and Developing Countries* (Washington, DC).

2. Expansionary Policy for Full Employment in the United States: Retrospective on the 1960s and Current Period Prospects

Robert Pollin and Elizabeth Zahrt

INTRODUCTION

As is by now thoroughly documented, the material well-being of the majority of people in the United States has been stagnating or declining for roughly a quarter-century. The USA has become an increasingly difficult place to find a secure job and to earn a living wage. Permanent jobs offering good benefits and training opportunities, organized mostly through internal labour markets, have increasingly been supplanted by contingent work arrangements established through employment contractors or leasing firms. Average incomes have correspondingly fallen and poverty has increased. At the same time, income and wealth have soared for the richest 1 per cent of households, as inequality has also risen sharply.[1]

Many factors have contributed to these trends, including increased global integration, technological change, and the undemocratic and inefficient features of many workplace arrangements. Associated with each of these factors as both cause and effect are two basic trends. These are the decline in the rate of output growth and the weakening of institutions, such as labour unions, which enable the benefits of growth to be equitably shared. We hold that no matter how the specific issues of global competition or technological change are dealt with, the worsening conditions for the majority will continue unless, within a relatively short time, the problems of output growth and distribution are successfully addressed. From the perspective of

We wish to thank the May 1996 Robinson College conference participants for their constructive comments, and especially the conference organizers and volume editors Jonathan Michie and John Grieve Smith for their careful reading of the chapter. We also wish to thank Eileen Appelbaum, Dean Baker, Jerry Epstein, and Dave Fairris for enlightening us on many of the issues we too hastily survey in this study. All errors unfortunately remain our own.

[1] A standard reference documenting these trends is Mishel and Bernstein (1994). See also Gordon (1996), especially his detailed analysis on real-wage trends in the appendix to ch. 1.

policy then, the most basic question to pose is how to improve growth and equalize income distribution both as quickly as possible and in a manner that is sustainable over time.

Of these two factors themselves, growth is the one most amenable to significant change in the short run, i.e. within one to two years. Changing the distributional patterns is no less important, but is unlikely to be done successfully in an environment of declining growth. This then brings us to the question of the chapter: are there ways to raise the rate of output growth in the short run that can also promote a more egalitarian income distribution, while also addressing the longer-term problems associated with global integration, technical change, and inequitable workplace organization?

It is widely acknowledged among economists that expansionary fiscal and monetary policy can produce higher growth and more jobs in the short run. The issue is whether such a policy-induced expansion would be sustainable. Over the past twenty-five years—that is, the period over which average living standards have been falling—the majority of the economics profession in the USA has argued that expansionary policy cannot yield a higher-growth, full employment path over the longer or even medium term (one and a half to four years). The reason is that the economy operates at something approximate to what Milton Friedman termed the natural rate of unemployment. That natural rate is said to be effectively zero when government does not interfere with market activity and all job seekers receive the wage that the market determines they deserve. According to this predominant view, government efforts to lower unemployment below its natural rate will only produce inflationary pressures and distort what would otherwise be optimal market outcomes.

The natural-rate argument first gained ascendancy in the USA as a result of the inflation associated with the escalation of the Vietnam War in the second half of the 1960s. But there is considerable irony in the way the economic legacy of Vietnam has been moulded into a cautionary tale on the failures of large-scale interventionist policies and the overriding dangers of inflation. Aside from any economic consequences, the war was, first of all, a horribly destructive imperialist venture. In terms of its domestic economic effects, it is also true that the escalation of the war beginning in 1965 was associated with a rise in inflation. But to focus on inflation alone ignores the other side of the war's domestic economic impact: that it contributed to the enormous advance in social and economic progress in the 1960s. The reason this occurred is that Vietnam spending, along with the conscious expansionary policies pursued through the 1964 Kennedy/Johnson tax cut, created a near fully employed labour market. Full employment brought in its train higher wages, better working conditions, and less job discrimination against women, African Americans, and other minorities. As Arthur

Okun, a member of the Council of Economic Advisors under President Johnson wrote about these years,

Prosperity has been the key to the reduction of the number of people below the statistical poverty line from 40 million in 1961 to 25 million in 1968. It has meant jobs for those formerly at the back of the hiring line . . . It has made economic security a reality to millions of middle-income families. (1970: 124)

In other words, the expansionary policies associated first with the 1964 Kennedy/Johnson tax cut and then with Vietnam managed to yield the sort of widespread economic benefits that the majority in the USA so badly need at present. The premise of this chapter is that there are lessons from this experience as to how an expansionary policy can be successfully implemented today. Operating from this premise obviously extends the discussion well beyond the constrictions of mainstream discourse on where exactly the NAIRU stands now or at any other time.

The main body of the chapter is divided into two parts. First we discuss the domestic economic experience during the Vietnam War years to consider both the benefits of the expansion-induced tight labour market and the problems associated with inflation. This is the logical place to consider the viability of an expansionary programme in today's environment if for no other reason than this was the last time the US economy operated under tight labour-market conditions.

We then consider whether the positive results due to the Vietnam experience can be replicated in the current period. To some extent, the experience during the Reagan Presidency—in which deficit-led fiscal expansions were much larger than the 1960s but growth, income, and employment patterns were nowhere near as favourable—makes clear that the results attained in the 1960s are not readily reproducible. We argue that the reason for this is that the economy has undergone substantial structural changes since the 1960s, including the much greater degree of global integration; the rising relative size and importance of financial-market activity, what we will term the 'financialization' of the US economy; and the worsening of income and wealth distribution. These factors have weakened the extent to which a given expansionary impulse can stimulate growth, employment, and incomes. This is because these changes have increased the likelihood that the multiplier and accelerator effects of the expansion will be diminished through import, saving, and what we will call 'speculative' leakages, this being the unproductive trading of existing assets rather than the creation of productive assets. These three leakages are in addition to the balance of payments, public debt, and inflation constraints that operate when the expansion is too forceful.

In the rest of the section, we therefore consider ways of designing an expansionary programme that can address all of the factors which have made an expansionary programme in the USA less viable than in the 1960s. Here we first consider the problem of controlling for inflationary pressures. We then discuss how to minimize both the leakages which weaken an expansion and the constraints that operate when it is too strong in terms of specific features of an expansionary programme. These include the alternative growth nodes that can be targeted, the alternative ways in which the expansion can be financed, and the extent to which such programmes would be affected by downward pressures on the dollar.

However, even if a programme is carefully designed to maximize the expansionary impulse, such gains will be unsustainable unless a longer-term restructuring process begins concurrent with the short-run programme. At least for the contemporary US economy, in other words, those who believe in a relatively unyielding NAIRU have a point about the ephemeral nature of government-induced expansion in the absence of longer-term restructuring. We therefore briefly consider the types of longer-term changes that need to be made in two spheres—the work process and labour market; and in financial institutions and markets. One point we wish to stress in including this discussion is our view that an expanding economy is the most favourable environment in which to make structural adjustments consistent with sustainable full employment.

The chapter concludes with a brief summary and some comments concerning one sphere of longer-term restructuring that we do not consider in the chapter's body, which is developing international co-operation around sustainable full employment policies. There is no doubt that such co-operation is highly desirable.[2] However, it is difficult to see any such agreements occurring without pressure first coming from political movements that are seeking to implement an expansionary programme within their domestic economies. We therefore operate from the premise that the programme we explore for the USA will operate within the existing global order that is basically hostile to expansionary initiatives. Operating within such an environment presents serious, but still less formidable constraints for the USA than other OECD countries. At the same time, the success of a US domestic expansion could generate powerful demonstration effects that will create pressure for comparable programmes elsewhere. In addition, a US expansionary programme will also increase world demand and engender a positive shift in investors' expectations world-wide. This is the context in which we would likely see pressure building for international co-operation to support expansionary policies.

---

[2] Succinct discussions as to why this is so are in Davidson (1996) and Eatwell (1994).

THE DOMESTIC ECONOMIC IMPACT OF VIETNAM[3]

A few basic indicators will initially make clear the extent to which the 1960s were a period of unequalled prosperity, especially in terms of the egalitarian spread of well-being. The average GDP growth rate for the decade was 4.1 per cent, compared with 2.8 per cent for the 1970s, 2.6 per cent for the 1980s, and 1.7 per cent between 1990 and 1994. The unemployment rate averaged 4.6 per cent in the 1960s, then rose to 6.1 per cent in the 1970s, 7.2 per cent in the 1980s. It did fall somewhat, to 6.5 per cent, over 1990 to 1994, but to a level still much higher than the 1960s.

The average real wage for non-supervisory workers increased in the 1960s at an annual rate of 1.4 per cent but, as mentioned above, has been falling since, declining by 0.3 per cent in the 1970s, 1.0 per cent in the 1980s, and 0.3 per cent again between 1990 and 1994. At the end of the 1960s, the average non-supervisory worker earned $465 a week in today's dollars while by 1994, she or he was earning only $396. As the introductory quote from Arthur Okun makes clear, the number of people in poverty also declined dramatically in the 1960s, from 40 to 24 million between 1960 and 1969, or from 22.2 to 12.1 per cent of the total population.

There were several factors which contributed to this boom period, not all of which were due to conscious expansionary or military-related policy initiatives. The most important of these was that the United States emerged from World War II as the unquestioned world leader in producing manufactured goods for exports, and this momentum carried into the 1960s. US exports were also greatly bolstered by policies, such as the Bretton Woods monetary system and the Marshall Plan, that promoted a US-led free-trade regime throughout the capitalist world.

Concurrent with this export boom was the development in the USA of new industries for both the domestic market and exports. As noted above, one major area of expansion came from industries growing out of World War II developments in aerospace, communications, and electronic products. A separate source of new industrial growth came from the expansion of the automobile industry and the allied sectors of oil, rubber, glass, road-building, and the development of suburbs. Another factor strengthening the USA in the 1960s was that the financial system was highly robust, as both businesses and households came out of World War II carrying little debt. This gave them considerable latitude in increasing their level of indebtedness to finance investment and household-durable purchases.[4]

Finally, the stated economic policy priority at that time, in the USA, as well as in other advanced capitalist countries, was to attain a full-

---

[3] This discussion summarizes that in Baker, Pollin, and Zahrt (1996).

[4] See Glyn, Hughes, Lipietz, and Singh (1990) and Brenner (1996) for contrasting discussions of the basic factors underlying the 1960s boom.

employment growth path. Throughout the West, it was considered incumbent upon governments to demonstrate that capitalist economies could achieve full-employment prosperity, and thus counteract the claims to superiority coming from the Soviet Union. After all, Nikita Khruschev's 1956 boast that the Soviet economy would 'bury' the West was then taken quite seriously, since the Soviet economy experienced no unemployment during the 1930s depression and had been growing at more than double the rate of the USA through the 1950s.

It was in this spirit that in 1962, Walter Heller, Chair of the Council of Economic Advisors under Kennedy, proposed a tax cut that would stimulate the economy by increasing the federal deficit, and thereby move the economy toward full employment. Due to the scepticism of the opinion élite—though not at this point the economics profession—it was not until 1964 that what was then the largest tax cut in history was signed into law. The economy responded quickly, as withholding rates on wages and salaries were reduced immediately rather than in stages.

Growth accelerated from 4.1 to 5.3 per cent between 1962 and 1964 and unemployment fell from 5.5 to 5.0 per cent. As a source of government stimulative spending, the rise in the military budget was an important factor contributing to the 1960s boom. However, prior to 1965, increases in the defence budget were not motivated by the situation in Vietnam, but rather the general post-Sputnik intensification of the Cold War.

There has been some confusion and associated controversy as to when the major escalation of military spending on Vietnam itself actually began.[5] As Weidenbaum (1967) showed soon after the escalation, the source of the confusion is the presence of lags between the time military orders are placed and when they are delivered and paid for. When such considerations are accounted for, Weidenbaum showed that the increase in defence orders actually began rising rapidly during the second quarter of 1965, from $51 to $55b. between the first and second quarters of 1965, then again to $59 and $62b. in the subsequent two quarters.

This escalation came on top of an already expanding economy, which is the central point for understanding the economic impact of Vietnam. Because of this, its effect was to push the utilization rates for both productive capacity and people beyond the point that had been experienced at any time over the post-World War II period. This is the sense in which a careful observer such as Otto Eckstein, working from his Data Resources econometric model, concluded that 'without the stimulus of the War expenditures, the economy would have entered a protracted growth recession in the spring of 1966', and more generally that 'from 1965 through 1971, the principal movements of the economy can be explained by the Vietnam war' (1978: 26).

---

[5] See, for example, Walker and Vatter (1982).

THE BENEFITS OF THE VIETNAM BOOM

We have made reference to the figures on aggregate unemployment, wage growth, and poverty during the 1960s. While these data are indicative of the gains of this period, there is much to be learned by considering some of the more detailed statistics tracking this period, as well as by following some contemporaneous accounts of developments in these years. We rely on *Business Week* magazine (hereafter *BW*) as a relatively neutral journalistic reference for the period.

Returning briefly to the aggregate data on unemployment, what does not emerge from the decade average figures is that the gains in reducing unemployment come entirely from the 1965–9 years, that is, after the start of the Vietnam escalation. Thus, the average unemployment rate for 1960–4 was 5.7 per cent, exactly the same as that for the full 1950–89 period. By contrast, over 1965–9, unemployment averaged a post-war low of 3.8 per cent.

But even these aggregate figures do not adequately convey the changes in labour markets that resulted from the Vietnam escalation. Some additional crucial developments include the following:

1. The dramatically improved employment conditions did not occur merely in a few regions with heavy concentrations of military-related industries. Rather, to an unprecedented extent, the prosperity was spread throughout the country. Thus *BW* reported on 17 December 1966 (p. 64) that 'The Labor Department's Bureau of Employment Security released a proud statistic this month: 65 major industrial centers are now classified as low unemployment areas, the largest number ever' ('low unemployment' means that the unemployment rate in the arca is less than 3 per cent).
2. The unemployment rate for African Americans and other minorities also reached a post-World War II low of 7.2 per cent during 1965–9. The figure for the first half of the 1960s was 10.8 per cent, which again, is the same average rate for the full 1950–89. In addition, the ratio of non-white to white median income rises sharply between 1965 and 1969, from 53.8 to 59.0 per cent, a five-year gain that has yet to be equalled. The rising employment opportunities for African Americans also led to a surge in Blacks joining integrated labour unions. This was occurring throughout the country, but especially in the South and, as *BW* noted on 21 November 1968 (p. 120), 'despite a rising tide of separatism in the ideology of the Negro movement'.[6]

---

[6] This is not to suggest that the Vietnam boom was solely responsible for the gains made by Blacks in the 1960s. Other important factors include the northern migration of southern Blacks, the gains in educational opportunities and the Civil Rights Act of 1964 and its subsequent enforcement. It is difficult to separate out the relative contributions of these and still

3. Not surprisingly, the most direct employment benefits of the Vietnam-led expansion flowed to young people, especially young men of military age. The number of men in the civilian labour market expanded by 33 per cent from 1964 to 1969, from 2.6 to 3.9 million. In addition to this, the military itself expanded its enlistments from 2.6 to 3.5 million in those same years. Poor people gained the most directly from this search for new enlistees as enlistment rates for young males living in poor communities was disproportionately high. In general, however, the Vietnam escalation had made young and inexperienced job-seekers increasingly valuable to employers.

4. We cannot overlook the less benign aspects of the opportunities created by the war-induced expansion. Most obviously is that because many young men, especially the poor, lacked other prospects, they were forced both to put their lives at risk and become legal killers in an immoral venture. For African Americans, an additional indignity was they faced patterns of discrimination in the military similar to those in the civilian labour market, as they were placed disproportionately in low-skilled jobs and received fewer opportunities for advancement.

FULL EMPLOYMENT, INFLATION, AND INCOME DISTRIBUTION

Given the widespread benefits of the war-induced boom, why is the Vietnam experience so widely viewed as having inflicted serious damage to the economy? The most common answer, of course, is that the war set off an

other factors, especially since many of them happened concurrently. However, the fact that the most rapid advances were begun and then sustained over the second half of the 1960s supports the notion of the Vietnam boom's central influence. By contrast, northern migration by Blacks had begun in earnest in the 1940s and its effects were more gradual. Improvements in educational opportunities similarly brought substantial gains, but over a period of decades. The Civil Rights Act was passed in 1965 but it produced only a legal framework in which Blacks could pursue employment opportunities. As has been seen increasingly since the 1960s, such legal claims to equal employment opportunity offer only limited benefits when the demand for labour is slack, especially for those with fewer credentials and connections. It is on the basis of this type of logic that an extensive survey by Smith and Welsh (1989) determined that of all the factors that have contributed to economic progress by African Americans over the post-World War II period, economic growth alone accounts for roughly half of the advances. They conclude their study by warning that 'until we restore the growth rates of the 1960s, further long-term improvements in Black economic status will not materialize' (p. 561). Other studies do assign far greater weight to other factors. For example, Donohue and Heckman (1991) acknowledge that the most rapid period of progress begins in 1965, but they argue that this was due to the passage and aggressive enforcement of civil rights laws, especially in the South. However, they make no attempt to disentangle the relative effects of the changing legal environment from the war-induced full-employment conditions which also emerged in 1965. Indeed they make no attempt at all to measure the contribution of full employment to the progress they observe.

inflationary spiral which could not be contained, leading to the stagflation and high unemployment of the 1970s. It is undeniable that inflation did accelerate in the second half of the 1960s. After having averaged only 1.2 per cent from 1960 to 1964, it rises to 1.9 per cent in 1965 and then averages 4.4 per cent from 1966 to 1969.

Assuming the war-induced full employment was a major cause of inflation, how serious were the problems that either led to the inflation or were caused by it?[7]

A first issue to consider is whether the boom created severe difficulties for businesses in finding qualified workers to hire. Certainly, the tight labour market forced businesses to be more aggressive in their methods of recruiting workers. In April 1966, for example, *BW* reports (p. 101) that 'U.S. employers are finding that the tight market for labor is forcing them to use gimmicks to lure sorely needed workers from other companies—and other countries as well.' Among the specific strategies employed, the story notes that 'Ford and other employers have combed Appalachia and the Ozarks, looking for workers among coon and squirrel hunters. They've come up with, at most, a handful.'

Over time, however, businesses became increasingly adept at operating in tight labour markets. Thus on 17 February 1968, *BW* ran a story (p. 41) headlined, 'A Tight Labor Market That Doesn't Really Hurt', that describes 'the proved talent of business for living in a tight labor market'. It reports that 'after three years with unemployment near or below 4 per cent, business knows how to get the labor it needs. Companies are importing, upgrading, and training labor with increasing facility and ingenuity.' The story details ways in which businesses are increasingly recruiting women, Blacks, and other minorities, expanding their job-training programmes, and providing more opportunities and incentives for promotion.

But what of the costs of the inflation emanating from the tight labour market? Despite the widespread opposition to even moderate inflation from central bankers and other élites throughout the world today, there is little evidence showing that overall economic performance is harmed by moderate rates of inflation. This view has been confirmed most recently in research led by Michael Bruno (1995), the Chief Economist of the World Bank. Studying the relationship between inflation and economic growth for 127 countries between 1960 and 1992, Bruno and colleagues found that average growth rates fell only slightly as inflation rates move up to 20–25 per cent.

---

[7] Some economists (e.g. Walker and Vatter 1982) argue that the Vietnam escalation could not have been responsible for the accelerating inflation of the late 1960s because, relative to the size of the economy, spending on the war was too small to have produced so large an impact. This view is simply a restatement of a more general position that assigns little significance to the war in explaining the boom of 1965–9. Because we believe the war-induced full-employment conditions did play a decisive role in fuelling the boom, we must then also acknowledge its role in generating inflationary pressures.

Of particular importance for our concerns here, Bruno found that during 1960–72, economic growth on average *increased* as inflation rose from negative or low rates to the 15–20 per cent range. This is because, as Bruno explains, 'in the 1950s and 1960s, low-to-moderate inflation went hand in hand with very rapid growth because of investment demand pressures in an expanding economy' (1995: 35).

Such growth-led 'demand-pull' pressures were clearly the source of the rise in inflation in the USA between 1965 and 1969. As we have seen, the benefits of this growth were widespread. Why then should the accompanying moderate inflation be regarded as a débâcle?

The real problems that were occurring in the second half of the 1960s were not inflation *per se*, but rather that the distribution of national income had shifted in favour of working people and the less wealthy and that the profitability of US businesses was declining. Yet these are not generalized problems for the economy as a whole; indeed, it is not obvious that they are problems at all for working people enjoying a rising share of national income. Moreover, these developments were only partially connected to the onset of inflation. Nevertheless, by focusing on inflation as such rather than the issues of income distribution and profitability, the priorities of a small segment of society—i.e. the wealthy—acquired the status of a nationally shared concern.

Capital income—including corporate and business profits, interest payments, and rent—rose throughout the second half of the 1960s, but the rate of increase was somewhat lower than earlier periods, despite the booming economy. Thus, in the latter half of the 1960s, working people made substantial gains in the distribution of income. Wages as a share of national income jumped from 68.1 per cent in 1965 to 72.4 per cent in 1969, an unprecedented increase and one that has not been equalled since. Overall income distribution among families also reflects this trend (Blinder 1980).

What is the relationship between these distributional shifts and inflation? To begin with, the distributional shifts did not result primarily from accelerating wage increases. The rise in real wages for non-supervisory workers between 1965 and 1969 was 1.2 per cent. This represented a decline in wage growth from the first half of the 1960s, when wages rose by 1.7 per cent, and the 1950s, when real-wage growth averaged 2.6 per cent.

There were, rather, three other sources of the distributional shift. The first was that full employment and the accompanying expanding labour market simply converted a higher proportion of the population into wage-earners. This change was connected with inflationary pressures only indirectly, inasmuch as full employment produced both the inflationary pressures and the relative increase of wage-earners in the labour market.

The second source of the distributional shift was more closely associated with inflation. When inflation is not anticipated, creditors will lose real

income relative to debtors since interest rates will not be indexed to inflation. The US credit market was not indexed to inflation in the 1960s, and
creditors experienced some real-income losses as a result.

The final cause of the distributional shift was that even though wages
were rising only slowly, the rate of profit of US businesses was, by a broad
range of measures, in actual decline. Could full employment or inflation
explain this profitability decline? We clearly cannot explain the profitability
decline by a wage squeeze alone since, as we have seen, real-wage growth
had slowed in this period. However, aggregate productivity growth did also
begin to decline in these years, and to the extent that productivity growth
was slower than wage growth, this would contribute to a profit squeeze.

The fully employed labour market may have played a role in generating
the productivity decline. First, the average level of job experience and skill
likely declines as the strong demand for labour induced new entrants into
the job market. In addition, full employment may have created an environment in which workers felt more secure in their jobs and consequently
reduced their level of effort.[8] But these explanations would suggest a pattern of declining productivity growth that is consistent across industries,
while in fact, the decline was heavily concentrated in utilities, transportation, and especially construction, which experienced an *absolute* decline in
productivity between 1966 and 1973. Thus, declining aggregate productivity relative to real wages did contribute to the fall in profitability, but it is
unlikely that full-employment conditions were primarily responsible for the
productivity decline itself.

A separate and more generally applicable explanation for declining profitability in the USA was that US dominance in export markets was starting
to erode by the mid-1960s. In particular, the West German and Japanese
economies had entered a phase of post-reconstruction boom, as productivity growth in both countries rose rapidly while wages were far below those
in the USA. Thus, even though real wages in US manufacturing did not
increase in this period, unit labour costs were growing in the USA at a rate
almost double those of Germany and almost triple those of Japan. As a
result, US manufacturers could not raise their prices as fast as their nominal wage payments and other nominal costs were rising. Thus, the rise of
foreign competition, beginning in the mid-1960s, produced a decline in
profit income in the USA.[9]

Note here that, though the fundamental problem was the inevitable
decline of US hegemony, one could conceive of a 'solution' to the problem
in which US wages would have fallen to a level comparable to those of
Germany and Japan, which in turn would have eliminated the economy's

---

[8] This is the argument advanced by, among others, Bowles, Gordon, and Weisskopf (1983).
[9] This account of the causes of declining corporate profitability draws from Brenner (1996).
Alternative perspectives on this question are developed in Moseley and Wolff (1992).

inflationary pressures. This would have entailed US workers relinquishing all the gains they had achieved throughout the entire post-war period. Certainly, eliminating the war-induced full employment as well as aggressively attacking labour unions would have been necessary to achieving these ends. In this sense, therefore, full employment could be held 'responsible' for the profitability decline.

In any case, the moderate inflation that emerged in the late 1960s was itself never the problem with the war-induced full employment economy. At least from the standpoint of manufacturing capitalists, financiers, and other capital-income receivers, the issue was rather their declining relative fortunes. Eliminating inflationary pressures by ending full employment may have helped eliminate these difficulties, but only by attacking the well-being of the great majority who were benefiting from full employment. Other solutions were feasible, but unfortunately never attempted.

WHY CONTROLS COULDN'T WORK

In the admittedly tepid form of wage/price guidelines, the Council of Economic Advisors under President Kennedy had sketched some initial outlines of an approach to sustaining full employment while addressing problems of distribution and competitiveness as well as inflation *per se*. The real breakdown of policy begins only when it becomes clear that such policies could not be made workable in the political environment dominated by Vietnam.

Kennedy's 1962 *Economic Report of the President* included a simple plan for controlling inflationary pressures while the government pushed the economy toward full employment. Because the Council of Economic Advisors believed that the rate at which aggregate productivity could grow in the economy was approximately 3.2 per cent per year, their 1962 *Report* argued that wage increases should also rise by no more than 3.2 per cent annually. Though productivity in some sectors of the economy would undoubtedly increase by more than 3.2 per cent, wage increases in those sectors could not exceed the economy-wide average, or else workers in the more slowly advancing sectors would also demand faster wage increases, which would then generate inflation.

The guideposts were widely regarded as having succeeded in reducing inflation by about one-third in the early 1960s, even though there were no legal enforcement mechanisms behind them.[10] But unemployment was relatively high in the early 1960s, and thus the ability of the guideposts to reduce inflationary pressures in a full-employment economy was not tested in these years.

[10] This estimate is reported by both Sheahan (1967) and Taylor (1974).

As the Vietnam boom gathered force, it became clear that such general and informal guidelines were incapable of dealing equitably with the distributional issues posed by the full-employment economy and the rise of Western European and Japanese competitiveness. A broad range of economists did recognize the inadequacy of the guidelines and the need for more comprehensive measures if full employment were to be sustained. Indeed, what is remarkable is the extent to which so broad a consensus of analysts, including many conservatives, were committed to at least thinking of how active government policy could serve to promote full employment with price stability.

An impressive piece of evidence in this regard is a volume from a 1966 conference on the wage/price guidelines (Schultz and Aliber 1966). The conference was held at the Graduate School of Business at the University of Chicago, then as now a bastion of conservative thinking on economic policy. The majority of participants at the conference were interested in exploring viable approaches to wage/price controls, given the understanding that their overriding concern was how best to sustain full employment. The one major dissident at the conference was Milton Friedman, who presented there (Friedman 1966) the initial statement of his 'natural unemployment rate' theory, a theme to which we return below.

The Johnson administration, for its part, also made some significant attempts to coalesce such initiatives. In the end though, all these efforts failed. Understanding the sources of this failure explains much about why the war-induced full-employment economy was unsustainable.

We must first of all dismiss the notion that there is something intrinsic to capitalism that led to the failure of the wage/price policies. It is true that for such policies to have succeeded, the fundamental issues of the relationship between full employment, income distribution, and international competitiveness needed to be seriously addressed. This implies that the government's involvement in the economy would need to expand to incorporate non-defence industrial policy and a more active role in influencing income distribution, these in addition to the government's then growing commitment in the area of macroeconomic growth and stability.

In fact, when the USA was first implementing wage/price guidelines in the early 1960s, more comprehensive approaches of this kind were being developed throughout Western Europe, as is made clear in the Schultz/Aliber conference volume.[11] In the Nordic countries in particular, wage/price guidelines were developed as part of a broad social contract over planning for full employment. Among other things, wage/price guidelines in the Nordic countries were not written and handed down by the equivalent of the US Council of Economic Advisors. These policies were rather the result

---

[11] See especially the essay by Ross (1966). Similar material is covered by Sheahan (1967).

of extensive negotiations by business and labour in addition to government representatives. Wage bargaining to sustain full employment, in short, became a central feature of the 'social corporatist' model that evolved among the Nordic countries and a few other countries such as Austria. The result was that these countries maintained near full employment throughout the 1970s and 1980s, long past the time when US policy was paying even lip service to full employment. The success of these policies was primarily due to the strength and sophistication of these countries' labour movements. As Rowthorn and Glyn write, the strength of the labour movement allowed the working class

. . . to develop coherent objectives and strike an advantageous bargain with other social groups. In particular, it allows this class to establish full employment as a major national priority. Not only is such a priority accepted by other social groups, but the working class in turn honors its own side of the bargain and accepts the sacrifices required to achieve its employment objectives. (1990: 254)

Within the USA, the equivalent political coalitions never existed to introduce a social corporatist policy approach. Capital opposed the guidelines for evident reasons. Experiencing the realities of full employment first hand, they saw little advantage to themselves of continuing it. Their perception was that full employment was cutting into their profits, and they tended to accept the assessment of an economist quoted in *BW* on 20 July 1968 (p. 112) that 'you have to keep unemployment high enough so that workers don't get too greedy'. This view prevailed despite the fact that real-wage growth had diminished by the mid-1960s, and wages were actually falling in manufacturing.

Labour was similarly unenthusiastic. To a significant extent, the attitude of labour was fostered by their experience in the first half of the 1960s. Over that period, profits were rising well beyond the 3.2 per cent guideline for wage increases, so much so that by mid-1966, Council of Economic Advisors' Chair Gardner Ackley had to warn business that 'labor cannot be expected to continue honoring the guidelines as well as it has when it sees prices and profit margins continually rising' (*BW*, 12 May 1966: 43). At the same time, labour had not attempted to involve itself broadly in the formation of economic policy. Unlike in the Nordic countries, the US labour movement did not articulate a desirable and feasible set of policies that would be needed to complement expansionary policies for full employment. In particular, if it were true that some degree of wage restraint was necessary in expansions, the labour movement never developed a view as to what types of quid pro quos to insist upon in exchange for wage restraint.

There was, finally, the problem of the war. Because full employment was the by-product of the war, it was difficult to conceive of full employment as having been a positive achievement of conscious government policy that might also be sustained by further policy interventions. Moreover, the natural supporters of full-employment policies on the left were also the strongest opponents of the war, and were therefore not well situated to consider how the existing war-induced full-employment conditions should be sustained. The war also divided the left from what would otherwise have been its natural allies in the labour movement, which had long supported the Cold War consensus on foreign policy.

EXPANSIONARY POLICY IN THE CURRENT PERIOD

What Impact Would a 1960s-Type Expansion Have Today

To a significant extent, the 1980s provides a good basis for testing the viability of this question, in that the Reagan administration's fiscal policy was also dominated by federal-deficit spending and a military buildup.[12] Some basic evidence makes clear that the effects were dramatically different. Thus, the federal deficits were a much larger 4.0 per cent of GDP on average in the 1980s relative to the 1960s figure of 0.8 per cent. Yet real GDP growth averaged 4.1 per cent in the 1960s but only 2.6 per cent in the 1980s, and fixed-investment growth followed a similar relative pattern.

Why didn't the far larger fiscal expansion of the 1980s yield a comparable boost to economic growth? We can point to three overarching and interrelated structural changes in the US economy responsible for this less-favourable outcome. The first is globalization—i.e. the increased integration of the USA into the world economy. The second is 'financialization', the extensive growth of financial-market activity relative to the size of the economy.[13] The third is the upward distribution of income and wealth. As we try to show briefly, these have weakened the impact of expansionary policy through four effects: an import, saving, and what we call 'speculative' leakage, as well as through imparting a deflationary bias in policy formation. These factors constrain expansionary policy just as do the more traditional factors generated from an excessively strong expansion, i.e. the balance of payments, public deficit, and inflation constraints.

Globalization

To date, the primary effects of globalization on the viability of expansionary policy have been through the trade account and financial-market

---

[12] This discussion follows some of the arguments made in Pollin (1993a).
[13] We borrow this term from Arrighi (1994), who considers this process in world historical terms.

patterns.[14] Considering trade, since the 1960s, the USA has moved from a persistent surplus to a persistent deficit position. Over the last full business cycle, 1982–90, the trade deficit averaged 2.5 per cent of GDP. The figure has fallen somewhat between 1991 and 1994 to 1.8 per cent but the basic pattern of significant deficits persists. Consistent with such a trade deficit is the fact that the income elasticity of imports in the United States is high. Hooper and Marquez (1995) estimate that between 1976 and 1992, this elasticity would mean that every dollar of increase would increase imports by nearly 30¢.

In terms of financial integration, foreign sources accounted for only 1.2 per cent of all funds available in the US financial market in the 1960s, but 7.2 per cent over the last full 1982–90 business cycle. This high degree of integration has meant that both foreign and domestic-market participants are able to move forcefully against an expansionary programme that would yield—or even that the market participants would expect to yield—significantly lower interest rates and/or a dollar depreciation. Correspondingly, the demise of the Bretton Woods system which prevailed in the 1960s has made co-ordination of global expansion more difficult, and thereby has contributed to the deflationary bias in the policy agenda of industrial countries.

Financialization

The collapse of Bretton Woods and more general global integration of domestic financial markets since the 1960s is an important aspect of the expansion of financial-market activity relative to GDP. But we can also observe financialization by other measures relating more specifically to the domestic market *per se*. For example, the growth rate of the domestic financial sector has vastly exceeded that for the overall economy. The value added in the sectors devoted exclusively to the issuing and trading of financial assets increased over 900 per cent in nominal terms in the years from 1971 to 1991, going from 0.4 per cent to over 1 per cent of GDP. The level of aggregate private borrowing, at 12.3 per cent of GDP also reached unprecedented levels over the most recent full business cycle. This figure is also a 46 per cent increase over the 8.4 per cent private borrowing GDP ratio in the 1960s.

There have been two major effects of financialization in terms of its impact on expansionary policy. First, the growth of speculative trading has imparted a short-term bias to corporate time horizons which has weakened the ability of expansionary policy to encourage long-term productivity

---

[14] The effects of the globalization of investment on the US economy have been less significant thus far, though this is likely to change due to the increasing openness to multinational corporations in both the developed and developing countries. These issues are discussed in Crotty, Epstein, and Kelly (1995).

enhancing investments. Thus, in a private consumption-led expansion, the impulse from the initial multiplier to the investment accelerator will be weaker, as firms look increasingly to expand through the purchase of competitors' assets or a more general competitive repositioning rather than through the expansion of their productive capacity.[15] Relatedly, these financial patterns have increased macroeconomic instability, such that upturns are less stable and downturns more severe.[16] These are the primary factors contributing to the speculative leakage on expansionary policy.

In addition to this speculative leakage, the relative growth of the financial sector has also contributed to the policy bias in favour of protecting the value of financial assets rather than expanding the output of new productive assets. Thus, the Reagan administration combined its highly expansionary fiscal position with the Federal Reserve's restrictive monetary stance. This contributed to the historically high real-interest rates of the period. It thereby also contributed to the relative attractiveness of asset transfers—in which returns on investment derive from interest-rate spreads, regardless of whether levels are high or low—over creating new productive assets, in which high interest-rate levels raise the hurdle rate of return on a project.[17]

Upward Redistribution

The increasing inequality of income and wealth referred to earlier contributes first to the traditional saving leakage. This is because the wealthy have much higher saving rates, and thus a correspondingly low marginal propensity to consume. Most US households, by contrast, are liquidity constrained, and therefore will consume a high proportion of an increase in income.[18] In addition, the high levels of concentrated wealth, combined with the increasingly active speculative financial markets, also then contribute to the speculative leakage.

In total, the effect of these structural changes mean that expansionary policy could only be successful to the extent that it addresses the import, saving, and speculative leakages that are an outgrowth of structural change; this, in addition to dealing with inflationary pressures more successfully than was done in the 1960s. It is to these matters that we now turn.

---

[15] The idea that the corporate takeovers of the 1980s served largely as a substitute for productive investments is developed in Pollin (1996a).

[16] See Pollin (1992) and Wolfson (1994) for development of these points.

[17] See the interesting empirical investigation of the causes of the 1980s merger and takeover wave in Blair and Schary (1994). Pollin (1996a) provides some critical perspective on their research findings.

[18] The distributional patterns of US saving behaviour are discussed in Bunting (1991) and Carroll and Summers (1991), the latter study providing evidence on other OECD countries as well.

INFLATION AND NAIRU

Can a short-term expansion promote sustainable full employment and growth? The most widely held view within the voluminous literature on the Phillips Curve and NAIRU is that expansionary policy can lower unemployment and increase real growth, but only at the cost of accelerating inflation.[19] Moreover, these short-term gains in employment and real growth will be temporary when the unemployment rate falls below the NAIRU rate. Efforts to lower unemployment below NAIRU will thus only succeed in raising inflation, with no sustainable benefits in terms of growth or unemployment.

This is not the place to address in depth the literature on NAIRU.[20] For our purposes here, it will be sufficient to make a few basic points. First, following the substantial critical literature on NAIRU, it is at least evident that any 'natural rate' or more precisely 'non-accelerating inflation rate' of unemployment is entirely dependent on the broader institutional setting in which expansionary policies are pursued. Otherwise, there would be no explanation for the widely disparate experiences with unemployment in different countries (see Rowthorn and Glyn 1990).

Second, it does not follow that if such supportive institutional structures are established, that we can then expect to have eliminated the likelihood of inflationary pressures resulting from expansionary policy. Inflation will normally rise as growth accelerates and unemployment falls. The real issue here is how much inflation will accelerate and what are the costs of such increased inflationary pressures. The preponderance of evidence, as with the Bruno study mentioned above, shows that as long as inflation remains moderate, the costs of such inflation are negligible.

Beyond this, the problem of inflationary pressures resulting from expansionary policies needs to be understood in political terms. As we saw in the 1960s, the reason full employment induces inflation is that it increases workers' bargaining power in labour markets and thus tends to bid up wages, and thereby shift the distribution of income in favour of wages. This then creates an incentive for capitalists to support the return to unemployment

---

[19] Of course, this view is not universally shared: indeed a fundamental contention of new classical economics is that because rational economic agents will adapt instantaneously to short-run government policy interventions, these adaptations will nullify any real effect of policy. However, this perspective has not been successful in demonstrating its empirical validity, and even early proponents of this approach have begun to retreat from its stronger assertions about applicability of the rational expectations assumption (e.g. Sargent 1993).

[20] Cross's edited collection (1995) presents a range of perspectives. Additional critical perspectives include Blanchard and Summers (1988), Gordon (1988), Ormerod (1994), and Eisner (1995).

as a means of disciplining labour and regaining a higher share of national income.[21]

On the other hand, everything else equal, capital will benefit from full employment inasmuch as capacity utilization rises. It therefore follows that at least certain sectors of capital will favour full employment, and even accept the shift in relative shares, as long as in absolute terms, profits are growing along with the rate of capacity utilization. This point is crucial in that it implies that a progressive government may well be able to find supporters among the capitalist class for an expansionary programme.[22]

At the same time, inflation is an instrument of redistribution from creditors to debtors to the extent that the financial market is not indexed to inflation. As such, in an unindexed financial market, rentiers will be adamantly opposed to an expansionary policy that generates accelerating inflation even if it increases the rate of capacity utilization. This is because rentiers' income will not rise with the rate of capacity utilization but will fall with inflation.

Should progressives embrace a system of wage/price controls as a component of their expansionary policy? As we saw in the 1960s, the fundamental problem with such an approach was that it forced labour to limit their wage claims at precisely the point of their maximum bargaining power. Whether they should be willing to do so should depend first, of course, on the level at which capital will agree to an administered division of national income. Given the fact that for twenty-five years average wages have been falling in absolute terms in the USA while productivity has risen, for capital to agree now to something akin to the 1960s guidelines of maintaining wage growth at a rate equal to that for aggregate productivity growth would constitute a clear victory for workers. But it would also be important that an agreement also address issues through which egalitarian growth could be sustainable. The critical concerns here would be issues around the labour process, the structure of financial markets, and the level and composition of investment, issues we take up below.

A less elaborate and therefore perhaps more readily acceptable approach to overcoming especially the rentiers' opposition to expansion is to establish a workable system of indexing financial instruments to the inflation rate. As of this writing, no US government bonds and only a small percentage of privately issued instruments are indexed to inflation in US

[21] Wolff (1979) shows that the inflation from 1969 to 1975 redistributed income downward. It does not necessarily follow that wage-earners will increase their relative share in a full-employment-induced inflation, as firms may succeed, in a wage/price spiral dynamic, in marking up their prices faster than the wage increase. Rowthorn (1977) provides a clear statement of this process, and Rosenberg and Weisskopf (1981) develop the point for the US experience.

[22] The relationship between utilization rates and profitability is examined analytically in Marglin and Bhaduri (1990) and specifically with respect to the US experience in Gordon (1995). Epstein and Schor (1990) discuss the evidence on the breakdown of support for expansionary policy among sectors of the capitalist class.

financial markets. However, the US Treasury did announce in May 1996 that it will begin issuing indexed bonds for the first time later in 1996. In other countries, bond indexation has generally worked successfully in that it has contributed to reducing the arbitrary income redistributions resulting from inflation. This includes countries experiencing hyperinflation such as Brazil in the 1960s, but even more pertinent for the US, countries in which inflation was relatively modest, such as the UK, Sweden, Australia, and Canada. The major argument against bond indexation is that, by weakening bondholders' opposition to inflation, some approximation of price stability will erode as a public-policy goal, which in turn will embed inflation as an inertial force in the economy. Another weakness is that it could be applied only to newly issued debt; outstanding bonds will still be equally vulnerable to inflation. But the indexation policy will also have collateral strengths. In particular, it should raise the government's credibility in pursuing an expansionary programme that does not encourage excessive inflation, since the burden of the newly issued government debt will no longer fall with inflation.[23]

Given the range of strengths and weaknesses of both an incomes policy and bond indexation, the most viable approach is that both instruments serve as complements to each other.

COMPOSITION OF EXPANSION

Expansionary policy initiatives can be divided according to whether they are consumption- or investment-led and according to whether they are centred on the public or private sectors. The simplest approach is to encourage private consumption through monetary expansion and/or a tax reduction. This of course was the strategy with the 1964 Kennedy/Johnson initiative. The multiplier effects of the consumption-led expansion then increased investment through the accelerator. However, the import leakage has weakened the effects of a private consumption-led expansion.

Relative to a 1960s-style private consumption-led expansion, a private investment-led expansion has the merit that it is directly targeting the economy's productive capacity for growth, and therefore raises the likelihood that long-term productivity will rise along with short-term expansion. The policy tools amenable to private long-term investment are, however, less

---

[23] A range of assessments of the viability of bond indexing include Tobin (1971), Friedman (1974), Steinherr (1978), and Fischer (1978, 1983), Munnell and Grolnic (1986), Weiner (1983), Shen (1995), and several essays in Dornbusch and Simonsen (1983). In announcing its plans to introduce indexed bonds, the US Treasury cited the standard argument that this will provide bond purchasers with another inflation hedge. At least publicly, it did not consider the possibility that this may also soften the resistance of the financial-market investors to an expansionary programme.

reliable than those with consumption. The Federal Reserve can reduce short-term interest rates, but it is uncertain what such a change would have on long-term rates, as demonstrated by the volatility of yield curves in recent years. It is further unclear that a fall in long-term interest rates will itself significantly boost investment, given the long-running evidence on the relative weakness of the interest elasticity of investment relative to other determinants of investment growth. Koepke's recent comprehensive econometric 'horse race' on the relative factors determining investment finds that accelerator and profit/cash flow effects are significantly more powerful than cost of capital/interest-rates changes.[24] This same finding has been supported by Fazzari's (1993, 1994) innovative micro-level research on the determinants of investment.

Using tax policy to promote private investment is, under most circumstances, an even weaker tool. For example, Karier (1994) finds that tax credits to stimulate private investment are highly inefficient: only 12 per cent of the credits are actually spent on new investment. The other 88 per cent are used to pay higher dividends, buy stocks or bonds, or otherwise reduce reliance on external sources of funds.[25] The case for capital-gains tax cuts to spur private investment is still weaker. Such a tax cut is not even targeted to reward new investment *per se*, but rather any increase in asset prices. Such asset price increases are at least as likely to result from short-term manœuvres to raise asset prices—such as increasing dividends or laying-off workers—as from an increase in long-term investment.

This brings us to public consumption and investment as foci for expansionary policy. A strong advantage of both public-spending-targets policy approaches is that the import leakage of the expansion can be minimized, which then strengthens the domestic multiplier and accelerator effects of the expansion.

Getting more specific, what is the difference between a public-consumption versus investment-led expansion? In fact, it is difficult in some cases to distinguish public consumption from investment goods. For example, park maintenance is clearly a consumption good while road construction is an investment good. But what about military spending or health care? We will simply distinguish them conceptually according to whether the spending can be assumed to promote productivity. This allows us then to argue that of the two options, a public-investment-led programme will have the advantage of also forging a strong link between short-term expansion and long-term productivity and sustainability. Thus, a public-investment programme will enable policy-makers to target employment-generating forms of invest-

---

[24] Koepke's research is summarized in Berndt (1991).

[25] This finding is consistent with earlier studies, such as Eisner (1973) and Chirinko and Eisner (1982).

ment, such as in education, health care, and public infrastructure.[26] In addition, through a public-investment expansion, the government can promote a 'transformational growth path' (Nell 1992) through which the economy shifts towards more environmentally benign production techniques. This will then reduce the environmental barriers to growth. Indeed, one of the most promising areas of public-investment expenditure has been in the LA region through the process of downsizing the military economy in that region. Public investments in military conversion have supported the technology and market for environmental, alternative transportation, intelligent vehicle, telecommunications, and mass-transit products, despite meagre support from such projects at the Federal level (Oden *et al.* 1996).

The overall point then is that a public-investment-led expansion is likely to be most effective both through minimizing import leakages and through meshing short and long-term goals of policy. This does not mean that the other targets of expansionary policies should be overlooked completely. Indeed, because each type of expansion path has weaknesses as well as strengths, there are benefits to including both private consumption (its speed of implementation) and public consumption (low import content) as features within an overall package of initiatives whose leading thrust is public investment.

A public-investment-led expansionary programme can, of course, open widespread opportunities for rent-seeking. The only way to control the problem is to create broad-based forms of democratic accountability as the expansionary programme is established. Thus, public investment should initially concentrate on smaller-scale, labour-intensive projects, such as expanding educational or health services, or smaller-scale construction. Such projects create the means for substantial local control over the allocation and management of funds. While this hardly guarantees that the funds will be well-spent, it does encourage the development of local institutions of accountability. By contrast, large-scale public works projects such as airports or subway systems are not only less labour-intensive, but they also create far more openings for large-scale corruption.

ALTERNATIVE STRATEGIES FOR FINANCING EXPANSION

The viability of any expansionary programme will depend to a large degree on how it is financed. It is crucial, of course, that the programme be

---

[26] There has been considerable research in recent years on the effects of public infrastructure investment in productivity growth. The weight of evidence supports the idea that large productivity gains could be achieved (e.g. Munnell 1990). However, even more sceptical analysts do not deny that positive supply-side effects would result (Gramlich 1994). These would be independent of the expansionary impact on the demand side.

financed in a way that minimizes the balance of payments, inflation, and public debt constraints. The programme will also have to minimize the import, saving, and speculative leakages. We consider now the various paths to achieving these ends.

Monetary Expansion

(i) *Money growth unlinked to composition of expansion.* Traditional monetary stimulus certainly cannot be dismissed as an expansionary financing tool, if for no other reason that it is the one instrument that US policymakers are still willing to regard as legitimate. But its limitations also need to be carefully recognized.

The direct relationship between monetary expansion and output stimulus has long ago broken down (Friedman 1988). Development of speculative/innovative financial markets and globalization are the primary factors in weakening the direct relationship between monetary expansion and output growth. As both currency and domestic financial markets are highly speculative, money is used for asset transfers to an increasing extent relative to output purchases (Schaberg 1995; Palley 1996). Moreover, these same factors have created more uncertainty in the relationship between movements in short-term interest rates, which the Fed can control, and long-term rates, which are determined by the market.

Given all this, there is considerable evidence that expansionary policy can stimulate increased activity in the short run. This operates primarily through sectors which are relatively more interest-rate sensitive, namely housing and consumer durables. A decline in short-term interest rates can lead to significant reductions in mortgage payments and in the purchase of consumer durables. In addition, monetary expansion can still act as a stimulant through the channel of dollar depreciation, though global financial integration means that there is increasing pressure for purchasing-power parity among currencies.[27] Finally, though monetary expansion is less successful at stimulating private investment via an interest-rate channel, Fazzari has argued that it can promote investment among liquidity constrained firms independent of interest-rate channels *per se*.

The problem with monetary expansion is that, at its best, the primary stimulus will still be targeted at private-consumption goods. This will mean that the expansion will be weakened by the import leakage. It also means that there is no explicit means of developing a link between short-run expansion and long-run growth.

(ii) *Monetizing government debt.* In this case, the monetary authority itself purchases the government bonds associated with an expansionary

---

[27] The evidence on these effects is summarized in Epstein (1993).

programme. Though some debt monetization now occurs on a routine basis, this is not usually regarded as a viable financing approach for an expansionary policy, though there is no intrinsic reason why this should be so.[28] Monetizing an increase in government spending has the distinct advantage that it will not create distributional problems nor will it increase the debt burden. At the same time, it could create inflationary and exchange-rate problems (which in turn may generate distributional effects). These problems would occur first to the extent that monetary expansion exceeds the growth rate of output. Such a mismatch in growth rates becomes more likely the greater are the import, saving, and speculative leakages from a demand stimulus. But this then means that all of these influences are minimized, at least in the first round of spending, when the monetary expansion is being used to finance explicit public-investment expenditures.

The more likely channel through which such policies can engender negative inflationary and exchange-rate outcomes is through their effect on expectations. The idea that government spending is being financed through monetary expansion will raise inflationary expectations, and thus strong opposition within the rentier class, even if the government spending is well targeted and the country has had a creditable record with similar such efforts.

In general then, though financing through monetization offers clear advantages, it is almost certainly too dangerous as a financing technique unless it is used as a subsidiary measure within a broader set of financing methods. Even then, to minimize the negative expectations resulting from such an action would first require that financial markets have been brought under some significant degree of regulatory control.

Taxation and a Balanced Budget Multiplier

The advantage of an expansionary programme financed through tax increases is that it will minimize the balance of payments, inflation, and public-debt constraints. But the real question is whether such a programme is capable of promoting aggregate expansion and jobs growth.

A balanced-budget programme can be expansionary if the government's tax and revenues are reconfigured to increase employment opportunities explicitly and raise aggregate demand. Three strategies for changing the methods of taxation in the USA seem promising in this regard.

---

[28] This was not always the case. Indeed, the related concept of a 'real bills doctrine' was the guiding idea behind Federal Reserve policy at its inception. It is true that this approach—in which bank notes are lent in exchange for 'real bills', i.e. titles to real value or value in the process of creation—proved itself to be impractical in a strong form (Green 1987). At the same time, the core idea of the doctrine—that central banks should seek to issue reserves in close concern with the non-financial sector's explicit needs for productive financing—remains valid.

The most obvious target for employment-enhancing tax reform is the payroll tax that finances the Social Security system and Medicare. This tax now accounts for 36.7 per cent of all federal receipts, exceeded only by the 43.2 per cent from individual income taxes. From the viewpoint of an employment-generating expansionary programme, this tax has two fundamental drawbacks. The first is that it raises the costs of employment and therefore acts as a disincentive to expand employment. The size of this disincentive is disputable, since it depends on the incidence of the tax, assuming that businesses can pass along at least part of the cost in higher prices. Nevertheless, it is safe to say that there would be positive employment effects if the direct costs of labour were allowed to fall through abolishing the tax. The payroll tax is also highly regressive, in that it allows no deductions or exemptions, it is limited to the portions of income under $61,200, and it only applies to labour income. Thus, substituting a more progressive tax for the payroll tax will redistribute income downward, and thereby weaken the saving leakage on expansionary policy.[29]

A second area that should be targeted would be to tax unproductive activities (that is, following Bhagwati's 1982 definition of 'directly unproductive profit seeking' as activities that may be privately profitable but do not directly increase the flow of goods and services). One example of this type of tax is a securities-transaction excise tax, which would both discourage unproductive speculative finance as well as raise revenue. The level of such a tax could be set according to whether priority is to be given to raising revenue or discouraging speculation. But in countries which have highly active speculative trading, even a low tax rate on such activities would generate substantial revenue. For example, in Japan, the securities-transaction tax raised 4.1 per cent of all government revenue in 1988. In the USA, a transaction tax of 0.5 per cent on equity trades which was then scaled down appropriately by maturity for all bonds and derivative instruments would raise roughly $30b. a year, assuming total trading were to fall by 50 per cent. There are several challenging issues involved in making such a tax neutral and workable, the most important of which is designing it such that domestic taxpayers cannot avoid the tax by moving their trading to alternative domestic markets or offshore. Clearly, the tax implemented in Sweden in 1984 and lifted in 1990 was not designed adequately for avoiding this problem. The tax was levied only on trades arranged by Swedish brokerage services and some assets, such as debentures, were exempt completely. This invited market participants to simply arrange their trading

---

[29] This discussion follows in part Eisner's (1996) proposal for a 'progressive flat tax'. Eisner notes that abolishing the payroll tax does raise concern over the fact that the funds are specifically earmarked to finance Social Security, and that therefore eliminating this source of funds may also then threaten the viability of the Social Security system. To address this, Eisner simply proposes that the requisite portion of the comprehensive income tax be permanently earmarked as a first spending priority for Social Security.

through non-Swedish brokers or to trade assets that were either exempt or traded by counterparties rather than brokers. Alternatively, the tax in the UK was a tax on the transfer of legal ownership of equity shares in the UK. With this much broader and more neutral basis, as Campbell and Froot argue (1993), the British tax has operated much more successfully than that in Sweden.[30]

The other way to support an expansionary programme through taxation would be through a highly progressive income tax or a wealth tax. Unlike a securities-transaction tax, this would not be targeted directly at unproductive activity. It would rather be directed at redistributing resources from high-income households toward the unemployed and working people. The marginal propensity to consume should rise as a result, which is to say that the saving leakage of an expansionary impulse diminishes.[31]

Overall, a well-designed fiscal realignment within a balanced federal budget could have a significant positive multiplier effect. However, it is unlikely that it would be sufficient on its own to generate a strong enough short-term expansion to bring the economy to full employment; it is more likely to be useful in sustaining full employment once it is achieved. It is therefore necessary to consider the much maligned instrument of deficit spending as the final financing source.

Deficit Spending

This is not the place to attempt an extended discussion of this wide-ranging and highly contentious issue. But let us briefly consider what are widely regarded as the two major constraints on such policies, namely 'crowding out' and the burden of the debt.

(i) *Debt burden.* Fiscal deficits can be self-financing in a purely demand-constrained economy. In such a case, the deficit will induce income expansion, which in turn will cover the increased debt burden. Thus, the debt would become burdensome only if the interest obligations rise faster than GDP, and this should not occur as long as the deficit spending is increasing demand by raising the utilization rate of existing capacity. But success at raising utilization rates depends on the import, saving, and speculative leakages: this was the difference in the effects of deficit spending between the 1960s and 1990s. Clearly then, the success of a deficit-financed expansion in the current environment will depend on the specific ways the expenditure programme is designed so as to minimize these leakages.

[30] Baker, Pollin, and Schaberg (1996) provide a discussion on the most effective ways of designing a neutral and broad-based tax in the USA.

[31] Wolff (1996) proposes a Swiss-type wealth tax for the USA for which the average tax rate on household wealth would be 0.2 per cent, and the top marginal rate would be 0.3 per cent. Such a tax would have raised about $40b. in 1994.

(ii) *Crowding out*[32]. The question here is whether borrowing by the federal government necessarily inhibits private firms from undertaking productive investments. There are separable real and financial channels through which this may occur. We have already touched on the real-side channels, as they are manifested through the issue of the Phillips Curve and NAIRU. Let us consider now the financial channel, through which government borrowing is said to absorb national saving to the extent that it makes credit for private investors unavailable or prohibitively expensive. Everything else equal, we can accept the premiss that an increase in the federal government's borrowing will exert some upward pressure on long-term interest rates. But what will be the outcome of this upward pressure? This will depend on the forces determining the supply and demand curves in credit markets. On the supply side of the market, the crucial influence will be the nature of the system of financial intermediation in place, and that system's capacity to innovate. A more innovative financial structure implies that, even with a given supply of national saving and no monetary accommodation, the credit-supply curve can either flatten or shift outward in response to an increase in credit demand. This would mean that the upward interest-rate pressure from an increase in government borrowing is more moderate than in the case when a financial structure is less flexible. Because of the flexibility of the contemporary US financial system, there is no clear direct impact of rising deficits on the level of interest rates.

The effects of the increase in government borrowing will also depend on the demand for funds by potential alternative users. That is, the effects on interest rates of an outward shift in the government credit-demand curve will depend on the level of demand coming from other sectors. For example, the equilibrium level of interest rates following an increase in government-borrowing will be lower if the government borrowing increase is accompanied by a reduction in private credit demand to finance speculative asset transfers. Thus, in some circumstances, a securities-transaction tax or some other policy instrument that discourages borrowing to finance speculative asset transfers might also then reduce any possible crowding-out constraint on government borrowing.

Finally, the full effects of any increase in interest rates due to government borrowing must be evaluated in terms of how much such an interest-rate increase will effect productive investment decisions relative to other factors influencing investment decisions, such as the accelerator, and the rate of profitability. As noted earlier, the preponderance of evidence (e.g. Berndt 1991; Fazzari 1993, 1994–5), finds that the interest elasticity of investment in the contemporary US economy is weak.

In short, the extent to which an increase in government borrowing exerts

---

[32] This discussion follows that in Pollin (1996*b* and 1997).

upward pressure on interest rates available to private investors, and whether such an effect will then 'crowd out' private investment, are both highly contingent. Moreover, the factors influencing both outcomes—e.g. the speculative demand for private credit—can also be influenced by policy initiatives. Finally, any upward interest-rate pressure generated by increased government borrowing can also be countered through monetary expansion. Overall then, deficit financing should be considered a highly effective expansionary tool if it is deployed with care within a broader programme that can maximize the multiplier and accelerator effects of the initial expansionary impulse.

HOW TO RESPOND TO AN EXCHANGE-RATE DEPRECIATION

Even if the types of measures considered above are taken to minimize the external constraint on expansionary policy, it is nevertheless unlikely that such external pressures can be avoided altogether. Financial-market investors are likely to view any egalitarian expansionary policy as an occasion to sell dollars. This will then put upward pressure on domestic interest rates (whether or not the condition of interest parity holds in full). Domestic inflationary pressures will also likely result.

Pressure on the exchange rate will be lowered in so far as the expansionary programme is tax financed, since a tax-financed programme will have no direct effect on the public-sector borrowing requirement or pressures for monetary expansion. Nevertheless, even a purely tax-financed programme is likely to encourage downward pressure on the dollar to the extent that both domestic and foreign rentiers would lose income through the substitution of progressive income tax for the payroll tax, or the imposition of a securities-transaction or wealth tax. In other words, the only type of progressive programme that would not encourage a dollar depreciation would be one that strictly redistributes from working people to the unemployed and very poor. But this programme will also carry no expansionary impulse, and therefore would deliver little to raise living standards or employment opportunities for working people. It is therefore reasonable to expect downward pressure on the exchange rate to accompany any egalitarian-policy agenda. The pertinent question is therefore how serious these pressures would be, and how to address them as they arise.

Given the size of the US economy and the importance of the dollar as a key currency, the nature of the problems it faces here would be unique. On the one hand, there will inevitably be less downward pressure on the dollar due to the vested interest other countries have in maintaining a stable dollar. This is due first of all to the fact that the US import market is so large that other countries will want to maintain the dollar high enough so that their US-bound exports remain competitive. Holders of dollar-denominated financial assets similarly will want to maintain the value of the dollar. These factors will engender policy initiatives by central bankers throughout the world to counteract any downward movement of the dollar. In addition, and probably more important, the foreign demand for physical and financial assets of the USA is likely to remain strong in the foreseeable future, especially given that its closest substitutes, Japanese and German assets, have significant problems of their own. Indeed, given the importance of the dollar and US assets for business, it is quite plausible that an expansionary programme initiated within the USA would provide the basis to initiate international co-operation to pursue expansionary programmes elsewhere. This, of course, would be the most desirable outcome, and it is one that US policy-makers should promote as a piece of their expansionary-policy arsenal.

Short of this, the most likely scenario is that the dollar will depreciate moderately as a result of the expansionary programme. This will then have a favourable effect on the US trade balance. According to Hooper and Marquez's recent study (1995), the elasticity of the US trade account given an exchange-rate depreciation is –1.0, meaning that the trade deficit will contract by 1 per cent for every 1 per cent fall in the dollar relative to the yen. At the same time, the depreciation will worsen the terms of trade for the US and thereby encourage domestic inflation. However, Bryant, Holtham, and Hooper's (1988) survey of econometric models on US trade issues finds that such inflationary effects are moderate. The average result for the models they survey is that a 25 per cent dollar depreciation would produce only a 5 per cent increase in the inflation rate. Overall then, US policy-makers would have little to fear from a moderate dollar depreciation following an expansionary initiative. In fact, the depreciation would moderate the rise of import demand that would result from the expansion of domestic incomes.

Because of the central role of the USA, there is, however, the danger that should there be a real move to dump the dollar and allow it to depreciate significantly, this could create a crisis of great severity. This is an unlikely scenario. However, the conditions that are most likely to encourage it would be if domestic inflation were to appear to be out of control.

In this regard, it is instructive to compare two recent periods—1976–9 and 1990–2—in which US interest rates declined significantly. In the 1976–9 period, the interest-rate decline precipitated a run on the dollar. This was the severe dollar crisis which eventually led to the installation of Paul Volcker as the Chair of the Federal Reserve and his imposition of a draconian policy of high interest rates. In the 1990–2 period, the fall in domestic interest rates did produce a fall in the dollar, but nowhere near to the previous extent. One important difference is that in the first experience, domestic inflation was much higher than in Germany, and in the second case it was not. More generally, in the first case, the US economy was perceived as weak relative to Japan and Germany, while in the second period overall, the US economy was relatively strong and stable.[33]

What this suggests is that pressure on the dollar should not reach a crisis stage in the USA as long as domestic inflation is not considered to be out of control. This conclusion would argue in favour of some form of incomes policy to prevent inflationary pressures from getting too strong during expansion. And as noted earlier, an incomes policy in the contemporary USA which linked wage increases to aggregate productivity growth would represent a significant gain for workers relative to the experience of the past twenty years.

LONG-TERM RESTRUCTURING TO SUSTAIN FULL EMPLOYMENT

Slow output growth has been a major cause of the rise of the contingent work-force of underemployed people. Lester Thurow writes that:

there are 8.1 million American workers in temporary jobs, 2 million who work 'on call' and 8.3 million self-employed 'independent contractors' (many of whom are downsized professionals who have very few clients but call themselves self-employed consultants because they are too proud to admit that they are unemployed). Most of these more than 18 million people are looking for more work and better jobs. Together these contingent workers account for 14 per cent of the workforce. (1996: 56)

A successful expansionary policy should provide the basis for reversing the trend toward contingent work arrangements. When labour markets tighten, competition intensifies among firms for workers at all skill levels. As we saw, this is what occurred during the Vietnam-led expansion of the 1960s, when *Business Week* reported that firms were 'importing, upgrading, and training labor with increasing facility and ingenuity', and that they were increasingly recruiting women, Blacks, and other minorities, expanding their job-training programmes, and providing more opportunities and incentives for promotion.

The more difficult question to raise is, once expansionary policy creates pressure to reconstitute the rudiments of an internal labour market, what form should such new work arrangements take? It is widely recognized that the system that operated in the first half of the post-World War II era was excessively hierarchical, inefficient, and, as such, a contributor to the

---

[33] This discussion follows Epstein (1993).

productivity slowdown that began in the late 1960s.[34] This system emerged initially as a result of the labour shortages resulting from World War I. The aim of firms was to retain workers in the tight market, thereby minimizing the costs of search and turnover. This led to the development of personnel departments of large firms that established clear hierarchies in the workplace. This enabled firms to monitor workers' performance more systematically, and thus to seek to minimize shirking that might otherwise occur when tight labour markets reduced the cost of job loss. Corresponding to this development was the spread of mass assembly-line production technologies, following Frederick Taylor's 'scientific management' production system. The assembly line/Taylorist system was premissed on the idea that production could be run efficiently with a few highly educated and skilled workers, with the majority of front-line workers having little more than basic literacy and numeracy skills. According to Taylor, the point was to give management almost complete control over the 'one best' production method, through allowing all challenging tasks to be performed by either management or machines.

Beginning with World War II, another period of tight labour markets, this system was developed further through the proliferation of the bureaucratic procedures associated with internal labour markets, that is, personnel departments, centralized employment procedures, rating systems, and seniority provisions. These bureaucratic procedures combined with the highly formal relationships established through labour law of labour unions with both firms and their members, including a highly bureaucratic, legalistic grievance procedure. The result was a rigid and alienating work environment.[35]

Thus, the demise of this system of internal labour markets is not to be mourned. To the extent that it still operates, its deficiencies are even more glaring in the contemporary world of advanced production systems and intensified global competition. This environment requires the ability to produce high-quality products and to alter the composition of output frequently to meet changing market demand. The really damaging effects of the slack labour markets of recent years is not therefore that it has undermined the old internal labour-market system. The problem rather is that contingent labour arrangements governed by the free market, that which has increasingly supplanted the old system, is an even worse alternative (Marshall 1996).

---

[34] However, as noted above, it is unlikely that this was the sole cause of the productivity slowdown since, among other things, the decline in productivity was not consistent across industries, as one would expect to observe if the cause of the slowdown was the generalized mode of work organization.

[35] Some basic references on this are Gordon, Edwards, and Reich (1982), Osterman (1984), Baron, Dobbin and Jennings (1986), Cappeli (1996), and Fairris (1997).

Given this, using expansionary policy to create a fully employed labour market will provide an opportunity not to recreate the old system but to produce a new 'high performance' system. The main elements of high-performance systems have been widely discussed, and indeed, are already operating in a small number of US firms, as well as being in much more widespread usage elsewhere. Among the new approaches to organizing and managing work are quality circles and continuous improvement in Japanese firms; worker participation in plant-level and strategic management decision-making in German companies; autonomous teams of workers who are responsible for decision-making in Swedish operations; and interfirm networks, which are responsive to changing market conditions, in Italian and German industrial districts (Appelbaum and Batt, 1994).

However, even in tight labour-market conditions, it does not follow that any version of a new internal-labour market will emerge spontaneously. This is first of all because managers remain highly resistant to relinquishing authority and privilege within a more democratic workplace (Gordon 1996). In addition, there are significant initial start-up investments to creating a high-performance work system, even while recognizing that these costs achieve long-term productivity gains in the longer run. These initial investments costs are not evaluated favourably by financial markets. This is in part the result of the general short-term bias emanating from the highly liquid capital markets in the USA. But in addition, financial-market analysts take a sceptical view of arrangements through which workplace power devolves away from managers. Thus, Appelbaum and Berg (1996) report on the results of a 1995 survey of senior line and human-resource executives at mid-sized and large US companies. The survey found that 98 per cent of respondents agreed that improving employee performance would significantly improve business results while 73 per cent said that their company's most important investment was in people. Still, when asked to rank a number of business priorities, the respondents put performance of people and investment in people near the end of the list, well below standard measures of financial performance.

As a result, even in a tight labour-market environment, it will require the strong intervention of public policy to create such a new internal labour-market model. The tight labour market will create the preconditions for such policy initiatives to be considered seriously. But if they are not implemented when the labour market is tight, it is almost certainly the case that a rising-wage/high-productivity/full-employment economy will not be sustainable.

FINANCIAL MARKET RESTRUCTURING[36]

As presently organized, the financial system in the USA does present formidable obstacles to the successful pursuit of national full-employment policies. As we have briefly discussed above, these include the rise of speculative finance and short-term bias in corporate-planning horizons; the increased instability of the financial system, which has made cyclical upturns less stable and downturns more severe than they would be otherwise; and the deflationary policy bias of rentiers and their political allies. Within this context, policies would be needed to accomplish three things: lengthen time horizons and reduce the tendency toward speculative finance; counteract the factors which weaken the effects of expansionary fiscal and monetary policy; and reduce the political power of the rentier class.

The policy interventions that would be most important for accomplishing these aims would include, first, a set of financial regulatory policies which 'levelled the playing field upward' among all financial intermediaries. A substantial inducement toward financial innovation has been simply to exploit differences in how intermediaries are regulated. A consistent regulatory environment would obviously eliminate such opportunities, and would therefore strengthen the impact of any given set of regulations.[37]

In addition, the most important set of policies would be those which increased incentives toward productive investment and employment creation and weakened those for speculative asset transfers. In addition to the securities-transaction tax mentioned above, several policy instruments could be used here, many of which are already part of existing law. One is the existing Community Reinvestment Act. This law obligates banks to lend for projects among under-served areas of the communities in which they are located. This law has not been seriously enforced by the Federal Reserve, the agency responsible for enforcement. But if the CRA were extended to include all intermediaries, not just banks, and were then seriously enforced on a uniform basis, it would have a significant impact on the composition of both lending and investment throughout the country.[38]

A similar approach could be taken with the investment of pension funds. Although pension funds are heavily subsidized by government policy, they are not required to consider the social rate of return on their investments. This is so, despite the fact that such a calculation is fully consistent with what Barber and Ghilarducci describe as fund participants' 'whole identities: as workers who need employment to accumulate retirement income, as citizens whose quality of life depends on the economic health of their com-

---

[36] This discussion follows that in Pollin (1996*b*).
[37] Discussion on this question began with the innovative work of D'Arista and Schlesinger (1993).   [38] See Campen (1993) on this question.

munities, [and] as parents who want their children to have as much or more opportunity than their parents had' (1993: 291). It is true that vexing problems stand in the way of implementing such an approach to pension-fund investing. For example, how would a single pension fund capture for its own community the social rate of return accruing to that funds' investments? But these problems are becoming less formidable as experience is gained with such investment strategies.

A third instrument of this kind could be Federal Reserve policy itself (see Pollin 1993*b*). For example, the Federal Reserve could use asset requirements for financial institutions to promote investments with high social rates of return, and discourage short-time horizons and speculation. Something like this has already been implemented on a large scale in the USA with, for example, the long-standing asset requirements that were applied to the Savings and Loan industry. Up until they were deregulated in 1980, the S&Ls were required to concentrate their lending almost entirely on individual family-home mortgages. These policies were extremely successful in promoting home ownership among the non-rich to an unprecedented degree. Comparable policies could be successful in promoting investments with high social rates of return, including high-employment multipliers, and to discourage speculative finance.

All of these policies would increase the power of government regulators over the financial system. It would therefore be necessary to increase the accountability of the regulators to the public, which would then also increase the accountability of the financial system more broadly. Several proposals for extending accountability have been formulated, including within the US Congress. One suggestion (in Pollin 1993*b*) calls for direct election of the Presidents of the regional Federal Reserve Banks. Such increased accountability would also address—though never entirely solve—the legitimate concerns that public-allocation policies would degenerate into rent-seeking and other hidden costs to the economy.

Overall, these financial-market policies, pursued in conjunction with a short-term expansionary programme, would be supportive of a sustained full-employment growth path in three ways:

1. Investments induced by the accelerator effects of expansionary policies would be channelled increasingly toward investments with high social rates of return, including high-employment multipliers, and away from asset transfers that absorb financial resources but do not increase output and income. This would reduce the 'speculative leakage' of expansionary policy.
2. Lowering the level of speculative activity will also reduce the amplitude of cyclical activity, and thus the need for policy interventions to stabilize cycles.

3. Creating more accountability within the financial system would weaken the power of financial capitalists in the system. This, in turn would reduce the bias against expansionary policies.

CONCLUSION

Can an expansionary government intervention bring full employment, rising wages, and greater equality to the United States? In part, the answer must necessarily be 'yes', since we have seen that the Vietnam-led expansion achieved these things in the 1960s. But of course, the more pressing question is whether these attainments of the 1960s could be reproduced in the current setting. Here the answer must be 'it depends'. Not all types of government-induced expansions will yield equally desirable outcomes. Indeed, a Reaganite expansion—one in which there are no constraints on imports, financial speculation, or upward income distribution and no efforts to link expansion with productive investment or employment growth—is clearly unsustainable. However, we have tried to show that a policy which does pay careful attention to the composition of expansion, the alternative forms of financing, and the longer-term needs for financial and labour-market restructuring can indeed yield results similar to those achieved in the 1960s.

Of course, the challenge would be less formidable if expansionary policies could be co-ordinated throughout the OECD. This would produce a virtuous growth cycle in which concerns over import leakages and the exchange rate would be reduced. However, we cannot expect that international co-operation in support of full-employment policies will occur in a political vacuum. That vacuum could be filled through the success of a domestic expansionary programme in the United States, and the positive demonstration effects this would have throughout the world. We have tried to show that this is not beyond our reach today.

REFERENCES

Appelbaum, Eileen and Batt, Rosemary (1994), *The New American Workplace: Transforming Work Systems in the United States* (Ithaca, NY: ILR Press).
—— —— and Berg, Peter (1996), 'Financial Market Constraints and Business Strategy in the U.S.', in J. Michie and J. Grieve Smith (eds.), *Creating Industrial Capacity: Towards Full Employment* (Oxford: Oxford University Press), 192–224.
Arrighi, Giovanni (1994), *The Long Twentieth Century: Money, Power and the Origins of our Times* (London: Verso Press).
Baker, Dean, Pollin, Robert, and Schaberg, Marc (1996), 'The Case for A Securities

Transaction Excise Tax: Taxing the Big Casino', MS, Dept. of Economics, University of California-Riverside.

—— —— and Zahrt, Elizabeth (1996), 'The Vietnam War and the Political Economy of Full Employment', *Challenge* (May–June), 35–45.

Barber, Randy and Ghilarducci, Teresa (1993), 'Pension Funds, Capital Markets, and the Economic Future', in G. Dymski, G. Epstein, and R. Pollin (eds.), *Transforming the U.S. Financial System: Equity and Efficiency for the 21st Century* (Armonk, NY: M. E. Sharpe), 287–320.

Baron, James N., Dobbin, Frank R., and Jennings, P. Devereaux (1986), 'War and Peace: The Evolution of Modern Personnel Administration in U.S. Industry', *American Journal of Sociology*, 92/2: 350–83.

Berndt, Ernst R. (1991), *The Practice of Econometrics: Classic and Contemporary* (Reading, Mass.: Addison-Wesley).

Bhagwati, Jadish (1982), 'Directly Unproductive Profit-Seeking Activity', *Journal of Political Economy*, 90/5: 998–1002.

Blair, Margaret M. and Schary, Martha A. (1994), 'Industry-Level Indicators of Free Cash Flow', in M. Blair (ed.), *The Deal Decade: What Takeovers and Leveraged Buyouts Mean for Corporate Governance* (Washington, DC: The Brookings Institution), 99–135.

Blanchard, Olivier and Summers, Lawrence (1988), 'Beyond the Natural Rate Hypothesis', *American Economic Review Papers and Proceedings*, 78: 182–7.

Blinder, Alan (1980), 'The Level and Distribution of Economic Well-Being', in M. Feldstein (ed.), *The American Economy in Transition* (Chicago: University of Chicago Press), 415–79.

Bowles, Samuel, Gordon, David M., and Weisskopf, Thomas E. (1983), *Beyond the Wasteland: A Democratic Alternative to Economic Decline* (New York: Anchor Press Doubleday).

Brenner, Robert (1996), 'Uneven Development and the Long Downturn', *New Left Review*, forthcoming.

Bruno, Michael (1995), 'Does Inflation Really Lower Growth?', *Finance and Development* (Sept.), 35–8.

Bryant, Ralph C., Holtham, Gerald, and Hooper, Peter (1988), 'Consensus and Diversity in the Model Simulations', in R. Bryant, D. Henderson, G. Holtham, P. Hooper, and S. Symansky (eds.), *Empirical Macroeconomics for Interdependent Economies* (Washington, DC: The Brookings Institution), 27–62.

Bunting, David (1991), 'Savings and the Distribution of Income', *Journal of Post-Keynesian Economics*, 14/1: 3–22.

Campbell, John Y. and Froot, Kenneth A. (1993), 'Securities Transaction Taxes: Lessons from International Experience', NBER Working Paper, No. 4587.

Campen, James T. (1993), 'Banks, Communities and Public Policy', in G. Dymski, G. Epstein, and R. Pollin (eds.), *Transforming the U.S. Financial System: Equity and Efficiency for the 21st Century* (Armonk, NY: M. E. Sharpe), 221–52.

Cappeli, Peter (1996), 'Rethinking Employment', *British Journal of Industrial Relations*, forthcoming.

Carroll, Chris and Summers, Lawrence (1991), 'Consumption Growth Parallels Income Growth: Some New Evidence', in B. D. Bernheim and J. B. Shoven (eds.),

National Saving and Economic Performance (Chicago: University of Chicago Press), 305–48.

Chirinko, Robert S. and Eisner, Robert (1982), 'The Effects of Tax Parameters in the Investment Equations in Macroeconometric Models', in M. Blume, J. Crockett, and P. Taubman (eds.), *Economic Activity and Finance* (Cambridge, Mass.: Ballinger), 25–84.

Cross, Rod (1995) (ed.), *The Natural Rate of Unemployment: Reflections on 25 Years of the Hypothesis* (Cambridge: Cambridge University Press).

Crotty, James, Epstein, Gerald, and Kelly, Patricia (1995), 'Multinational Corporations and Technological Change: Global Stagnation, Inequality, and Unemployment', MS, University of Massachusetts-Amherst.

D'Arista, Jane and Schlesinger, Tom (1993), 'The Parallel Banking System', in G. *Dymski, G. Epstein, and R. Pollin (eds.), Transforming the U.S. Financial System: Equity and Efficiency for the 21st Century* (Armonk, NY: M. E. Sharpe, 157–200).

Davidson, Paul (1996), 'The Viability of Keynesian Demand Management In an Open Economy Context', *International Review of Applied Economics*, 10/1: 91–106.

Donohue, John J. III and Heckman, James (1991), 'Continuous versus Episodic Change: The Impact of Civil Rights Policy on the Economic Status of Blacks', *Journal of Economic Literature* (Dec.), 1603–43.

Dornbusch, Rudiger and Simonsen, Mario Henrique (1983) (eds.), *Inflation, Debt, and Indexation* (Cambridge, Mass.: MIT Press).

Eatwell, John (1994), 'The Coordination of Macroeconomic Policy in the European Community', in J. Michie and J. Grieve Smith (eds.), *Unemployment in Europe* (London: Academic Press), 209–19.

Eckstein, Otto (1978), *The Great Recession* (Amsterdam: North-Holland).

Eisner, Robert (1973), 'Tax Incentives for Investment', *National Tax Journal*, (Sept.), 397–401.

—— (1995), 'A New View of the NAIRU', unpubl. MS, Dept. of Economics, Northwestern University, Ill.

—— (1996), 'Tax Reform: A Progressive Flat Tax', in T. Schafer and J. Faux (eds.), *Reclaiming Prosperity: A Blueprint for Progressive Economic Reform* (Armonk, NY: M. E. Sharpe), 79–92.

Epstein, Gerald (1993), 'Monetary Policy in the 1990s: Overcoming the Barriers to Equity and Growth', in G. Dymski, G. Epstein, and R. Pollin (eds.), *Transforming the U.S. Financial System: Equity and Efficiency for the 21st Century* (Armonk, NY: M. E. Sharpe), 65–100.

—— and Schor, Juliet (1990), 'Macropolicy in the Rise and Fall of the Golden Age', in S. Marglin and J. Schor (eds.), *The Golden Age of Capitalism: Reinterpreting the Postwar Experience* (New York: Oxford University Press), 126–52.

Fairris, David (1997), *Shopfloor Matters* (New York: Routledge), forthcoming.

Fazzari, Steven (1993), 'Monetary Policy, Financial Structure and Investment', in G. Dymski, G. Epstein, and R. Pollin (eds.), *Transforming the U.S. Financial System: Equity and Efficiency for the 21st Century* (Armonk, NY: M. E. Sharpe), 35–64.

—— (1994), 'Why Doubt the Effectiveness of Keynesian Fiscal Policy?', *Journal of Post-Keynesian Economics*, 17/2: 231–48.

Fischer, Stanley (1978), 'The Demand for Indexed Bonds', in Marshall Sarnat (ed.), *Inflation and Capital Markets* (Cambridge, Mass.: Ballinger), 213–42.

—— (1983), 'Welfare Aspects of Government Issue of Indexed Bonds', in R. Dornbusch and M. Simonsen (eds.), *Inflation, Debt, and Indexation* (Cambridge, Mass.: MIT Press), 223–46.

Friedman, Benjamin (1988), 'Lessons of Monetary Policy from the 1980s', *Journal of Economic Perspectives*, 2/3: 51–72.

Friedman, Milton (1966), 'What Price Guidelines?', in G. Schultz and R. Aliber (eds.), *Guidelines, Informal Controls and the Market Place: Policy Choices in a Full Employment Economy* (Chicago: University of Chicago Press), 17–40.

—— (1974), 'Monetary Correction', in his *Essays in Inflation and Indexation* (Washington, DC: American Enterprise Institute).

Glyn, Andrew, Hughes, Alan, Lipietz, Alain, and Singh, Ajit (1990), 'The Rise and Fall of the Golden Age', in S. Marglin and J. Schor (eds.), *The Golden Age of Capitalism: Reinterpreting the Postwar Experience* (New York: Oxford University Press), 39–125.

Gordon, David M. (1988), 'The Un-Natural Rate of Unemployment: An Econometric Critique of the NAIRU Hypothesis', *American Economic Review Papers and Proceedings*, 78: 117–23.

—— (1995), 'Growth, Distribution and the Rules of the Game: Left Structuralist Macro Foundations for a Democratic Economic Policy', in G. Epstein and H. Gintis (eds.), *Macroeconomic Policy After the Conservative Era: Studies in Investment, Saving and Finance* (Cambridge: Cambridge University Press).

—— (1996), *Fat and Mean: The Corporate Squeeze of Working Americans and the Myth of Managerial 'Downsizing'* (New York: Free Press).

——, Edwards, Richard, and Reich, Michael (1982), *Segmented Work; Divided Workers* (Cambridge: Cambridge University Press).

Gramlich, Edward M. (1994), 'Infrastructure Investment: A Review Essay', *Journal of Economic Literature*, 32/3: 1176–96.

Green, Roy (1987), 'The Real Bills Doctrine', in J. Eatwell, M. Milgate, and P. Neuman (eds.), *The New Palgrave Dictionary of Money and Finance* (London and Basingstoke: Macmillan), 101–2.

Hooper, Peter and Marquez, Jaime (1995), 'Exchange Rate, Prices and External Adjustment in the U.S. and Japan', in P. Kenen (ed.), *Understanding Interdependence: The Macroeconomics of Open Economies*, 107–68.

Karier, T. (1994), 'Investment Tax Credit Reconsidered: Business Tax Incentives and Investments', Public Policy Brief no. 13 (Annandale-on-Hudson, NY: Jerome Levy Economics Institute of Bard College).

Marglin, Steven and Bhaduri, Amit (1990), 'Profit Squeeze and Keynesian Theory', in S. Marglin and J. Schor (eds.), *The Golden Age of Capitalism: Reinterpreting the Postwar Experience* (New York: Oxford University Press).

Marshall, Ray (1996), 'Work Organization', in T. Schafer and J. Faux (eds.), *Reclaiming Prosperity: A Blueprint for Progressive Economic Reform* (Armonk, NY: M. E. Sharpe), 79–92.

Mishel, Lawrence and Bernstein, Jared (1994), *The State of Working America* (Armonk, NY: M. E. Sharpe).

Moseley, Fred and Wolff, Edward N. (1992) (eds.), *International Perspectives on Profitability and Accumulation* (Brookfield, Vt.: Edward Elgar).

Munnell, Alice (1990) (ed.), *Is There a Shortfall in Public Capital Investment?*, Conference Series no. 34 (Boston: Federal Reserve Bank of Boston).

—— and Grolnic, Joseph B. (1986), 'Should the U.S. Government Issue Index Bonds?', *New England Economic Review* (Sept./Oct.), 3–21.

Nell, E. (1992), *Transformational Growth and Effective Demand* (London: Macmillan).

Oden, Michael, Markusen, Ann, Flaming, Dan, and Drayse, Mark 'Post Cold War Frontiers: Defense Downsizing and Conversion in Los Angeles', Working Paper no. 105, Center for Urban Policy Research (New Brunswick, NJ: Rutgers University).

Okun, Arthur M. (1970), *The Political Economy of Prosperity* (Washington, DC: The Brookings Institution).

Ormerod, Paul (1994), 'On Inflation and Unemployment', in J. Michie and J. Grieve Smith (eds.), *Unemployment in Europe* (London: Academic Press), 45–60.

Osterman, Paul (1984) (ed.), *Internal Labor Markets* (Cambridge, Mass.: MIT Press).

Palley, Thomas (1996), 'The Demand for Money and Non-GDP Transactions', *Economic Letters*, forthcoming.

Pollin, Robert (1992), 'Destabilizing Finance Worsened This Recession', *Challenge*, 35/2: 17–24.

—— (1993*a*), 'Budget Deficits and the U.S. Economy: Considerations in a Heilbronerian Mode', in R. Blackwell, J. Chatha, and E. J. Nell (eds.), *Economics as Wordly Philosophy: Essays in Political and Historical Economics in Honour of Robert L. Heilbroner* (New York: St. Martin's Press), 107–44.

—— (1993*b*), 'Public Credit Allocation through the Federal Reserve: Why It Is Needed: How It Should Be Done', in G. Dymski, G. Epstein, and R. Pollin (eds.), *Transforming the U.S. Financial System: Equity and Efficiency for the 21st Century* (Armonk, NY: M. E. Sharpe), 321–54.

—— (1996*a*), 'Borrowing More but Investing Less: Economic Stagnation and the Rise of Corporate Takeovers in the U.S.', MS, Dept. of Economics, University of California-Riverside.

—— (1996*b*), 'Saving and Finance: Real and Illusory Constraints on Full Employment Policy', in J. Michie and J. Grieve Smith (eds.), *Restoring Full Employment: Rebuilding Industrial Capacity* (Oxford: Oxford University Press), 254–88.

—— (1997), 'Financial Intermediation and the Variability of the Saving Constraint', in R. Pollin (ed.), *The Macroeconomics of Finance, Saving and Investment* (Ann Arbor: University of Michigan Press), forthcoming.

Rosenberg, Sam and Weisskopf, Thomas E. (1981), 'A Conflict Theory Approach to Inflation in the Postwar U.S. Economy', *American Economic Review*, 71/2 (May), 42–7.

Ross, Arthur M. (1966), 'Guideline Policy—Where We Are and How We Got There', in G. Schultz and R. Aliber (eds.), *Guidelines, Informal Controls and the Market Place: Policy Choices in a Full Employment Economy* (Chicago: University of Chicago Press), 97–142.

Rowthorn, Bob (1977), 'Conflict, Inflation and Money', *Cambridge Journal of Economics*, 1/3 (Sept.), 215–39.

—— and Glyn, Andrew (1990), 'The Diversity of Unemployment Experience since 1973', in S. Marglin and J. Schor (eds.), *The Golden Age of Capitalism: Reinterpreting the Postwar Experience* (New York: Oxford University Press), 218–66.

Sargent, Thomas (1993), *Bounded Rationality in Macroeconomics* (Oxford: Clarendon Press).

Schaberg, Marc (1995), 'Fluctuations in the Velocity of Money: What Puzzle?', MS, Dept. of Economics, University of California-Riverside.

Schultz, George and Aliber, Robert (1966) (eds.), *Guidelines, Informal Controls and the Market Place: Policy Choices in a Full Employment Economy* (Chicago: University of Chicago Press), 97–142.

Sheahan, John (1967), *The Wage–Price Guideposts* (Washington, DC: The Brookings Institution).

Shen, Pu (1995), 'Benefits and Limitations of Inflation Indexed Treasury Bonds', *Federal Reserve Bank of Kansas City Economic Review*, 80/3: 41–56.

Smith, James P. and Welsh, Finis R. (1989), 'Black Economic Progress After Myrdal', *Journal of Economic Literature* (June), 519–64.

Steinherr, Alfred (1978), 'Indexation of Monetary Assets and Credit Instruments', in Marshall Sarnat (ed.), *Inflation and Capital Markets* (Cambridge, Mass.: Ballinger), 149–78.

Taylor, Jim (1974), *Unemployment and Wage Inflation with Special Reference to Britain and the USA* (New York: Longman).

Thurow, Lester (1996), 'The Crusade that's Killing Prosperity', *The American Prospect* (Mar./Apr.), 54–9.

Tobin, James (1971), 'An Essay on the Principles of Debt Management', in his *Essays in Economics*, i: *Macroeconomics* (Chicago: Markham), 378–455.

Walker, John F. and Vatter, Harold G. (1982), 'The Princess and the Pea: Or the Alleged Vietnam War Origins of the Current Inflation', *Journal of Economic Issues* (June), 597–608.

Weidenbaum, Murray (1967), *Economic Impact of the Vietnam War* (Washington, DC: Center for Strategic Studies, Georgetown University).

Weiner, Stuart (1983), 'Why Are So Few Financial Assets Indexed to Inflation?', *Federal Reserve Bank of Kansas City Economic Review* (May), 3–18.

Wolff, Edward (1979), 'The Distributional Effects of the 1969–75 Inflation on Holdings of Household Wealth in the United States', *Review of Income and Wealth*, 25: 195–207.

—— (1996), *Top Heavy: A Study of the Increasing Inequality of Wealth in America* (New York: The Twentieth Century Fund).

Wolfson, Martin (1994), *Financial Crises: Understanding the Postwar U.S. Experience* (Armonk, NY: M. E. Sharpe), 2nd edn.

3. Effective Demand and Disguised Unemployment

John Eatwell

COMMON AND DIVERGENT FACTORS DETERMINING UNEMPLOYMENT

Two issues have dominated the employment experience of the major industrial countries over the past twenty years: first, the common rise in unemployment throughout the G7; second, the diversity in the scale and content of that rise as between the countries of the European Union (i.e. the twelve member states as in 1994) on the one hand, and Japan and North America (particularly the United States) on the other. A satisfactory analysis of the rise in unemployment should encompass both the common and the diverse aspects of the problem.

In Eatwell (1995) I examined the common experience of the G7 countries. All G7 countries' long-term trends in unemployment since the War show a distinct break at some time around 1970. Up to that time unemployment rates were at historically low levels in all G7 countries. So low that it is not unreasonable to talk of a period of 'full' employment, or of a 'Golden Age', as the major capitalist economies grew faster than they had ever before, or have ever since (Marglin and Schor 1990). But after the early 1970s unemployment levels show a distinct rise in all G7 countries (see Table 3.1).

Table 3.1. Unemployment in the G7, 1964–1973 and 1983–1992

	A. 1964–73	B. 1983–92	B/A
Canada	4.23	9.64	2.28
France	2.23	9.70	4.35
Germany	0.79	6.03	7.63
Italy	5.48	10.13	1.85
Japan	1.22	2.71	2.22
UK	2.94	9.79	3.33
USA	4.46	6.69	1.50

Note: Annual standardized unemployment rates as percentage of the labour-force, averaged for each 10-year period.

Source: OECD, *Main Economic Indicators*.

The common increase in unemployment has been accompanied by considerable diversity in the scale and composition of that increase. Not only
has the increase in unemployment in the United States, Canada, Japan, and
Italy been relatively low, but this was at a time when these countries (other
than Italy) experienced relatively rapid labour-force growth.

The high rates of labour-force growth in North America and Japan have
been matched by high rates of job creation. In North America there has
been an 80 per cent increase in the number of jobs since 1960. In Japan the
number of jobs has increased by 40 per cent. In the European Union
employment has increased by only 10 per cent. Of course, comparing rates
of 'job creation' does not mean very much. It would have been impossible
for the European Union to 'create' as many jobs as North America, simply
because the European rate of population growth was so much lower. The
fundamental question is not why European job creation has been low in
absolute terms, but why job creation in Europe did not keep pace with its
(slower) rate of population growth.

The *OECD Jobs Study* (1994a: 13) argued that 'The high incidence of
long-term unemployment in most EU countries is associated with low
inflow rates into unemployment. The opposite relationship—low incidence
of long-term unemployment and high inflows into unemployment—holds
for N. America.' In Japan inflows and long-term unemployment were both
low. The result of all these changes is that while Japan has remained a country with very low unemployment, the European Union, which in the 1960s
had average unemployment rates a little over 50 per cent of those in North
America, now has unemployment rates which are almost 150 per cent of
American rates.

There are, of course, a wide variety of factors which may affect these
trends, including the age structure of the population, government employment schemes, 'labour-hoarding', and employment in the 'black economy'.
I have argued that whilst these effects may have some influence, the most
important determinant of the *common* experience of growing unemployment
has been the slow-down in the growth of aggregate demand in the 1980s
throughout the G7 (Eatwell 1995). In this chapter I will suggest that the
differential experience of the G7 countries is attributable to the interaction
between changes in the growth of effective demand and national labour-
market structures.

The emphasis in this chapter on the role of the growth of effective
demand makes the approach quite different from that adopted in conventional analyses of employment (e.g. Drèze and Bean 1990; Layard, Nickell
and Jackman 1991; Bean 1994; OECD 1994a). The conventional approach
seeks to explain the differential employment experience of Europe and
North America primarily in terms of imperfections in the operation of
the labour market. The clear implication is that if the labour-market

imperfection were absent then the economy would converge to full employment.[1] It should be noted that this argument typically embodies a serious theoretical error, namely in presuming that a 'well-behaved' labour market is sufficient to ensure full employment. Suppose, for example, that the volume of investment is totally inelastic with respect to the interest rate, and that the propensity to save is positive. Then even a perfectly well-behaved labour market will not ensure full employment.

The analysis which follows adopts a simple Keynesian perspective. The level of effective demand is taken as an independent variable (at least in what will be identified as the 'advanced' sector of the economy), and accordingly unemployment is not attributable to the presence of imperfections, but to the fact that the level of effective demand (or, over time, the rate of growth of effective demand) is too low.[2]

Whilst the behaviour of effective demand is the key to the common growth in G7 unemployment, the characteristics of national labour markets are important in the analysis of their differential experience. For, as will be shown, it is the impact of labour-market policies which determine whether there is any employment *in excess of that which might be expected from the growth in effective demand.* The factors influencing this 'additional' employment will be the main focus of this chapter. It will be argued that the additional employment is likely to be greater wherever unemployment benefits are either low or of short duration, or where low-productivity employment is subsidized or protected. The scale of additional employment is determined by the supply of labour. The activities undertaken by the additionally employed will be characterized by significantly lower productivity than is typical of the advanced sector of the economy. This additional employment is, in fact, disguised unemployment, in the precise sense that a higher level of effective demand would result in workers being reallocated to jobs with much higher productivity per person employed. In this chapter I will both analyse the origins and structure of disguised unemployment, and provide an illustrative estimate of the magnitude of disguised unemployment from 1979 to 1990.

---

[1] For a critical review of theories of unemployment which are based on 'imperfections' which inhibit the operation of a market mechanism which would otherwise ensure the maintenance of full employment, at least in the long run, see Eatwell and Milgate (1983).

[2] Nor is the level of effective demand itself regarded as a function of relative prices. The role of market imperfections (typically rigid wages or prices, but including the impact of 'uncertainty' or 'false conjectures') in models of unemployment is examined in some detail in Eatwell and Milgate (1983). The objective of this chapter is to present a positive interpretation of the unemployment experience of the G7. Hence critical analysis of alternative explanations is at a minimum.

DISGUISED UNEMPLOYMENT: ANALYSIS

The approach adopted in this chapter is based on ideas first developed by Joan Robinson (1937). She argued that the level of employment in the economy was determined as the sum of the employment determined by effective demand (taken as an independent variable) and the level of *disguised unemployment*. She defined disguised unemployment in the following manner:

In a society in which there is no regular system of unemployment benefit, and in which poor relief is either non-existent or 'less eligible' than almost any alternative short of suicide, a man who is thrown out of work must scratch up a living somehow or other by means of his own efforts. And under any system in which complete idleness is not a statutory condition for drawing the dole, a man who cannot find a regular job will naturally employ his time as usefully as he may. Thus, except under peculiar conditions, a decline in effective demand which reduces the amount of employment offered in the general run of industries will not lead to 'unemployment' in the sense of complete idleness, but will rather drive workers into a number of occupations—selling match-boxes in the Strand, cutting brushwood in the jungles, digging potatoes on allotments—which are still open to them. A decline in one sort of employment leads to an increase in another sort, and at first sight it may appear that, in such a case, a decline in effective demand does not cause unemployment at all. But the matter must be more closely examined. In all those occupations which the dismissed workers take up, their productivity is less than in the occupations that they have left. For if it were not so they would have engaged in them already. The wage received by a man who remains in employment in a particular industry measures the marginal physical productivity of a similar man who has been dismissed from it, and if the latter could find an occupation yielding him a better return, he would not have waited for dismissal to take it up. Thus a decline in demand for the product of the general run of industries leads to a diversion of labour from occupations in which productivity is higher to others where it is lower. The cause of this diversion, a decline in effective demand, is exactly the same as the cause of unemployment in the ordinary sense, and it is natural to describe the adoption of inferior occupations by dismissed workers as *disguised unemployment*. (Robinson 1937: 83–4)

Joan Robinson went on to argue that the disguised unemployed would typically have a marginal propensity to consume equal to 1. Hence any diversion of demand from 'the general run of industries' to the products of the disguised unemployed would be offset by the extra demand which their expenditures add to the system. Accordingly, the potential scale of disguised unemployment is independent of the level of effective demand for the products of 'the general run of industries'.

In effect, Joan Robinson portrays a dual economy. In one sector, the advanced sector (A), the level of employment is determined by effective demand. In the other, the backward sector (B), the level of employment is determined by the supply of labour to that sector. The distinction between the sectors might be reinforced by deploying the arguments embodied in theories of segmented labour markets. But this would obscure the core point: the *potential* productivity of labour in the two sectors is exactly the same. It is effective demand which is lacking. Those who are working in sector B are measured as 'employed' in the employment statistics. But given the insufficient level of effective demand they are 'disguised unemployed'. If only effective demand were higher, sector B jobs would disappear, and with them disguised unemployment:

. . . we may say that unemployment is present when an increase in the output of capital goods (not offset by an increase in thriftiness) would lead to an increase in the output of consumption goods.

Let us apply this criterion to disguised unemployment. If a revival of investment were to occur, dismissed workers would be called back from the hedgerows and the street-curbs into their normal occupations. The wages they now receive represent a command over consumption goods which they prefer to the product of their former hand-to-mouth efforts. The output of consumption goods, as evaluated by consumers, has therefore increased. Hence, according to our definition, unemployment existed before the revival of investment took place, even though every individual worker was busy all day long. There has been no increase in employment reckoned by heads, but there has been an increase in employment reckoned in terms of output, because efficient methods of production have been substituted for inefficient methods. (Robinson 1937: 85–6)

Hence Joan Robinson anticipated the phenomenon of 'jobless growth'.

This analysis has been simplified by the assumption of a homogeneous labour-force. In circumstances in which effective demand is increasing this assumption is likely to be more viable in the medium term than in the short term. In the short term an expansion of effective demand may run up against a barrier of relatively unskilled sector B workers, whose prior exclusion from sector A has eroded their potential productivity in sector A employment. In the medium term the desire to meet growing demand will induce companies to invest in the expansion of sector A work-force. The most dramatic example of the medium-term flexibility of the labour-force was the increased employment of women in Britain during World War II. In response to the very high demand for labour the total employed population increased by 2.9 million (14.5 per cent) between 1939 and 1943. Eighty per cent of that increase consisted of women who had not been previously employed or who had been housewives (Parker 1957: 482). Yet levels of productivity comparable to, or even exceeding, the levels achieved by the earlier, predominantly male, labour-force were rapidly achieved.

This example suggests that the definition of disguised unemployment should be extended to cover inactivity, i.e. to include the participation rate, where the participation rate is a function of the level and rate of growth of effective demand. The persistence of high levels of male unemployment in Britain over the past fifteen years has resulted in a large number of men withdrawing from the labour-force altogether.[3] The high level of male unemployment and non-employment has also been a major stimulus to an increased supply of female labour in an attempt to balance family budgets. The demand for part-time labour has in turn increased the supply of part-time workers. Surveys of 'discouraged workers' and of 'involuntary part-time work' are designed to capture something of this variety of disguised unemployment.

The components of the analysis of G7 unemployment are, therefore:

1. the factors affecting the level of aggregate demand, and in turn defining the *common* experience of the G7 countries;
2. the factors affecting the level of disguised unemployment, and hence defining the differential experience of the G7 countries.

DISGUISED UNEMPLOYMENT: EVIDENCE

Identification of disguised unemployment will require an examination of both the levels and rates of change of output and employment between and within sectors of the economy. This raises a number of significant statistical difficulties.

It is, for example, extremely difficult to identify disguised unemployment *within* an industry, yet this makes an important contribution to disguised unemployment. The widespread growth of self-employment may be an indication of growing sector B employment within relatively dynamic industries. But sorting out type A and type B employment within an industry will require detailed micro and survey analysis which goes beyond the scope of this chapter.

A further major difficulty is the traditional problem of measuring the growth of output and productivity in service industries. No difficulty is presented in comparing the value of output per head as between, say, manufacturing and services, as is appropriate in defining sectors A and B. But any dynamic analysis of the impact of productivity growth on employment presents the problem of measuring the 'real' output. In many services, this can only be done by measuring the incomes of those working in the industry, an approach which necessarily weakens any conclusions about rates of

---

[3] Jonathan Wadsworth (1994) has shown that the *inactivity rate* amongst males aged 16–64 has risen from 3 per cent in 1975 to 12 per cent in 1993. The sum of unemployed men and inactive men gives a total of nearly 4 million men, one in four, out of work. Moreover, Wadsworth shows that the inactivity rate falls when there are sharp upturns in the employment rate.

productivity growth (but not, of course, the increase in peculiarly low-paid jobs). In this study employment and output in public-sector services are excluded from the analysis, even though public-sector employment may be an important 'sponge' in some circumstances.

I use the data on sectoral outputs provided in the OECD *National Accounts* for four sectors, Agriculture, Manufacturing, Construction, and Services, and one sub-sector, Services excluding finance, insurance, real estate, and business services (or Services excluding finance for short). Employment is defined as 'all persons active in the sector', not just 'employees', in order to include the self-employed and all forms of casual work in the identification of B sectors. The analysis is conducted over the (roughly) peak-to-peak trade cycle, 1979 to 1990.

Identification of disguised unemployment requires first, an examination of benefit levels and their likely impact on sector B employment; second, the identification of employment in sector B; and third, an estimate of 'true' unemployment, that is, measured unemployment plus disguised unemployment.

(i) *The reservation wage*

Wage flexibility, the freedom for real wages to adjust to equate the demand for labour to the supply of labour, is a central concept in the OECD *Jobs Study*:

Both theory and empirical evidence suggest that lower labour costs stimulate employment in the private sector, and all measures which reduce wage pressures at a given level of unemployment ultimately show up in better labour market performance. (OECD 1994c: 51)

Nowhere in the *Jobs Study* is there an explicit consideration of the theoretical 'evidence' cited. Indeed, one of the peculiarities of the *Study* is this lack of theoretical specification. For example, despite its overt concern with the problem of aggregate unemployment, virtually all the analysis is conducted at the level of *partial* equilibrium. There is no consideration of the fact that, as was argued above, even within the neoclassical model which is the underlying motivation of the argument, wage flexibility is not a sufficient condition for the attainment of full-employment. If an increase in employment is to be sustained then increased investment must absorb the increased savings which the higher level of activity will produce. If for any reason investment fails to increase then the higher level of employment cannot be maintained, even though wages are perfectly flexible. Despite the key role of investment in the determination of the level of employment, there is in the *Jobs Study* no sustained analysis of the determination of the level of investment, and of the relationship between investment and employment.[4]

By contrast, in this chapter it is presumed in Keynesian fashion that, given technological conditions, the level of effective demand determines the level of employment in sector A. In sector B employment is determined by the supply of labour to sector B activities. This supply of labour to sector B, and hence sector B employment, is determined by the reservation wage. A major influence on the level of the reservation wage is the level of social security benefits available to the unemployed.

Table 3.2.   Benefit replacement rates, and benefit coverage, 1991

	Average replacement rate	Beneficiaries/unemployed
Canada	28	129
France	37	98
Germany	28	89
Japan	8	36
Italy	3	—*
UK	18	71
USA	11	34

* No comparable statistic is available for Italy. However an EC survey of benefit recipients suggests that the Italian figure would be low.

Notes: The average replacement rate measures the average benefit entitlement before tax as a percentage of previous earnings before tax. The beneficiaries/unemployed ratio expresses the ratio of the number of unemployment beneficiaries to the total number unemployed as measured by the ILO Labour Force Survey.

Source: OECD (1994c) Jobs Study, Evidence and Explanations, Part II.

If, for example, there is no social security benefit then the only unemployed will be those who can live off the earnings of someone else. Other than in this case, anyone without a job in sector A must find some way of scraping by.

The provision of social security benefits will provide a choice between scraping by and unemployment.[5] Since the reservation wage is related only to sector B employment, there is no reason to expect any relationship between benefit levels and aggregate employment. In fact there is, if anything, a negative relationship between benefit levels and unemployment:

[4] In a recent cross-section study Robert Rowthorn (1995) has found a strong positive relationship between investment and employment in manufacturing, and a positive relationship between investment and employment in the service sector. He interprets the role of investment as loosening capacity constraints, and hence lowering the level of unemployment at which inflationary pressures will emerge. This interpretation could be extended to encompass the dual role of investment: creating capacity and creating demand.

[5] Some sector B employment may be permitted as a supplement to benefit.

countries with higher benefit-replacement rates tend to have lower unemployment (OECD 1994c: 172–8).

Leaving the case of Italy aside for the moment, the data suggest a sharp differential between mainland European levels and coverage of benefits, and the levels and coverage of benefits in Japan and the United States, with the UK lying between mainland Europe and the USA. On this basis it might be expected that in the USA and in Japan the reservation wage would be low, and therefore in those countries there would be a tendency for declines in sector A employment to lead to increases in sector B employment, not increases in overt unemployment. In mainland Europe, higher benefit levels would be associated with higher unemployment. An OECD analysis (1994c) of trend changes (i.e. changes between trade cycles) in benefit entitlements and changes in unemployment is consistent with the hypothesized positive relationship. The elasticity of the unemployment rate with respect to the mean benefit level is estimated as being equal to 1. The elasticity above the mean is greater than 1.

The Italian case is an oddity in the G7, with very low benefit rates being associated with relatively high levels of unemployment. Clearly, alternative means of subsistence must exist in Italy, which enable the unemployed to survive. It has been widely suggested that this consists of a larger 'black economy', i.e. higher sector B employment which is not officially recorded, than is typical of other G7 countries. It should be remembered that the proportionate increase in unemployment in Italy was the lowest of the European members of the G7 (from a high base).

Table 3.3. Trends in lowest decile wages relative to the median, 1973–1991

	First year	Final year	M_f/M_1
Canada (1973–90)	0.52	0.44	109
France (1973–91)	0.62	0.66	119
Germany (1980–90)	0.67	0.71	127
Italy (1979–87)	0.67	0.75	104
Japan (1979–90)	0.63	0.61	118
UK (1973–91)	0.68	0.59	134
USA (1975–89)	0.41	0.38	96

Notes: The terms 'First year' and 'Final year' refer to the data for the first and final years shown after the specification of the country. The third column is the real median income in the final year relative to the real median income in the first year. The figure in the third column for Japan is the relative level of real compensation per employee in the business sector in 1990 relative to 1979.

Source: OECD, *Employment Outlook*, 1993.

The OECD *Jobs Study* (1994c: 175) finds that the trend slow-down in the growth of aggregate demand has been overlain by cycles in demand in which changes in the level of unemployment have been smaller the lower have been benefit levels. It is through the cycle that the expansion and con-traction of sector B employment might be expected to dampen the impact of changes in effective demand.

A further indication of the impact of forces determining the reservation wage and the supply of labour to sector B has been the change in the dis-persion of wages. In Canada, the UK, and the USA, wages paid to the low-est decile have diverged from the median wage. In the USA the median wage itself has fallen, precipitating a fall in real wages of more than 1 per cent per year between 1980 and 1989.

In France, Germany, and Italy, growth of real wages for the lowest decile has been greater than the increase in the median real wage. In Germany this has meant an increase in real wages for the lowest paid of over 2.5 per cent per year between 1983 and 1990. In Japan the relative position of the low-est paid was virtually unchanged. In the UK a rapid increase in median real wages was accompanied by a sharp increase in inequality, whilst in Canada and the USA an already unequal distribution of income has become even more unequal. The widening of the distribution of earned incomes in North America suggests a lowering of lower decile wages which may be associated with the growth of sector B unemployment, particularly in the face of low USA benefit levels. Something of the same phenomenon may be emerging in the UK as income inequality increases sharply. The Japanese case is very different. Low benefit levels would suggest a low reservation wage. But the relatively egalitarian distribution of earned incomes suggests that B sector employment may none the less be relatively well remunerated. The evidence suggest that levels of sector B employment are likely to be high in Canada, the USA, Italy, and Japan.

(ii) *Sector B*

Disguised unemployment is defined as employment in very low productiv-ity sectors. The benchmark is the performance of the German economy. With high benefits and broad coverage it might be expected that disguised unemployment would be low in Germany. Or, to put it another way, that the dispersion of the levels of value-productivity per head would be less in Germany than in other G7 countries. This is indeed the case. Other than in agriculture, the value of output per head is almost invariably at least 80 per cent of the value of output per head in manufacturing. So, as a rule of thumb, for each country 'very low' is defined as being a level of output per head less than 80 per cent of output per head in national manufacturing industry.

Table 3.4. Value of output per head relative to manufacturing, 1979

	Agriculture	Manufacturing	Construction	Services	Services(X)
Canada*	78	100	125	73	52
France	52	100	75	110	86
Germany	43	100	83	113	89
Italy	42	100	89	120	91
Japan	26	100	77	89	68
UK	83	100	99	114	84
USA	86	100	81	97	76

* Canada 1980.

Notes: Private sector employment as a proportion of total employment. Services(X) = private services excluding the financial sector.

Sources: OECD, *National Accounts*, 1979–91; Annual Abstract of Statistics, 1993; *Survey of Current Business*, Nov. 1993.

Tables 3.4 and 3.5 illustrate the rationale for separating non-financial services from the rest of the services sector. The high value of output per head in the financial sector seriously biases the overall output figures in services.

Particularly striking are the very low levels of productivity in agriculture generally, and in Japanese and (in 1990) Italian agriculture in particular. Very low levels of output per head are also found in Canadian, Japanese, and USA non-financial services. Equally striking is the high level of output per head in services within the European Union (including Italy), with only British non-financial services sliding into sector B at the end of the period, as wage differentials in Britain widened. More generally there has been a fall in relative productivity in non-financial services in all G7 countries as unemployment has increased.

Table 3.5. Value of output per head relative to manufacturing, 1990

	Agriculture	Manufacturing	Construction	Services	Services(X)
Canada	57	100	105	67	46
France	53	100	65	110	83
Germany	45	100	80	120	95
Italy	32	100	81	111	84
Japan	22	100	87	84	63
UK	80	100	101	97	68
USA	70	100	69	90	69

Notes: Private sector employment as a proportion of total employment. Services(X) = private services excluding the financial sector.

Sources: OECD, *National Accounts*, 1979–91; *Survey of Current Business*, Nov. 1993.

However, an important distinction must be drawn between what has happened in low-productivity agriculture and what has happened in low-productivity non-financial services. Whilst aggregate unemployment has increased, in agriculture absolute employment has fallen, whilst in non-financial services both absolute employment and the share of employment have risen (and in the UK has risen very sharply). Given that disguised unemployment is conceived as a 'sponge' which absorbs workers who lose sector A jobs and are unable to acquire satisfactory benefits, it may be unreasonable to classify employment in sectors with falling employment as disguised unemployment. Of course, it could be argued that without the 'disguised', low-productivity effect, employment in agriculture would have fallen even more rapidly than it did. Without a clear-cut means of differen-tiating between these two cases, disguised unemployment will be estimated, first including all sectors in which productivity is less than 80 per cent of productivity in manufacturing, and second, excluding those sectors in which employment is falling.

Tables 3.6, 7, 8, and 9 provide detailed information on the pattern of the value of output per head for each year 1979–90 for Germany, Japan, the UK, and the USA. The German experience is totally different from that in the other three countries. In Germany there has been no tendency whatso-ever for sectoral value productivity to diverge (apart from a brief episode in German construction, 1984–9). Yet such a divergence has occurred in each of the other three countries, though the changes are most pronounced in the UK and the USA and least pronounced in Japan. In Japan the value of out-

Table 3.6. Value of output per head relative to manufacturing, Germany 1979–1990

	Agriculture	Manufacturing	Construction	Services	Services(X)
1979	43	100	83	113	89
1980	42	100	89	118	93
1981	43	100	87	120	93
1982	48	100	84	121	92
1983	42	100	81	120	91
1984	43	100	78	120	90
1985	39	100	74	117	88
1986	40	100	75	113	86
1987	37	100	77	116	90
1988	41	100	77	116	90
1989	46	100	79	116	90
1990	45	100	80	117	93

Note: Services(X) = private services excluding the financial sector.

Source: OECD, *National Accounts*, 1979–91.

Table 3.7. Value of output per head relative to manufacturing, Japan 1979–1990

	Agriculture	Manufacturing	Construction	Services	Services(X)
1979	26	100	77	89	68
1980	23	100	76	90	69
1981	23	100	80	89	69
1982	23	100	77	87	68
1983	24	100	71	87	68
1984	24	100	71	87	66
1985	24	100	72	88	67
1986	24	100	75	88	71
1987	23	100	81	86	65
1988	22	100	82	86	64
1989	22	100	85	86	64
1990	22	100	87	84	63

Note: Services(X) = private services excluding the financial sector.

Source: OECD, *National Accounts*, 1979–91.

Table 3.8. Value of output per head relative to manufacturing, UK 1979–1990

	Agriculture	Manufacturing	Construction	Services	Services(X)
1979	83	100	100	116	84
1980	87	100	100	113	83
1981	88	100	98	107	79
1982	87	100	94	101	74
1983	76	100	95	99	71
1984	86	100	92	95	69
1985	71	100	88	91	67
1986	74	100	89	96	71
1987	74	100	91	93	68
1988	70	100	96	92	69
1989	73	100	93	88	63
1990	76	100	91	90	64

Note: Services(X) = private services excluding the financial sector.

Source: OECD, *National Accounts*, 1979–91.

put per head in non-financial services, already low, has tended to decline further relative to manufacturing in the late 1980s. Japan also has the highest proportion of the labour-force working in non-financial services (45 per cent), other than in Canada (53 per cent). In the UK and the USA there have been sharp declines in relative productivity in non-financial services

Table 3.9. Value of output per head relative to manufacturing, USA 1979–1990

	Agriculture	Manufacturing	Construction	Services	Services(X)
1979	86	100	81	97	76
1980	71	100	82	99	77
1981	80	100	76	97	75
1982	70	100	76	96	74
1983	54	100	73	95	73
1984	68	100	73	94	73
1985	68	100	74	95	73
1986	63	100	76	95	73
1987	62	100	74	92	70
1988	59	100	72	91	70
1989	67	100	71	91	69
1990	70	100	69	90	69

Note: Services(X) = private services excluding the financial sector.

Sources: OECD, *National Accounts*, 1979–91; *Survey of Current Business*, Nov. 1993.

over the whole period. Both countries have also experienced sharp increases in the proportion of the labour-force working in non-financial services. In the USA the proportion of such employment has increased from 39 per cent in 1979 to 43 per cent in 1990. In the UK the increase has been even sharper, from 31 per cent in 1979 to 38 per cent in 1990.

(iii) *Disguised unemployment and 'true' unemployment*

The analysis of the preceding section provides the material for the calculation of disguised unemployment and for the determination of 'true' rates of unemployment, that is the rates of unemployment measured as the sum of published unemployment rates and disguised unemployment. Having classified sectors as belonging to category B, the next task is to measure disguised unemployment. Disguised unemployment is defined as the number of jobs which would need to be lost if a sector is to attain a level of value productivity per head equal to 80 per cent of the level of productivity in manufacturing, i.e. the typical relationship in Germany. As noted above, this calculation will be conducted both including and excluding those sectors in which employment is falling. The estimates of disguised unemployment are set out in Table 3.10. The time-series pattern of disguised unemployment for Germany, Japan, the UK, and the USA is illustrated in Fig. 3.1.

The highest levels of disguised unemployment are, as expected, in Canadian services, in Italian and Japanese agriculture, and in American,

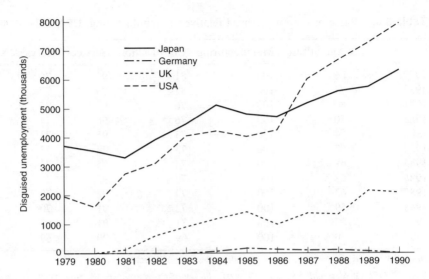

Fig. 3.1.   Disguised unemployment in the G7 countries, 1979–1990.

Japanese, and British non-financial services. The high level of disguised unemployment in UK non-financial services in 1990 has emerged despite the well-known high rate of productivity growth in retail services. This may be a result of the rapid growth of low-productivity self-employment in the service sector in recent years.

The scale of disguised unemployment in Japan is extraordinary, and totally transforms the traditional employment picture of the economy.

In Table 3.11 the figures for disguised unemployment are added to published unemployment figures to give what may be called the 'true' unem-

Table 3.10.   Disguised unemployment in the G7 countries, 1979 and 1990 (thousands)

	Agriculture		Manufacturing		Construction		Services		Services(X)	
	1979	1990	1979	1990	1970	1990	1979	1990	1979	1990
Canada*	15	154	—	—	—	—	554	1,285	1,860	2,769
France	678	447	—	—	117	300	—	—	—	—
Germany	652	224	—	—	—	—	—	—	—	—
Italy	1,446	1,342	—	—	—	—	—	—	—	—
Japan	5,384	4,391	—	—	218	—	—	—	3,442	6,216
UK	—	—	—	—	—	—	—	—	—	1,510
USA	—	376	—	—	—	868	—	—	1,422	7,007

* Canada 1980 and 1990.
Notes: Disguised unemployment in *italic type* occurs in sectors in which employment is falling. Disguised unemployment in roman type occurs in sector in which employment is rising.

Table 3.11. 'True' unemployment rates

	1979			1990		
	Published	'True'	(B−A)/B	Published	'True'	(B−A)/B
(a) *including sectors with falling employment*						
Canada*	7.4	24.0	0.69	7.5	29.0	0.74
France	6.0	9.5	0.37	8.9	11.9	0.26
Germany	2.9	5.1	0.43	4.9	5.5	0.11
Italy	7.8	14.5	0.46	11.1	16.5	0.33
Japan	2.1	18.3	0.88	2.1	18.7	0.89
UK	4.5	4.5	0.00	5.9	11.6	0.49
USA	5.8	7.1	0.19	5.5	12.1	0.55
(b) *excluding sectors with falling employment*						
Canada*	7.4	24.0	0.69	7.5	27.9	0.73
France	6.0	6.0	0.00	8.9	8.9	0.00
Germany	2.9	2.9	0.00	4.9	4.9	0.00
Italy	7.8	7.8	0.00	11.1	11.1	0.00
Japan	2.1	8.7	0.76	2.1	11.8	0.82
UK	4.5	4.5	0.00	5.9	11.6	0.49
USA	5.8	7.1	0.19	5.5	10.3	0.47

* Canada 1980 and 1990.

Notes: $(B-A)/B = \dfrac{(\text{'True'} - \text{Published})}{\text{'True'}}$.

Sources: OECD, *National Accounts*, 1979–91; OECD, *Employment Outlook*, 1993; and own calculations.

ployment rates. One significant result is that the supposed superiority of the North American labour market immediately disappears. Instead, the 'true' unemployment rate in North America greatly exceeds the rate of unemployment in Germany, and is comparable to that in France and the UK. The Japanese 'true' unemployment rate is the second highest in the G7. If the identification of disguised unemployment is correct, these high rates of 'true' unemployment are the consequence of the slow-down in the rate of growth of effective demand.[6]

By far the greatest proportion of disguised unemployment is to be found in Japan and in Canada. In the UK and the USA disguised unemployment in 1990 is nearly half 'true' unemployment, i.e. 'true' unemployment is double the published rate. In mainland Europe, disguised unemployment is around a third of 'true' unemployment, and vanishes altogether if those sectors with falling employment are excluded from consideration. Moreover, whereas disguised unemployment is increasing as a proportion of 'true'

[6] The expression 'true' rate of unemployment refers here only to the addition of disguised unemployment to the published rate of unemployment. It does not involve any adjustments to allow for other concerns which have been expressed about the published rate.

unemployment in Canada, Japan, the UK, and the USA, in mainland
Europe it is falling as a proportion of 'true' unemployment.

DISGUISED UNEMPLOYMENT OR 'FLEXIBILITY'

The OECD *Jobs Study* attributes the low measured rate of unemployment
in North America to the flexibility of labour markets, particularly in the
USA, as measured by low rates of worker protection. The OECD policy
conclusion is that steps should be taken to increase labour-market flexibility in Europe by weakening worker protection, lowering minimum wage levels, reducing unemployment benefits, and so on.

The analysis presented in this chapter suggests a quite different interpretation of the data. It attributes the low measured rate of unemployment in
North America and in Japan to the presence of very high levels of disguised
unemployment. Disguised unemployment is growing in Britain as benefits
are cut and inequality increases. The disguised unemployment which exists
in mainland Europe is predominantly due to the subsidization of inefficient
employment in European agriculture.

In effect, there are three strategies being pursued within the G7 in reaction to growing unemployment, the mainland European 'benefits strategy',
the USA and (increasingly) UK 'impoverishment strategy', and the
Japanese 'protection' strategy. It may well be argued, of course, that disguised unemployment at low wages is superior to unemployment on relatively high benefits, and reasonably well-paid employment in protected
sectors is, in social terms, best of all.

But whatever the circumstances in individual G7 countries, the policy
conclusion is the same. The rate of growth of effective demand is every-
where too low relative to the growth of sector A productivity, and steps
should be taken to remove the constraints to the expansion of demand by
an appropriate mix of fiscal and monetary policies. If measures to expand
demand were implemented throughout the G7 the expansion could prove
contagious.[7] Constraints may be imposed by the fear of inflation, or by
international financial considerations, or both. But if most B sector employment has persisted for a long time, the most important constraint may be
the difficulty of transferring labour from sector B to sector A. This is akin
to the familiar problem of returning the long-term unemployed to the

---

[7] It is often argued that a co-ordinated expansion of demand is required. The problem is
that whilst it is widely agreed that a co-ordinated expansion of demand is desirable, it never
happens. There are a number of good reasons for this which are surveyed in Eatwell (1994).
It is important to note that the Bretton Woods system did not work by means of macroeconomic co-ordination. Instead, it worked because of a framework of circumstances which permitted governments to pursue national macroeconomic policies without too much fear of
international financial disruption.

labour-force, but is typically overlooked given that sector B labour is disguised unemployment.

Increased flexibility, in the sense of the removal of workers' protection, is likely to do little to increase employment in sector A. Indeed, figures for 'true' unemployment suggest that the highly regulated German labour market is the most efficient in the G7. However, elimination of unemployment benefit would reduce the level of measured unemployment to very low levels, if not eradicate it altogether. This would be because the unemployed would be forced into disguised unemployment.

An increase in disguised unemployment is clearly a waste of resources, since labour is working at a level of productivity below its true potential. Moreover, high levels of disguised unemployment when associated with very low wages may discourage productivity-boosting innovation in other sectors, so slowing down the overall rate of productivity growth. The experience of Japan, where disguised unemployment is associated with a relatively egalitarian structure of wages, and where productivity growth is relatively high even in sector B industries, is instructive in this respect.

The analysis outlined in this chapter suggests that G7 unemployment is not due to rigidities in the labour market, but to those factors, international and domestic, which inhibit an increase in the rate of growth of effective demand. There is substantial surplus labour, either openly unemployed or hidden in disguised unemployment.

REFERENCES

Bean, C. (1994), 'European Unemployment: A Survey', *Journal of Economic Literature*, 32 (June), 572–691.

Drèze, J. and Bean, C. (1990) (eds.), *Europe's Unemployment Problem* (Cambridge, Mass.: MIT Press).

Eatwell, J. (1994), 'The Co-ordination of Macroeconomic Policy in the European Community', in J. Michie and J. Grieve Smith (eds.), *Unemployment in Europe* (London: Academic Press).

—— (1995), 'The International Origins of Unemployment', in J. Michie and J. Grieve Smith (eds.), *Managing the Global Economy* (Oxford: Oxford University Press).

—— and Milgate, M. (1983) (eds.), *Keynes's Economics and the Theory of Value and Distribution* (London: Duckworth).

Keynes, J. M. (1936), *General Theory of Employment, Interest and Money* (London: Macmillan).

Layard, R., Nickell, S., and Jackman, R. (1991), *Unemployment* (Oxford: Oxford University Press).

Marglin, S. and Schor, J. (1990) (eds.), *The Golden Age of Capitalism* (Oxford: Oxford University Press).

Michie, J. and Grieve Smith, J. (1995) (eds.), *Managing the Global Economy* (Oxford: Oxford University Press).

OECD (1994*a*), *The OECD Jobs Study: Facts, Analysis, Strategies* (Paris: OECD).

—— (1994*b*), *The OECD Jobs Study, Evidence and Explanations*, Part I: *Labour Market Trends and Underlying Forces of Change* (Paris: OECD).

—— (1994*c*), *The OECD Jobs Study, Evidence and Explanations*, Part II: *The Adjustment Potential of the Labour Market* (Paris: OECD).

Parker, H. M. D. (1957), *Manpower* (London: HMSO).

Robinson, J. V. (1937), 'Disguised Unemployment', in *Essays in the Theory of Employment* (London: Macmillan).

Rowthorn, R. (1995), 'Capital Formation and Unemployment', *Oxford Review of Economic Policy*, 11/1: 26–39.

Wadsworth, J. (1994), 'The Terrible Waste', *New Economy*, 1/1: 25–7.

Part II

Unemployment and Inequality

4. Economic Functioning, Self-Sufficiency, and Full Employment

Roger Tarling and Frank Wilkinson

INTRODUCTION

Few economists would disagree that a central object of economic policy should be achieving and sustaining full employment; what they debate is how this can be achieved. Economists have traditionally argued that the labour market cleared; anyone can get a job if they are prepared to accept a market price which declines as the level of unemployment rises. Keynes identified over-saving as a cause of unemployment and introduced the idea that full employment required government intervention to establish and maintain a sufficiency in effective demand. Persistent inflation in the post-war period led to the re-establishment amongst economists of pre-Keynesian beliefs in a monetary explanation of inflation and a clearing labour market and established the notion of an equilibrium 'natural' level of unemployment at which inflation stabilizes. Monetarism rules out a macroeconomic intervention route to full employment and directs policy attention towards reform of the supply side of the labour market as the generator of jobs. However, despite seventeen years of continuous labour market deregulation and cutbacks in social welfare to sharpen work incentives in Britain, unemployment, depending on how it is measured, is currently between two to four times higher than it was in the 1970s.[1]

Explanations for this increase vary but the conventional wisdom amongst economists is that the natural rate has shifted. Increases in real (i.e. relative to product prices) raw material prices, capital goods prices, interest rates, and exchange rates have been identified as reducing profit rates and thereby lowering the demand for labour. The restoration of profits requires a compensating cut in wages relative to productivity and the refusal of labour to concede this has shifted the natural rate of unemployment upwards. Factors on the supply side of the labour market including asset values, interest rates, and social-welfare benefits are identified as raising out-of-work income and hence the asking price of labour. High levels of the natural rate

---

[1] For discussion of the evolution of inflation theory in the post-war period see Wilkinson (1997).

of unemployment are also attributed to trade unions, legal minimum wages, high non-wage labour costs, restrictive labour and employment legislation, population increase, labour-saving technical progress, the slow adjustment to external shocks, and the effects on the skills and work motivations of the unemployed of long spells of joblessness. Unemployment has therefore been increasingly regarded as resulting from the failure of wages to adjust downward to the falling demand price for labour and/or to the growing unemployability of the increasing proportion of the work-force through lack of skill and/or work motivation. Consequently, even to many economists who would regard themselves as Keynesian, unemployment is seen as voluntary or 'structural' and not amenable to macroeconomic stimuli; diagnoses which lead to such policy recommendations as a determined effort to reduce wages, the introduction of state-provided 'citizens income' designed to remove the disincentive effect of the means testing of benefits, and the subsidization of employment by tax relief (Meade 1995). The requirement is that workers become lower paid and therefore less self-sufficient, and/or more dependent on the state.

As opposed to this, this chapter argues that the ability of individuals to function economically so as to achieve and maintain self-sufficiency is critical to the achievement of full employment and a high road to economic growth. Economic functioning however is only in part determined by the individual's own efforts and decisions, the other main factors being embedded in the economic, social, and political systems within which the individual is located. These systems structure the incentives, disincentives, and barriers which increase or restrict the quality and quantity of economic and social participation of individuals and hence their capacity for self-sufficiency. For example, the segmentation of labour markets, resulting from the exercise of individual and collective power, leads to systematic differences in the valuation of the labour of groups located in the different segments and this reinforces and is reinforced by power inequalities within households and more widely in society.

The chapter further argues that attempts to increase employment by widening the distribution of income and deregulating the labour market have in reality created policy traps which reinforce and exacerbate inequalities and are counter-productive in terms of employment creation. This has put pressure on resources to compensate for the inequalities and to protect the stability of the existing structures. Common sense would recognize that the removal of labour market and other forms of undervaluation to reduce pre-tax income inequality will yield high returns in terms of economic and social progress by enabling those currently undervalued to increase their own economic functioning and self-sufficiency. Hence the chapter argues for a better understanding of what needs to be changed, not only for reasons of social equity and justice but also for the purposes of effective economic policy. Before doing that it is necessary to explain what we mean by economic functioning and self-sufficiency.

RESOURCE ENDOWMENTS, CAPABILITIES, AND ECONOMIC FUNCTIONING

Lancaster (1966) maintained that it is the *characteristics* of a product that make it attractive. Sen (1985) argued that characteristics are latent in products and require the appropriate *capabilities* to make them functional. He pointed out (ibid. 10), that it is the physical capabilities of the cyclist which makes functional the transportation characteristic of the bicycle; but then so does the state of the roads, whether the cyclists can afford their own bicycle pump and so on. There are therefore many dimensions to capability and hence to functioning. In this section the concepts of capability and functioning will be developed within the context of a discussion of the effective mobilization by individuals of the resources at their disposal as the means of becoming and remaining self-sufficient.

The resource endowments of individuals include their labour power, accumulated assets, and entitlements (net of contributions) to private and public transfers.[2] Resource endowments vary widely in both levels and composition between individuals and over an individual's lifetime. For example, the resource endowments of children consist mainly of their claim to intra-household transfers based on their family affiliation and public transfers in the form of child benefits, education, health, and other social provisions. In early adult life the most important part of individuals' resource endowment is usually their labour power and they have probably become net contributors to the tax/benefit system and possibly to private transfers. The importance of labour power and net contributions to public and private transfers increase with cohabitation and the formation of families but as individuals grow older their net contribution to private transfers can be expected to decline as their children leave the household, and when eventually they retire their resource endowments become mainly state transfers, accumulated private assets (including private pension rights), and, possibly, private transfers. There are, however, wide variations between individuals around this stylized lifetime profile of resource endowment related to time spent in education, age at cohabitation and family formation, types of household, participation in the labour market, and other socially and economically determined factors.

Given their resource endowments the economic functioning of individuals is determined by what can be described as their capabilities. Capabilities,

---

[2] The most important private transfers are within the household; others include private intra-community income-sharing, inter-generational transfers, and charities.

in the sense used here, depend on the personal efficiency and energy of individuals but also on the opportunities they have to utilize their resources to the best advantage. The capabilities of individuals in the labour market, for example, depend on employment opportunities and terms and conditions of that employment as well as on the effectiveness and intensity of work effort. Capabilities in domestic and other forms of non-market production also have important institutional and organizational dimensions. There are, for example, significant economies of scale in cooking, caring, cleaning, and other forms of household production and in the sharing of accommodation, heating, and other aspects of communal living. Capabilities also include individuals' knowledge and experience of systems of private and public transfers including, for example, their ability to take advantage of the tax/benefit system by minimizing the payment of the former and maximizing the receipt of the latter. Together with their resource endowment the capabilities of individuals determine their economic functioning, the flow of income at their disposal, and therefore their ability to maintain themselves and accumulate resources.

ECONOMIC FUNCTIONING AND THE WORKING OF LABOUR MARKETS[3]

In conventional economic theory the initial resource endowments of individuals are taken as given and capabilities are seen as being determined largely by personal qualities. Labour markets are more or less competitive and within them wages reflect the quality of individuals' labour-power endowment (their human capital) and their personal efficiency and energy. That these result in a wide dispersion of labour-market rewards, some of which may be insufficient to sustain a reasonable standard of life, is a demonstration, it is argued, of how widely dispersed are individual resource endowments and capabilities (Hirsch and Addison 1986). Within the household the allocation of members' labour between domestic production and internal transfers are regarded as a consequence of rational choice based on the relative values of individual members' domestic and labour-market employment and made by households operating as a single unit. The redistribution of income by the state through a tax and benefit system is recognized as necessary, particularly when the economic functioning of individuals is insufficient to yield some minimum standard of life. But this is qualified by an emphasis on the potential negative incentive effects of lowering the net market income of the taxpayer and of raising the non-market income of the benefit recipient.

[3] This sections draws heavily on Wilkinson (1991).

Conventional economics recognizes that although inequalities in resource endowment may exist these are essentially external to market processes. Therefore, given resource endowments, the economic functioning of individuals is largely determined by how productive they are and how effective market incentives are in mobilizing that effort so that wage differences largely reflect relative worth. In contrast to this conventional view, labour-market segmentation theorists recognize the importance of relative power in influencing wage differences. In particular, relationships in the labour market are permeated by inequalities of bargaining power, by structural barriers to mobility and by institutionalized discrimination, which together lead to the systematic *undervaluation* of the labour of disadvantaged groups. This focuses attention on the external and internal forces structuring the labour market and how these impact on the capabilities of individuals located in its different segments.

Out-of-Market Segmentation

Inter-community and inter-family differences in wealth, expectations, and information give individuals variable degrees of access to socialization, educational and training processes, and to job opportunities which enhance the resources and capabilities of the privileged and reduce those of the deprived whatever their inherent qualities. Household organization also serves to reduce the capabilities of women. Unequally distributed responsibility for domestic labour inhibits the labour-market activities of women to extents depending on the collective resource endowment of the household members and the willingness of other members to use their resources (either labour or capital) to provide substitutes for the cooking, cleaning, child care, and other domestic services traditionally provided by women. The greater the domestic responsibility of a woman (and hence the greater her transfer to others in her household) the less favourable are likely to be her labour-market opportunities. At one extreme, in resource-poor households highly dependent on the domestic services of female members (female-headed, single-parent households provide good examples) women will find it extremely difficult to realize their full capability on the labour market whatever skills they might have. At the other extreme, in households with access to ample resources to replace female domestic labour, women members will be strongly placed to exploit fully their labour-market assets.

The state represents the third major force differentially influencing the economic functioning of individuals by its labour, industrial and social welfare legislation, and by providing child- and other forms of care. The growth of the welfare state can be regarded as counteracting social, economic, and other disadvantages and therefore breaking down the barriers to effective labour-market participation. However, whether individuals can take advantage of education and training to enhance their resource endowment will depend on the willingness and ability of households to support non-economically functioning members and their experience, expectations, and information about education, training, and labour-market opportunities, all of which can be expected to discriminate in favour of the resource-rich households (Bowles and Gintis 1976). Moreover, whilst the resource endowment of the better-off can be expected to be enhanced by state education and training provision, social security (the elements of state expenditure to which the worse-off have greatest recourse) works to impair their economic functioning. For example, the capabilities of social-welfare recipients are reduced by means-tested benefits which are reduced as incomes rise. This effectively imposes high marginal taxes on the low-income households and ensnares them in the poverty trap (Parker 1995).

In-Market Segmentation

Within the labour-market professional associations, sectional trade unions, and other formal and informal organizations and networks exercise control over entry to particular labour-market segments and to training and other forms of in-market advancement restricting access to and the use of human capital. Labour-market disadvantages such as sex, race, age, low social status, and poor educational achievement are exacerbated by the difficulties such groups experience in forming or joining effective in-market organizations. The hiring, training, and labour-management policies of firms interrelate with supply-side factors in further differentiating job opportunities. Hiring rules adopted by firms rest on signals transmitted by social characteristics (age, sex, race, education and training qualification, dress, deportment, etc.) which are only partially objectively based but which are taken to measure the relative worth of job applicants (Spence 1973). The technical and organizational structure of the firm, the related systems of labour management and collective bargaining (or its absence) structure job opportunities within firms, and training and promotion policies regulate the allocation of workers within this internal labour market. Firms with a range of abilities to pay offer widely different levels of wages for comparable jobs so that promotion prospects—in terms of job content and/or pay—exist both within and between firms (Horrell, Burchell, and Rubery 1989). Successful progression within this job structure enhances the labour-market status of individuals whereas redundancy and other involuntary quits, periods out of the labour market for domestic reasons, and spells of unemployment have the opposite effect. Thus job prospects of individuals can be continuously modified from the supply side by their own employment experience and from the demand side by such factors as plant closures, industrial restructuring and changes in hiring and training rules adopted by employers.[4]

The structuring of job opportunities and related differences in the terms and conditions of employment are further reinforced by variations in incidence and effectiveness of collective bargaining and protection afforded by the law. Collective agreements reflect the bargaining power of labour and the ability of firms and industries to pay, and so their benefits can vary widely. In some European countries these disadvantages are offset by legally enforceable labour standards. In Britain, however, minimum-wage legislation is now non-existent and legally enforceable conditions of employment usually provide a floor of rights significantly below those secured by collective bargaining. Moreover, the employees of small firms, part-timers, workers on temporary and other non-standard contracts, and others whose employment status is ambiguous are frequently excluded from the scope of both collective bargaining and protective legislation (Deakin and Morris 1995).

The general characteristics of labour markets are, therefore, that access to jobs is generally carefully controlled, and the higher the pay and status the more restrictive the rules of entry. Rules of exclusion operate on all groups at all levels and are mutually re-enforcing in the sense that workers in each labour-market group, excluded from better jobs, more carefully protect those within their control. However, the ability to exclude others can be expected to decline at successively lower levels in the labour-market hierarchy. At the bottom end of the labour market jobs tend to be classified as unskilled whatever their job content, trade unionism is weak or non-existent, and the law offers little, if any, protection. As a result, terms and conditions of employment are poor, work is often casualized, and non-standard forms of labour contracts are common. Individuals are trapped in this segment by their lack of transferable and/or socially recognized and credentialized skills, by the many forms discrimination takes, and by the priority they are obliged to give to domestic and other responsibilities. At this level, jobs tend to be much more open to anyone and therefore regular employees are thrown into competition with students and others who want temporary jobs to top up their income from other sources and who are therefore prepared to accept wages below that necessary for self-sufficiency.

Interaction Between Internal and External Segmentation

There are virtuous and vicious cycles built into the interaction between the resource endowment of individuals, their capabilities, and hence their

---

[4] For detailed analyses of the dynamic effects of industrial restructuring and changes in hiring, training, and other aspects of labour management on the supply- and demand-side structuring of the labour market see the collection of articles in *Labour and Society,* Oct. 1988.

economic functioning. Ample resource endowment creates labour-market privilege which enhances capability and economic functioning and increases resource endowment. By contrast, paucity of resource endowment interacts with reduced capabilities in reinforcing poor economic functioning in two separate ways. Lack of resources militates against the development of the human capital of deprived individuals and possibly their personal qualities and hence their capabilities. This defines what might usefully be called the *out-market* undervaluation of the labour of socially deprived individuals. This is compounded by what can be called the *in-market* undervaluation which results from the structuring of labour markets by social, organizational, and legal forces which relegates the socially disadvantaged to labour-market segments where their capabilities are further reduced because wages are low relative to the real value of labour input.

The segmentation of labour markets and the social and economic deprivation it engenders has significant macro- and microeconomic implications. The *out-market* undervaluation of labour reduces the overall productive potential of an economy whilst *in-market* undervaluation leads to further waste to the extent that it permits the continued existence of outmoded techniques and inefficient managerial practices. *In-market* undervaluation of labour also leads to a more unequal distribution of income than would be warranted by the distribution of what Marshall called *efficiency* earnings— 'earnings measured with reference to the exertion of ability and efficiency required of the workers' (Marshall 1947: 549). The beneficiaries of this unequal distribution of income may be either those in receipt of profits or more advantaged groups in the labour market depending on whether, and the extent to which, the cost advantage of employing undervalued labour is passed on to the customer (Marshall 1947: 549). For example, the availability of undervalued labour is one way by which retail traders and food and drink caterers compete to the price advantage of the customers. In other cases, the redistribution is more direct and here the provision of domestic and other labour services by disadvantaged workers to the more privileged provides an obvious example. This latter resource transfer becomes more indirect but none the less as real when mediated by local and central government and made possible by the low pay of public-sector workers. Finally, the unequal degrees of bargaining power of different groups of workers employed by the same firm provide a way by which the relative undervaluation of some workers can benefit others by reducing the conflict between their wage claims and profits. Thus there are a wide range of direct and indirect ways by which the wage share is distributed unequally in which both relative wages, prices and the system of taxation play a part which enhances the resources endowment and capabilities of some and reduces those of others.

The interaction between out-market and in-market segmentation is also a major obstacle to the effectiveness of labour-market policies. This double jeopardy strengthens the barrier between unemployment and employment by undermining the ability and willingness of individuals to take up and participate in labour-market schemes. It also threatens the effectiveness of even the best-designed measures to secure lasting employment opportunities. The resulting failure of policy initiatives has the additional negative effect of wasting the reserves and resources of the disadvantaged and of nullifying the potential benefits of the resource transfers embodied in the public-sector financing of labour-market measures. Such outcomes generate disillusionment amongst providers and the provided-for and encourages their withdrawal of support and commitment to structures and frameworks for the delivery of active labour-market policy whatever their potential value.[5]

SELF-SUFFICIENCY AND POWER RELATIONS

Individuals can be said to be self-sufficient if they can function economically so as to at least sustain throughout their life some minimum customary standard of life. The ability to achieve this objective will depend on both resource endowment and capabilities. It has been argued above that the effectiveness by which labour and material assets can be accumulated and utilized to achieve the customary standard of life will be determined both by the personal qualities of the individual and their relative power in market and non-market activities. Power relations also play an important part in influencing the pattern of contributions to and benefits from private and public transfers. In the traditional family, for example, male dominance structures the flows of income and real-service transfers. In the case of public transfers the importance of power in structuring resource endowment will depend on how the transfers are organized. Where the public-welfare system is based on the insurance principle, rights to benefits are established by contributions so that obligations and rights are clearly related. On the other hand, if transfers are made from current taxation, the effective status of the beneficiary is much closer to that of a supplicant dependent on the benevolence of the taxpayers expressed through their tolerance to taxation.[6] Therefore transfers out of current taxation are determined more

[5] For a discussion of these effects, see ERGO Programme, Phase Two, Final Report. (European Commission/Cambridge Policy Consultants).

[6] Individuals usually have the status of taxpayers and benefit recipients, but not always at the same time. They also may not give equivalent weight to the taxes they pay and the benefits they receive. For example, current taxpayers may resist the taxes needed to fund the education for other people despite the fact that they had earlier benefited from education. Moreover, benefit recipients are also taxpayers, but these are more likely to be the indirect taxes which are less politically sensitive if for no other reason they bear down most heavily on the poor.

directly by power relationships than transfers resulting from an insurance principle.[7]

In conventional economics, the obstacle to a redistribution of income intended to widen self-sufficiency, either by narrowing wage differentials or increasing transfers, is the risk of a reduction in the overall level of economic performance. By contrast, the recognition of the importance of power inequalities in the market and non-market processes underlying the distribution of income, leads to the possibility that a reduction in the undervaluation of labour, a greater equality within households, and a shift to a system of benefits based on the insurance principle can be expected to increase rather than reduce incentives and thereby increase productivity. The important point is that, in a system where differential economic and political power result in the failure of individuals to achieve self-sufficiency, the removal of this disadvantage by a narrowing of the power differentials can be expected to increase the overall economic performance. As a result the powerful can expect to be compensated at least in part for relinquishing part of the pie as the less powerful begin to function more effectively, as the pie expands and as part of this growth trickles up the income distribution.

ECONOMIC THEORY, ECONOMIC POLICY, AND ECONOMIC PERFORMANCE

The period from the 1930s to the mid-1970s can be viewed as a period when in both economic theory and economic policy there was a recognition of the need for state intervention to improve economic performance at both the micro- and macro-level by the reduction of inequality. More recently and particularly since the mid-1970s there has been a growing emphasis on the importance of inequality in improving economic performance. A comparison of these two periods should therefore serve to illustrate the dynamic processes underlying economic performance.

The experience of unemployment and poverty during the interwar years and the social accord engendered by World War II triggered a revolution in economic theory and policy practice which ushered in a commitment by governments to full employment and the welfare state. In the following three decades these changes seemed to have been justified by the high rates of economic growth, increasing levels of employment, declining levels of unemployment, and a progressive elimination of poverty as a growing proportion of the population of advanced industrial countries became increasingly self-sufficient.

---

[7] What has been called the fiscal crisis of the state is an example of taxpayers' exercise of their power.

Expanding UK government expenditure and increased state intervention in the labour market found wide justification amongst economists who encouraged the government to expand education and training in the interest of a larger and better qualified labour-force. Better social-welfare provision, greater job security, and improved labour standards secured by collective bargaining were also welcomed because, it was argued, these measures contributed to human-capital formation, facilitated job search, and generally increased the efficient utilization of human resources. Thus economic, social, and political pressures combined in the upgrading of the labour force in such a way as to benefit particularly those at the lower levels of the job hierarchy. The position of those who remained trapped, or who were drawn into, the lower reaches of the labour market was improved by an extension and strengthening of the regulatory framework to accommodate their needs. The combined effect of high and increasing employment, a consensus across the political spectrum on full employment and the need for a welfare state, and the strengthening of trade-union organization was to reduce the extent of the in-market and out-market undervaluation of labour and helped redress the power imbalance in state provision. Consequently, the more equal distribution of income, wider educational and training opportunities and more job choice improved the resource endowment and capabilities of hitherto deprived individuals. This improved economic performance by enhancing labour input, underpinned economic progress from the demand side by encouraging the diffusion of new products and thereby raised the customary standard of life and facilitated the labour market upgrading process (Wilkinson 1988). Thus, both at the level of the individual and the economy, increasing resources and improving capabilities interacted in a virtuous cycle of rising economic performance.

From 1975

From the early 1970s the cumulative process of economic and social progress has been replaced by a downward cumulative process of increasing inequality and growing poverty. This was precipitated by rising inflation, growing unemployment, progressive de-industrialization, and increasing government expenditure. This burgeoning economic crisis served to discredit the economic and social theories which had directed policy during the Golden Age leading to a re-emergence of pre-Keynesian orthodoxy in economic theory and eventually into economic policy (Wilkinson 1997). High inflation was attributed to a failure to control the money supply, unemployment to imperfection in the labour markets and over-generous welfare provision, and the responsibility for poor industrial performance was laid at the door of organized labour and the erosive effect of high taxation on entrepreneurial initiative. In 1976, under pressure from the oil crisis and the changing conventional wisdom in economic theorizing, the British government abandoned its commitment to full employment. Since 1979, control of monetary variables has dominated anti-inflationary policy whilst labour-market deregulation and reforms of the benefit system to increase work incentives have been allotted the task of securing full employment.

There can be little doubt that, measured by unemployment levels, these experiments with pre-Keynesian economics have failed. But if, as explained by its apologists, the natural rate of unemployment has shifted because of changes in supply- and demand-side conditions in the labour market, unemployment is not a good indicator of economic performance. However, other indicators give as little support to the claim that the introduction of monetarist macroeconomics or labour market deregulation policies have had their predicted beneficial effect. Between the peak years 1979 and 1990, output per head in manufacturing grew by 3.8 per cent per year but, as manufacturing output increased at less than 1 per cent per year, employment in manufacturing fell at an annual rate in excess of 3 per cent. Investment as a proportion of GDP increased from 17.5 per cent to 19.5 per cent between 1979 and 1990. This was due to a boom in real-estate investment in the distribution and financial sectors. Manufacturing investment fell from 3.1 per cent of GDP to 2.6 per cent. The failure of manufacturing output to expand at the same pace as the economy (which grew at 2.2 per cent per year) resulted in a surge of imports, so that Britain became a net importer of manufactured goods for the first time since before the Industrial Revolution. As a consequence of this, the balance of payments on current account deteriorated from a surplus of 1.3 per cent of GDP in 1979 to a deficit of 2.8 per cent of GDP in 1990. The scale of the inflow of capital necessary to sustain the high and growing current-account deficit without a collapse of sterling forced up real interest rates. The real short-term interest rate (treasury bill yield-adjusted for manufacturing-output prices) rose from 2.7 per cent in 1979 to 8.8 per cent in 1990. The only real success of the 1980s was the increase in consumption, which grew in real terms from 57.2 per cent to 63.1 per cent of GDP between 1979 and 1990.

The boom of the late 1980s was brought to an end by a severe credit squeeze. By 1992, GDP was 2.5 per cent below its 1990 level, manufacturing output was 6 per cent lower, manufacturing investment had fallen to 2.2 per cent of GDP, but the balance of payment deficit was still 2.4 per cent of GDP. The economy was stimulated by the British withdrawal from the ERM in September 1992 and the subsequent devaluation and cuts in interest rates. By 1994 GDP was 6 per cent higher than its 1992 level. At very best the latest up-turn in the economy has been weak. Manufacturing output failed to recover its late 1980s peak by 1994 when manufacturing investment was 2 per cent of GDP. Exports responded to the 1992 devaluation, but imports continued to grow strongly, so that the 1994 balance of payments deficit on current account remained as high as 1.6 per cent of GDP. The budget deficit also posed a threat to the recovery. Under the pressure of high levels of unemployment and growing poverty, it proved impossible to contain government expenditure which increased from 39.1 to 43.3 per cent of GDP between 1990 and 1994, with social-security spending alone rising from 11.4 to 14.8 per cent of GDP. In early 1995, the supply constraint tightened and price increases in the supply chain began to accelerate. Materials purchased by manufacturing increased in price by 9 per cent between April 1994 and April 1995 and over the same period the prices of metal manufactures, chemicals, and man-made fibres, all major industrial inputs, increased by 14, 7.3 and 9.3 per cent respectively. These price increases and the fall in the official unemployment count were interpreted as signalling a future increase in the general price level, and the government increased interest rates. Higher interest charges were added to increasing costs and the increase in output stalled. Interest rates have since been reduced but as yet there are few signs of a recovery in manufacturing and there is nothing to guarantee that if that happens supply-shortage-induced cost inflation will not take off again.

The implementation of pre-Keynesian macroeconomic policies and labour market deregulation (Wilkinson 1997) have resulted in the re-emergence of mass unemployment of interwar proportions, a deep restructuring of labour markets away from full-time secure employment, and a dramatic increase in inequality of income. Measuring the unemployment consequences of the policy shifts of the 1980s and 1990s raises major problems. Since 1979, no fewer than thirty changes have been made to the way unemployment is officially counted, all but one of which have reduced recorded unemployment. The official definition of unemployment has also been changed from persons registered as unemployed to the current definition of those out of work claiming unemployment benefits of various kinds. Between 1979 and 1993, claimant unemployment increased from around 1 million to 2.8 million. The Unemployment Unit has estimated that on the basis of those registered as unemployed, unemployment increased from around 1.4 million in 1979 to more than 4 million in 1993. These estimates receive support from a study by Wells (1994) which shows a level of unemployment in early 1994 'closer to the Unemployment Unit's total of 4 million than to the official claimant count of under 3 million'.

The record of deregulatory policies is no better if employment, rather than unemployment, is taken as the measure of success. It is a myth that the policies pursued in the 1980s and 1990s have led to substantial job growth in comparison to previous decades. Official figures show that by 1983 total employment—a figure which includes employees, the self-employed, and members of the armed forces—had fallen by 1.7 million from its 1979 peak. It then recovered slowly, but after 1989 a second intense depression again reduced the number of jobs, to 0.6 million below its 1979 level by the middle of 1993. Employment was also restructured during this period, with a decline in the number of full-time, secure jobs. Between 1979 and 1993, male full-time employment fell by 2.3 million; this was only partly compensated for by an increase of 0.5 million in male part-time jobs. Meanwhile, female employment increased by 1.3 million, although only 196,000 of these jobs were full-time. Overall, in this period the number of employees fell by 1.7 million and self-employment increased by 1.1 million (0.4 million of whom were part-time). Much of the 'new' self-employment resulted from government incentive schemes for the unemployed, and is very low-paid (Joseph Rowntree Foundation 1995: 53).

As unemployment has grown and employment has become increasingly part-time and/or casual, pay, and more generally income, has become more unequally distributed. Between 1977 and 1992 the average real wages of the bottom 10 per cent of male earners were static; the median or mid-point increase was 27 per cent; while for the top tenth of earners, the average increase was 44 per cent (Goodman and Webb 1994). During this period the earnings of non-manual workers rose more quickly than those of manual workers and full-timers' earnings rose more quickly than those of part-time workers. Of the self-employed in 1993, more than 20 per cent had incomes which were below half the average income for all households (Department of Social Security 1995). The rise in inequality of earnings, together with cuts in social security provision, has contributed to a sharp increase in household poverty. Official sources show that between 1979 and 1993 the lowest decile of households saw no increase in their income before housing costs are taken into account, whereas the highest decile had a rise of 45 per cent. When housing costs are taken into account, the lowest decile had a drop in real income of 17 per cent, compared to an increase of 62 per cent for the highest decile (ibid).

The degree of job insecurity and dissatisfaction arising from these developments is not easy to measure. Some part-time jobs are stable and secure, and some individuals may welcome the flexibility offered by part-time work and self-employment. Conversely, many full-time jobs pay very low wages and offer only partial guarantees of continuing employment. The essential question here is how insecurity affects different groups and to what extent it is growing. There is little doubt that an ever-growing number of workers are affected by insecurity. One recent assessment (Coutts and Rowthorn 1995) is that 13.5 million workers in the British economy are now in a 'primary' sector of the labour-force which, on the whole, enjoys secure and well remunerated full-time employment, with a further 6.5 million in an 'intermediate' category of those who, while not having a full-time job, are nevertheless relatively well-paid and secure. This leaves a further 9 million 'disadvantaged' workers without secure or well-paid employment. Of this 9 million, 4.9 million are in employment and 4.1 million are without employment. Thus 'around seventy per cent of the labour-force are financially comfortable and reasonably secure, while thirty per cent live in either insecurity or comparative poverty' (ibid). This analysis, if anything, errs on the side of caution; it does not seek to assess how many of those in the 'primary' segment, who are apparently secure, perceive their position as being under threat, as more firms use redundancy as a measure of first and not of last resort. The important point is that the ratio of disadvantaged to advantaged has increased over the past fifteen years and continues to do so, and this is undermining the economic functioning of the work-force as a whole.

POLICY AND THE FOUR TRAPS

The consequence of the reversal of policy from the mid-1970s has been a growing economic and social polarization. The rapid increase in the resource endowment of households at the top end of the income distribution has combined with improved capabilities as multi-earner households have become the norm and as job opportunities have widened for women. At the bottom end, high unemployment, the disappearance of well-paid male jobs, increased casualization of work, the growth of part-time work, declining relative pay, and cuts in social welfare have served to impede the economic functioning of the relatively poor by reducing their resource endowment and their capabilities. The outcome of policy and the resulting labour-market restructuring has sprung four closely interrelated traps: the Keynesian unemployment trap, the low-wage trap, the fiscal trap, and the social-exclusion trap.

The Keynesian Unemployment Trap

The impact of abandoning the full-employment objectives in the late 1970s was to increase the involuntary unemployment and lower effective demand. The resulting deep depression in the early 1980s reduced investment in productive industries and impeded its recovery by dampening expectations. This exacerbated the long-term de-industrialization of the British economy and, as a consequence, the supply side proved incapable of fully responding to the credit-induced boom of the 1980s and the resulting trend increase in the propensity to import added to the deflationary bias.[8] The ability of

---

[8] By 1990, the balance of payments on current account was in deficit to the extent of almost 2.8 per cent of GDP; in the same year manufacturing investment was 2.6 per cent of GDP.

the economy to generate full-employment effective demand was further weakened by a redistribution of income from the poor, most of whose income is consumed, to the rich who save a high proportion of their income and who have a relatively high import propensity. The negative Keynesian employment effects were disguised in the late 1980s by the high levels of speculative real-estate investment and debt-financed consumer expenditure. But they were revealed and reinforced in the 1990s by the effects of debt overhang, negative equity, the threat of unemployment and general pessimism on consumer expenditure, and by the effects of the 1980s over-investment in commercial building (the concrete overhang), high real-interest rates, and depressed expectation on investment.

The Low-Wage Trap

The official supposition is that employers and the economy will respond positively to lower wages and less restrictive employment conditions. But low wages and poor working conditions also offer a means by which firms can compensate for their own weaknesses and shortcomings. The growing availability of undervalued labour allows firms to compensate for organizational and managerial inadequacies, delay the scrapping of obsolete capital equipment, and engage in destructive price competition. The absence of wage discipline means that technologically and managerially backward firms can survive, and this helps prevent more progressive firms from expanding their share of the market. The overall effect is a lower average level of productivity and a slower rate of introduction and diffusion of new techniques and products.

More generally, the growing availability of undervalued labour and high unemployment create the environment in which entrepreneurship takes the form of cutting pay, worsening the conditions of employment, and the exploitation of low-paid labour. This can be expected to crowd out the 'high road' to competitiveness requiring product and process innovation and a highly skilled, well-motivated and co-operative work-force. Competition based on the development of new products has the effect of continuously shifting product-market boundaries. If firms fail to respond, they are trapped in declining market niches. Although they may remain viable by cutting labour costs and capturing a larger share of a reduced demand, this can only be a short-term expedient. The long term depends on product-based competition rather than price competition, and this requires an emphasis on research and development, product design, and quality. Yet this strategy is discouraged by low-wage competition and its continuous downward pressure on profit margins ruling out long-term considerations, encouraging cost-paring which threatens quality standards, and discouraging co-operation within and between firms designed to improve performance and foster product and process innovation.

The Fiscal Trap

The deflationary impact of macro-policy lowers the tax-take and increases the social-welfare bill while offsetting any incentive tax reductions may have on economic activity and hence the size of the tax-base. The use of the tax/benefit system to counter unemployment by subsidizing wages risks throwing subsidized labour into competition with unsubsidized. This can be expected to drive down wages and increase the incidence of wage subsidy. These Speenhamland effects are already in evidence. In April 1989 there were 285,000 claims for the in-work family credit at a cost of around £7m. per week (around £350m. on an annual basis). By January 1994 family credit had become more generous, the hours conditions had been relaxed, the number of claims for family credit had increased to 521,000, and the annual cost had risen to more than £1bn. (Department of Social Security 1995). There are further costs to the policy of promoting 'non-standard' forms of work. The proliferation of part-time work at low rates of pay and self-employment means that the direct tax-base is being eroded. In construction, which saw a considerable increase in self-employment in the 1980s, both (lawful) tax avoidance and (illegal) tax evasion have become widespread. The resulting loss to government revenues has been estimated at between £2 and £4bn. annually. The tax regime for construction has also contributed to a policy of cut-throat competition based on labour costs which is undermining quality standards and training which is creating serious skill shortages.[9]

The Social-Exclusion Trap

Unemployment and the increase in the number of jobs which are low-paid, insecure, and with poor working conditions has created a widening gap between the increasingly deprived and excluded 'under' class and the affluent 'contented' class (Galbraith 1992). But the boundary between the included and excluded has proved to be by no means permanently fixed. Many of the previously protected white-collar and managerial jobs have become increasingly precarious, as large-scale redundancies and casualization penetrate deeper into the 'primary' employment sectors. Growing poverty and cutbacks in welfare provision have aggravated social trends towards, for example, more single-parent families increasing the incidence of destitution in such households. There is also growing evidence of a causal

[9] M. Harvey (1995), *Taxed into Self-Employment: The Unique Case of the UK Construction Industry* (Institute of Employment Rights).

link between, on one side, unemployment, poverty, and social exclusion and, on the other, rising crime and declining physical and psychological health. These trends have deepened the vicious cycle of inadequate resources, impaired capabilities, and poor economic performance in which an ever growing number of individuals and households are trapped.

The Four Traps, Economic Functioning, and Self-Sufficiency

The Keynesian unemployment, low-wage, fiscal, and social-exclusion traps are mutually reinforcing. The economy is caught in the fiscal trap because of the exchequer cost of the Keynesian unemployment trap and competitive failure due to the low-wage trap. Similarly, individuals caught in the Keynesian unemployment trap can be expected to be in the low-wage and/or the social-exclusion traps. Moreover, unemployability (either actual or imagined by employers) and the lack of education, skill, and motivation can be seen as both causes and consequences of being caught in the low-wage and social-exclusion traps.

The separate and combined effects of the four traps has been to trigger a cumulative downward spiral in the resource endowments and capabilities of individuals and hence their ability to remain self-sufficient. The value of labour power has been eroded by the effect of de-industrialization and in-adequate retraining opportunities whilst capabilities have been devalued by unemployment, the casualization of work, and declining relative pay. The detrimental effects of this on economic functioning are compounded by the growing importance in the resource endowments of poor households of means-tested social-welfare benefits, the removal of many young people from the scope of social welfare, the changing sexual composition of employment, and the relatively low pay of women. This has changed the pattern of intra-household dependency, increased the burden of sharing within households exacerbating the trend towards more frequent family breakdown, and radically increased the incidence of private inter-household income transfers, obligations which are particularly difficult to enforce. The end of resource-sharing with the break-up of households further reduces economic functioning. The capabilities of single parents are reduced by the additional costs of managing small households and the effect of unshared responsibility for child-care on labour-market activities. The capabilities of young people are severely limited by the absence of a secure domestic base and the resulting poverty rules out the possibility of securing one. The effects of these cumulative downward spirals in economic functioning and self-sufficiency are a large part of the explanation of progressive social and economic degeneration of Britain at both the macro- and micro-levels.

REVERSING DECLINE

The single greatest obstacle to adopting policies designed to close the four traps and to reverse the cumulatively economic and social decline is the current conventional economic wisdom and its implementation in policy. This can be called the policy trap: the fifth, and arguably the deepest trap.

The Origins of the Policy Trap

Monetarism and the belief in a causal link between the PSBR and inflation seriously limit the ability of governments to borrow to finance public expenditure. NAIRU, the idea of an inverse causal relationship between levels of unemployment and price inflation, is now so firmly entrenched that central bankers look with deep suspicion at any downward movement of unemployment from any level as signalling potential inflation and the need to increase interest rates.[10] The neo-liberal notion that the relatively rich required higher incomes to provide incentives for investment and entrepreneurship, whilst reduced welfare and wages are needed to generate employment for the poor, provided the justifications for a more unequal distribution of income and cuts in tax and benefits. The adoption of these views as the conventional economic wisdom lifted responsibility for unemployment and poverty from the government and shifted it to the jobless and the poor. The idea that a more unequal distribution of income is superior on efficiency grounds also formed the basis for an opportunistic alliance between vote-seeking political parties offering tax cuts and market deregulation and the rent-seeking *contented classes*—special-interest groups and voters who stood to benefit from the tax cuts, the availability of low-paid labour, and the opportunities for profits created by deregulation (Galbraith 1992). The alliance between the state and the contented classes has been subsequently strengthened by four reinforcing processes. First, the victims of the downward economic and social spiral triggered by policy change have become increasingly alienated from the 'democratic' process so that political exclusion has been added to economic and social exclusion. Secondly, this political exclusion has been progressively reinforced as political parties of the left have abandoned their traditional class allegiances and embraced the new economic and social orthodoxy to compete for the so-called political centre ground. Thirdly, the growing problems of long-term unemployment, poverty, crime, and social dislocation over the past two decades have increasingly polarized society and the contented classes have found themselves more and more threatened by the 'dangerous classes'. Fourthly, those

---

[10] NAIRU thereby becomes a mechanism by which expected inflation is converted into actual unemployment by policy intervention.

promoting the conventional economic wisdom to practitioners have continued to justify their failed predictions by developing theories explaining
unemployment, underemployment and poverty in terms of labour-market
imperfections, welfare-state dependency, and the low quality and poor motivation of the unemployed, the underemployed and the working poor.[11] By
doing so they have provided continued justification for damaging economic
and social policies by the age-old expedient of blaming the victim (Ryan,
1971).

It is now virtually impossible for political parties to propose any radical
alternatives to those supported by the conventional wisdom. There is general consensus across political parties that the problem of unemployment is
a supply-side issue to be addressed by training or by such expedients as subsidizing jobs; that fiscal and monetary prudence is the essence of macroeconomic management; that the welfare state breeds dependency and needs
modification to reinforce employment incentives; that labour standards
other than a low minimum wage threaten jobs; and that union organizations
and collective bargaining are outdated forms of labour-market institutions.
Meanwhile, any party in opposition advocating policies with implications
for additional taxation are at grave electoral risk and any party in power
contemplating monetary and/or fiscal policies designed to reduce unemployment and alleviate poverty risks opposition from the increasingly independent central bankers and the threat of financial crises in increasingly
unregulated capital markets.

Closing the Policy Trap

As Galbraith noted when considering the conventional wisdom in social sci-
ences: 'Ideas are inherently conservative. They yield not to the attack of
other ideas but to the massive onslaught of circumstance with which they
cannot contend' (1969: 19). The conventional wisdom he had in mind was
the pre-Keynesian orthodoxy and the massive onslaught of circumstances
was the growing poverty and unemployment of the interwar years which
played no little part in the rise of Fascism and the developments leading up to
World War II. The new conventional wisdom was Keynesianism and welfare-
state theorizing. These ideas were developed to their fullest in the social
corporatist states of Europe where increasingly the right to jobs, skills, and
effective social welfare became recognized as citizen rights and whose governments proved most resistant to the neo-liberal theorizing and its regressive consequences. Increasingly, however, they are under the threat of
destructive competition from global competitors benefiting from deregulated labour and capital markets, and from the effects of the deflationary

[11] See for example Layard, Nickell, and Jackman (1991); Snower (1994); Phelps (1992,
1994).

macroeconomic policies, imposed at least partly in response to monetarist-inspired Maastricht restrictions on government borrowing. As a result, the core economies of the European Union are beginning to renege on their citizens' economic and social rights and are embarking on the degenerative neo-liberal policy path pioneered by the USA and Britain. Perhaps this will create the 'massive onslaught of circumstances' necessary for a U-turn towards a new conventional wisdom. To be successful such a development will need to embrace the national and international cohesiveness of the policy development which laid the foundation for the post-1945 revival of Europe.

Closing the Keynesian Unemployment, Low-Wage, Social-Exclusion, and Fiscal Traps

Labour standards have a central part to play in reforms of the social-security system and making successful policies to increase labour-market participation. As currently constituted, the poorest working families have little to gain from higher wages because increases in income are captured by the state by reductions in means-tested benefits. The unemployed are trapped both because the means-testing of benefits makes the effective tax rate on their marginal income very high and because job opportunities for the unemployed are generally low-paid and unstable. Consequently, although out-of-work benefits are low they can at least be relied upon, whereas that income certainty is sacrificed by participation in segments of the labour market where neither jobs nor pay levels are secure (McLaughlin *et al.* 1989). Improved wage and employment standards would therefore both help lift poor families out of the poverty and unemployment traps and increase the incentive for their members to increase their pay by seeking out better jobs, acquiring training, or by other means. Improved wage and employment standards would also contribute to the efficiency of social policy by preventing low-paid employment subsidized by social-welfare benefits and by ensuring that increased state provision of nursery schools and other measures designed to increase job opportunities result in their beneficiaries enjoying secure, well-paid jobs rather than providing undervalued labour to low-paying employers.

Such reforms are designed to increase the resources and the capabilities of individuals and reduce the risk of poverty and social exclusion. The most efficient way of achieving this at the micro-level is to increase the economic functioning of individuals so that they have more employment-generated income. Much has been learned by local action across the European Union about what constitutes good practice in assisting individuals who are long-term unemployed or exposed to social exclusion.[12] However, the

[12] See ERGO Programme, Phase One, Final Report.

requirement is for much greater co-operation and co-ordination between social-welfare, state, and voluntary organizations helping the disadvantaged, and the labour-market organizations responsible for designing and implementing labour-market policies directed at assisting individuals. Without this, individuals who are most disadvantaged will not receive the breadth and continuity of assistance essential for raising their capabilities. Therefore, a new consensus is necessary at national level to ensure that resources from the different areas of policy are available to support the primary objective. But this consensus must include the macroeconomic policy-makers. Raising the supply potential of the available labour-force may be a necessary but it is not a sufficient condition of full employment. Ultimately, the success of policies aimed at raising the functioning of individuals will depend on the availability of jobs; on dismantling the Keynesian unemployment trap.

This in turn will depend on an improvement in competitive performance requiring a closing of the low-wage trap by means of an effective system of regulation designed to raise labour standards and to reduce inequality. High and equitable terms and conditions of employment will require employers to improve management, technology, and products; encourage them to make better use of their workers by improved training and personnel policy; and create an environment in which workers have the long-term security necessary to benefit from the improved job opportunities. High labour standards also have an important part to play in securing a co-operative work environment now widely recognized as essential for securing worker co-operation in technical development, product enhancement, and continuous quality control. Worker involvement is the key to such development, but this cannot be relied on where workers have no long-term prospects and when there is no assurance that workers' interests will not be summarily sacrificed to those of other stakeholders in the firm, such as shareholders and creditors. The effectiveness of the modern business enterprise depends on providing workers with rights which give them a voice alongside those of other stakeholders. This, along with other aspects of effective labour regulation, requires that workers have independent representation and collective bargaining, underpinned by a floor of legal rights to minimum terms and conditions of employment. However, if such policies are to be effective in closing the low-wage trap they will need to be supported by measures to ensure the successful redeployment of workers displaced by technical progress and changing consumer demand. This will require effective, universal and equitable social-welfare provision; adequate and widely available facilities for retraining and the relocation of workers; the minimization of barriers to entry into different occupations, a strategy for working time; the provision of high-quality child care and effective anti-discrimination policies. Such measures are required to maintain demand in the labour market and to reduce structural unemployment so as to prevent the establishment and expansion of disadvantaged social and labour-market segments.

The cumulative effects of the policies outlined above will do much to close the fiscal trap (see Kitson, Michie, and Sutherland 1996, and this volume). The fiscal benefits of high levels of employment and improved labour-market standards are clear. Full employment and a more equal income distribution of income before tax would broaden the tax base, reduce the aggregate social-welfare payments and reduce the cost of redistributing income through the expensive tax/benefit network. Good labour-market standards would have the added advantage of ensuring that best use was made of government expenditure by removing the risk that any attempt to help the working poor would merely provide wage subsidies for inefficient employers and lead to declining pay levels, increasing employment insecurity, growing poverty, and burgeoning social-welfare expenditure.

A more permanent measure to close the fiscal trap and remove the cumulative spiral of increasing unemployment, social deprivation, and rising budget deficits would be to remove much or all social welfare from the government income and expenditure equation. This could be achieved by a switch away from a social-welfare system funded out of current taxation towards mutual insurance schemes by which rights to benefits were established by contributions. For this to be effective a way would need to be found of ensuring that individuals not active in the labour market—for example, the providers of household services—were credited with contributions. But this broader recognition of what constitutes economic activity would be central to any reforms designed to increase self-sufficiency and economic performance. A major advantage of mutual insurance schemes would be the removal of public transfers from the arena of power politics where the poor are particularly vulnerable. For this to be completely successful would probably require that the responsibility for such a scheme be vested in an institution constitutionally protected from short-term political expediency. To ensure such a scheme's viability, procedures would be needed by which adjustments could be made to such variables as levels of contributions and benefits, age at retirement to accommodate unpredicted increases in the average length of lifetime, and other factors influencing the cost of provision. These schemes would also need to go hand-in-hand with high and relatively stable rates of employment and measures to prevent labour undervaluation to ensure that the actuarial uncertainties of future job loss or low pay did not undermine the validity and viability of the schemes.

CONCLUSIONS

It cannot be pretended that this policy transition or its implementation will be easy. There are already examples in Britain of concentrations of social exclusion where two or more generations of households have had no contact with the labour market. Economic functioning for these groups has no meaning. They attract transfers until their eligibility expires or their entitlement is withdrawn, but then the costs of subsequent alienation, crime, ill health, and social disruption, replace transfers as a continuing cost on the state and the wider population. Having people outside the systems which maintain and encourage economic functioning is a dead-weight on macro-policy—a permanent fiscal trap. Hence a rational view is to make the systems all-inclusive.

The micro aspects of integration into full economic functioning fall broadly into two groups: first, the combination of work, welfare, and social inclusion, and second the pathways to integration into the core labour market and into self-sufficiency. The constraints on the first stage of integration are the cost burdens of the socially excluded and the difficulties of including the excluded groups into the support structures which are no longer part of their community culture. Recovery for these groups requires raising their capabilities to a level at which they can and will participate and succeed in labour-market measures aimed at facilitating economic functioning, but this is expensive and will only be partially self-financing in the short period. Hence, one constraint is the cost burden but another constraint is the difficulty in building a co-operative approach to the socially excluded which involves contributions from a wide variety of state departments and programmes (e.g. labour measures, social welfare, health, education).

Full integration will require continuing support to maintain participation. There are a wide variety of services that need to be provided as a package for individuals, including guidance, counselling, personal-problem solving, basic skills, vocational skills, work experience, and placements into jobs which have a regular contractual status in the labour market and pay the rate for the job. There are several constraints, including: the need to establish and reproduce an infrastructure of trainers and providers who have the skills appropriate to delivering the complex assistance required; the need to obtain involvement, commitment, and changed attitudes among employers and trade unions to ensure quality-employment opportunities; and, full assimilation into the workplace and associated collective bargaining arrangements.

The key to effective micro processes is that the value of participants in programmes is fully recognized and their needs met and that the expectations of outcomes are realistic, both for providers and participants. This requires co-operation between different providers (including the state, local actors, employers, and social partners) and between providers and their participants based on a consensus about objectives and a relationship of trust. Overall, policies and structures for welfare, labour-market support, health, education, collective bargaining, labour-market regulation, and social protection need to be complementary and mutually reinforcing. This is the major constraint on how effectively the micro- and macroeconomy can be made consistent, because it requires political and social, as well as economic, consensus and agreement over the rights and responsibilities of all parties. These conditions are constraining and there is potential for significant conflict between the micro and macro requirements. Moving from a situation in which the four traps are operating to one where they have been removed requires careful phasing of changes which show a net gain in economic functioning relative to the absorption of resources at each stage, and which are based on an agreed and accepted change in the balance of power in the labour market and more widely in society.

REFERENCES

Bowles, S. and Gintis, H. (1976), *Schooling in Capitalist America* (New York: Basic Books).

Coutts, K. and Rowthorn, R. (1995), 'Employment in the United Kingdom: Trends and Prospects', *Political Quarterly*, Special Issue (Oxford: Blackwell).

Deakin, S. and Morris, G. S. (1995), *Labour Law* (London: Butterworth).

Department of Social Security (1994), *Social Security Statistics 1993–1994*, tables A1.01, A1.02.

ERGO Programme, *Phase One, Final Report*, Commission of the European Communities, Directorate-General for Employment, Industrial Relations and Social Affairs, DG V/A/1, Apr. 1992.

—— *Phase Two, Final Report*, Commission of the European Communities, Directorate-General for Employment, Industrial Relations and Social Affairs, DG V/A/1, 1996.

Galbraith, J. K. (1969), *The Affluent Society* (London: Hamish Hamilton).

—— (1992), *The Culture of Contentment* (Boston: Houghton Mifflin).

Goodman, A. and Webb, S. (1994), 'For Richer, for Poorer', *Institute for Fiscal Studies Commentary*, 42.

Harvey, M. (1995), *Taxed into Self-Employment: The Unique Case of the UK Construction Industry* (London: Institute of Employment Rights).

Hirsch, B. T. and Addison, J. T. (1986), *The Economic Analysis of Unions: New Approaches and Evidence* (Boston: Allan and Unwin).

Horrell, S., Rubery, J., and Burchell, B. (1989), 'Unequal Jobs or Unequal Pay?', *Industrial Relations Journal*, 20/3: 176–91.

Joseph Rowntree Foundation (1995), *Inquiry into Income and Wealth*, ii (York: Joseph Rowntree Foundation).

Kitson, M., Michie, J., and Sutherland, H. (1996), 'The Fiscal and Distributional Implications of Job Generation', ESRC Centre for Business Research Working Paper 37, University of Cambridge, and forthcoming, *Cambridge Journal of Economics*, 1997 21/1 (Jan.).

Lancaster K. J. (1966), 'A New Approach to Consumer Theory', *Journal of Political Theory*, 43.

Layard, R., Nickell, S., and Jackman, R. (1991), *Unemployment, Macroeconomic Performance, and the Labour Market* (Oxford: Oxford University Press).

McLaughlin, E., Millar, J., and Cooke, K. (1989), *Work and Welfare Benefits* (Aldershot: Avebury).

Marshall, A. (1947), *Principles of Economics* (London: Macmillan), 549.

Meade, J. E. (1995), *Full Employment Regained*, Dept. of Applied Economics, University of Cambridge, Occasional Paper 61 (Cambridge: Cambridge University Press).

Parker, H. (1995), *Taxes, Benefits and Family Life* (London: Institute for Economic Affairs).

Phelps, E. S. (1992), 'A Review of Unemployment', *Journal of Economic Literature*, 30: 1476–90.

—— (1994), 'Low-Wage Employment Versus the Welfare State', *American Economic Review*, Papers and Proceedings, 84/2: 54–8.

Ryan, W. (1971), *Blaming the Victim* (New York: Pantheon Books).

Sen, A. (1985), *Commodities and Capabilities* (Amsterdam: North Holland).

Snower, D. J. (1994), 'Converting Unemployment Benefits into Employment Subsidies', *American Economic Review*, Papers and Proceedings, 84/2: 65–70.

Spence, M. (1973), 'Job Market Signalling', *Quarterly Journal of Economics* (Aug.), 355–74.

Wells, J. (1994), 'The Missing Million', *European Labour Forum* (Summer).

Wilkinson, F. (1988), 'Real Wages, Effective Demand and Economic Development', *Cambridge Journal of Economics*, 12/1: 179–90.

—— (1991),'The Structuring of Economic Deprivation and Social Deprivation and the Working of the Labour Market in Industrial Countries', *Labour and Society*, 16/2: 119–38.

—— (1997), 'Changes in the Notions of Unemployment and What That Means for the Poor', in P. Arestis, G. Palma, and M. Sawyer (eds.), *Relevance of Keynesian Economic Policies Today* (London: Macmillan).

5. Unemployment, Wage Dispersion, and Labour-Market Flexibility

Brian Henry and Kevin Lee

INTRODUCTION

The question of whether the UK can grow in the future at a high enough rate to give significant increases in employment without the increasing inflation which accompanied previous expansions concerns two separate, but interrelated, issues. On the one hand, it concerns the extent to which the growth in productive potential has improved, or whether the long-run rate of unemployment associated with constant inflation (i.e. the NAIRU) has fallen. And, on the other hand, it concerns the degree to which the process of adjustment to this long-run position has changed, influencing the extent of any trade-off between inflation and unemployment which might exist during transition to the long-run position. These issues, in turn, touch on the vigorous debate—which has been in train for some time—about possible links between macroeconomic performance and the operation of supply-side institutions, including bargaining structures, corporate organization, and institutional intervention in the labour market (loosely 'corporatism'). The argument is that such institutions determine the extent of labour-market flexibility, and that this provides the key to understanding how some countries have been able to achieve relatively low unemployment rates with moderate inflation. For example, in one strand of this literature, either very decentralized wage bargaining on the one hand, or highly centralized bargaining between national union and employer organizations on the other, are believed to be a reason for real wage flexibility and the better employment and inflation experiences of countries like Japan and the USA ('decentralized') and Sweden, Norway, and Austria ('centralized'). (See, for example, Calmfors and Driffell 1988).

Partly due to general arguments of this sort, the UK introduced widespread changes to labour-market arrangements over the 1980s, aiming to improve its flexibility. Have they worked, in the sense that quantifiable effects on the NAIRU or on the inflation–unemployment trade-off are now

Financial support from the ESRC (grant no. L116251016) is gratefully acknowledged. Thanks are also due to James Mitchell for assistance in producing the tables used in the chapter.

visible? Opinions differ, with pessimistic views expressed by Metcalf (1994), and Barrell *et al.* (1994), but more optimistic views found in the OECD *Annual Survey for the UK* (OECD (1995), Bootle (1996), and in Minford (1994). The latter, in particular, reaches bullish conclusions about the effects of the 1980s reforms on the labour market, arguing that they have produced a fall in the natural rate from about 12 per cent (which he calculates as the level for the early 1980s), to about 2 per cent in the early 1990s.

This chapter provides a discussion of recent labour-market experiences in the UK, considering whether labour-market reforms have had an impact on wage-setting and employment behaviour. We briefly set out below some of the developments in the UK labour market over the last decade or so, placing these in a comparative setting (both historically and internationally). Then we discuss more formally what is meant by 'labour-market flexibility' in order to evaluate how it might, or might not, have been affected by the reforms, first setting out the issues in a broad macroeconomic context, before considering the microeconomic foundations of this analysis in a little more detail. We then review some recent empirical work carried out by the authors which aimed to evaluate the effects of the reforms upon labour-market performance, amongst other things. This review considers whether there is evidence that the behavioural relationships which determine wage and employment levels have altered due to recent reforms and, in providing answers to this question, pays close attention to the interplay between wage-setting, unemployment levels, and wage dispersion. Our analysis favours the pessimistic school in the debate over whether or not the UK has experienced an improvement in its supply-side institutions during the last ten to fifteen years. It suggests instead that recent labour-market behaviour can more readily be interpreted as an (unchanged) response to unprecedentedly high unemployment rates experienced over a protracted period. We conclude with a further discussion of those commentators who take a more optimistic view of labour-market developments.

THE BACKGROUND

The analysis of the unemployment–inflation problems in the UK must start from an assessment of labour-market trends in the wider setting of the main industrialized countries. The diverse behaviour of the European and the US economies is very informative since the former are typically characterized as having labour markets in which institutional restrictions are pervasive, while the latter is seen as an example of a labour market free from institutional intervention. The labour-market reforms implemented in the UK over the recent past represent an attempt to move the UK further in the direction of the US model and away from the continental European model.

Fig. 5.1 provides details of employment, unemployment, and real-wage developments in the UK, USA, and three of the UK's Continental neighbours since 1960. Fig. 5.1(a) shows that, in the aftermath of the first oil-price shock, European unemployment increased from levels which were lower than those in the USA to levels comparable to those of the USA by the end of the 1970s, and subsequently outstripped USA levels in the 1980s (in the wake of the second oil-price shock and attendant recessions). Unemployment in the EU fell modestly in the 1990s boom, whereas in the USA unemployment almost halved. Most recently, unemployment rose to 12 per cent in the EU (by 1994), whereas it was just 6 per cent in the USA. The contrasting experiences of the USA and European economies is also shown in Fig. 5.1(b) which shows that employment in the USA grew on average by 1.6 per cent per year during the 1980s, whereas it grew by 0.5 per cent over the same period in the EU. And Fig. 5.1(c) documents the experiences of these same countries in terms of their real-wage growth, showing that real wages have not grown in the USA while there has been a general tendency for real wages to rise in the economies of the EU; a tendency which does not seem much affected by adverse real shocks and high unemployment levels.

As well as differences in employment and real-wage experiences, there were also inter-country differences in changes in participation ratios over the 1980s. In most countries falling male participation rates and increasing female participation rates were a common characteristic. Participation rates for males fell least in the USA and in Italy, and by more in Germany, France, and the UK where they changed by similar orders of magnitude. Female participation rates increased most strongly in the USA, followed by Italy. (See Table 5.1.).

Obviously, the issue is not the facility or otherwise of countries to decrease unemployment, but whether this can be achieved without increasing inflation. Hence the inflation experience in the UK and other European economies, relative to the USA, is significant. From 1986 to 1990, the UK's

Table 5.1.   Participation rates (percentages)

	Male			Female		
	1979	1983	1992	1979	1983	1992
France	82.6	78.4	74.7	54.2	54.4	58.7
Germany	84.9	82.6	78.9	52.2	52.5	58.6
Italy	82.6	80.7	79.1	38.7	40.3	46.5
UK	90.5	87.5	84.5	58.0	57.2	64.8
USA	85.7	84.6	84.8	58.9	61.8	68.9

Source: OECD, *Employment Outlook 1994*.

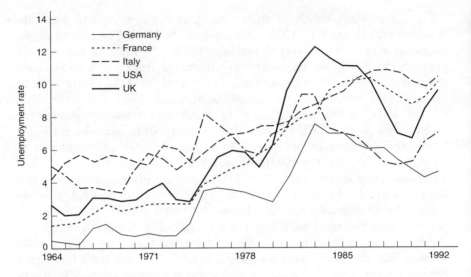

Fig. 5.1(a).   Unemployment rates.

Source: OECD (MEI). Rate defined as unemployed as % of labour-force.

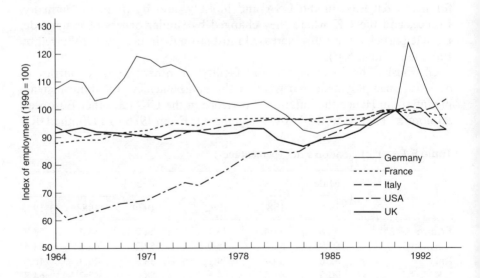

Fig. 5.1(b).   Employment.

Source: OECD (MEI). Total employment indices, 1990 = 100 (German series based on manufacturing only).

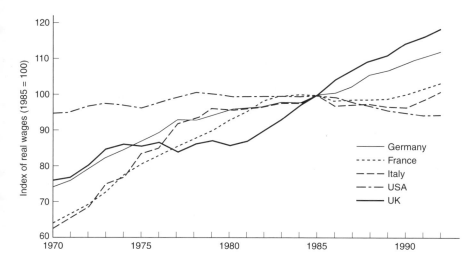

Fig. 5.1(c). Real wages.

Sources: OECD (MEI) and World Bank. Nominal wages measured by hourly earnings (manufacturing) in Germany, US, UK; and by hourly earnings (industry) in France and Italy. Deflated by GDP deflator to obtain real wages.

RPI inflation more than doubled, rising from about 3 per cent to 10 per cent. In the USA after falling unevenly in the early 1980s, CPI inflation rose from less than 2 per cent in 1986 to nearly 5.5 per cent in 1990, so it more than doubled there also. However, inflation in the USA was brought down to about 3 per cent by 1992–3, without much change in unemployment. So it seems that, until fairly recently, it was appropriate to describe the problem in the UK and in Europe more generally, as not simply one where the level of unemployment has increased, but where the *trade-off* between inflation and unemployment has apparently worsened. (See Jackman (1994) on this point.)

Clearly, in terms of employment creation and the elimination of unemployment without generating high inflation, the evidence above provides a priori evidence to support the view that the USA model outperforms the European alternative. In contrast with the USA, it appears that in EU countries, successively higher levels of unemployment are required to stabilize inflation at a given rate (i.e a rising NAIRU). For the UK, the NAIRU has been estimated to have increased substantially over the 1980s. The increase, reported in Layard, Nickell, and Jackman (1991), from just over 5 per cent to nearly 8 per cent from the late 1970s to the mid-1980s is a good representation of the sort of changes many—though by no means all—researchers have been reporting.[1] The *issue* of increasing employment

[1] NAIRU analysis of the labour market is increasingly being questioned as an empirically valid explanation of higher unemployment. (See for example Coulton and Cromb 1994.)

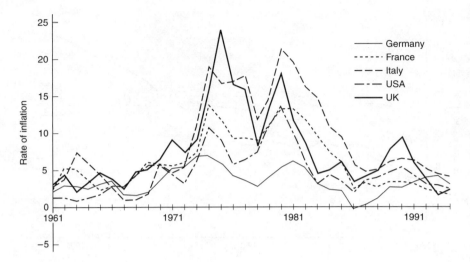

Fig. 5.2.   Rate of inflation.
Sources: OECD (MEI) and ETAS. 'All items' CPI used except in UK (RPI).

without increasing inflation is clearly a central one for policy-makers. Moreover, it is generally agreed that structural reforms can affect the trade-off between inflation and unemployment, even if there is less agreement on what these reforms should be and what their effects are.[2]

In fact, the UK experiences of the last decade provide an interesting forum in which to consider the role of supply-side reform in influencing macroeconomic performance. Recently, a number of commentators have expressed the view that the UK labour market has been transformed by changes in industrial relations and other labour-market reforms (OECD (1995) is a clear example of this view). These reforms were undertaken over the 1980s and include, *inter alia*: easing restrictions on hiring and firing; initiatives aimed at encouraging decentralized wage bargaining (through the government's own public pay policies, through the abolition of wages councils, and so on); employment law reform; training initiatives and other active labour-market policies; and significant changes to the benefit system.[3] Moreover, it is clear that, in terms of the recent employment/unemployment experiences of the European economies, the UK does indeed stand out. In the second half of the 1980s, UK employment growth matched that of the USA, and unemployment fell from about 11 per cent in the early 1980s to about 6 per cent toward the end of the 1980s. Again, these changes are com-

[2] See, for example, Calmfors and Driffell 1988; Nickell 1995; and Henry and Snower 1996.
[3] See Brown and Wadhwani 1990; Metcalf 1994; Anderton and Mayhew 1994; and Henry and Karanassou 1996.

parable to those in the USA, and are in contrast to the relatively stable unemployment rates achieved in other European countries over the same period. Further, these achievements have been made in the presence of low levels of inflation since, although inflation began to rise at the end of the 1980s, it has averaged about 2.5 per cent since early 1993. Superficially at least, there may appear to be evidence that the trade-off between inflation and unemployment has improved in the UK relative both to what it previously experienced, and relative to other European countries. But is it actually the case that the labour-market reforms have led to an improved trade-off in the UK? Or is it that recent performance is due to the combined effects of the experience of high unemployment rates over a protracted period, coupled with the benefits of low inflation in other industrial countries? If the latter, what we are witnessing is not a change in the underlying behaviour of wage and employment determination, but an (unchanged) response to unprecedented high unemployment.

Before considering the ways in which labour-market reform might have improved labour-market flexibility, and the evidence on whether this has indeed occurred in the UK, it is worth commenting at this stage on a further empirical similarity between the recent experiences of the UK and those of the USA. This relates to the marked widening in earnings differentials in the UK observed over the last decade and a half. As Fig. 5.3 shows, this has

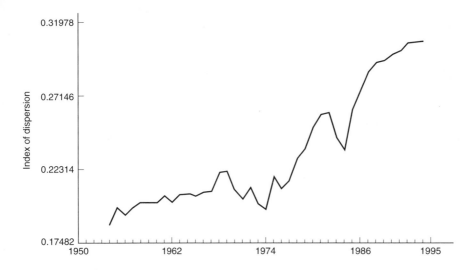

Fig. 5.3.   Real-wage dispersion.

Source: Lee and Pesaran (1993). Real-wage dispersion measured by ratio of standard deviation of sectoral real wages to average sectoral real wage, using data for sixteen industrial sectors.

widened by about 50 per cent measured in terms of the median wage, since 1979. This stylized fact is at the heart of the other main issue we take up: namely, the interplay of high unemployment, widening differentials and wage-setting behaviour.

A more formal account of these interactions is provided below. Here, however, we simply note that a widening dispersion of wages is often interpreted as reflecting improved labour-market flexibility, in that it provides greater scope for inter-industry, inter-group factor substitution (Freeman 1988). Whether this type of flexibility is the result of reform or as a response to high unemployment is clearly a question of some interest. Certainly others have noted a link between the effects of widening wage dispersion and of high unemployment rates on wage-setting. For example, Barrell, Morgan, and Pain (1995) note that unemployment duration effects on wages seem only to operate in countries where earnings dispersion has increased. This suggests that it might be difficult to distinguish between a 'long term unemployment' effect in wage equations (often thought of as a form of hysteresis) and the effects of widening dispersion as identified by Freeman (1988).[4]

FLEXIBILITY: THE ISSUES

The term 'labour-market flexibility' is often used loosely; a sin of which, up to now, we are also guilty. In the Appendix to this chapter, we set out a stylized model of the macroeconomy to help define what we mean by labour-market flexibility, and to consider how labour-market reforms might help influence flexibility and why such flexibility is an important determinant of macroeconomic performance. The model illustrates the importance of *real* and *nominal* rigidities in the operation of the macroeconomy. Real rigidities relate to the (lack of) responsiveness of prices (given wages), based on firms' decision-making, and of wages (given prices), based on wage-setters' decisions, to the level of activity in the economy.[5] Nominal rigidities, on the other hand, relate to the speed with which prices adjust to changes in costs (e.g. wage costs) and to the speed with which nominal wages adjust in response to price change in wage-setting decisions.

In the model of the Appendix, there is a level of output (and hence unemployment) at which firms' decisions on the price/wage mark-up are

[4] In this chapter, we do not pursue the important issue of the links between wage differentials and income inequality. Freeman's (1995) analysis of the US labour market provides a compelling description of the way in which rising wage inequality translates into falling living standards for the less-skilled, rising crime and incarceration rates, rising child poverty, and rising homelessness.

[5] Equivalently, real rigidities relate to the (lack of) responsiveness of firms' price/wage mark-up and of wage-setters' real wage demands during periods of expansion and recession.

consistent with wage-setters' decisions on real-wage levels, and at which there is a long-run consistency of price and wage expectations with actual price and wage outcomes. When this situation is achieved with constant inflation, the corresponding level of unemployment is frequently termed the 'NAIRU'.[6] The size and extent of real and nominal rigidities are shown to be important, however, in a number of ways:

(i) The NAIRU falls as rigidities fall;

(ii) In the model, unemployment falls below the NAIRU in the presence of a continual planned expansion in nominal demand due to the presence of nominal and real rigidities, and despite the fact that agents form expectations rationally. There therefore exists a trade-off between inflation and unemployment, and the greater is the extent of the rigidities, the more favourable the trade-off becomes (in the sense that lower unemployment is obtained for a given level of inflation);

(iii) The presence of real and nominal rigidities suggests that even a once-and-for-all increase in nominal expenditure (which has no long-run consequences on inflation) can have effects on real magnitudes for protracted periods;

(iv) Conversely, output stability (around the level associated with the NAIRU) is improved through reductions in real and nominal rigidities.

The comments above, and the stylized model of the Appendix, help us to relate the policy debate on labour-market flexibility with macroeconomic performance. While the term 'labour-market flexibility' is used in connection with a wide variety of changes in the labour market, in fact these reforms concern very different aspects of the labour market, and their impact on real and nominal rigidities is sometimes ambiguous. Let us consider some of the changes in the labour market which have been implemented to improve labour-market flexibility in turn:

(a) *Measures to reduce hiring and firing costs.* This legislation was concerned primarily with influencing the speed of adjustment of employment. Clearly reforms which facilitate the hiring and firing of employees reduce the costs of employment adjustment, and the outcomes of firms' decisions will be achieved more rapidly as a result. Note, however, that although such legislation would influence the dynamics of adjustment, it is unlikely to influence real rigidities (which are associated with the *long-run* real wage elasticity of the demand for labour). Absent any reasons for believing that

---

[6] In what follows, we shall also use this term, although more strictly we mean the level of unemployment (and corresponding output level) achieved when there is a long run consistency of price and wage expectations with actual price and wage outcomes.

this real-wage elasticity had altered, reforms involving the speed of employment adjustment will not have altered the NAIRU;

(b) *Measures to encourage movement from industry to single-employer bargaining* (see Brown and Wadhwani 1990). Changes in the extent of decentralization in wage bargaining can have complex off-setting effects on wage settlements: Calmfors and Driffell's analysis (1988) provides explanations for why decentralization of wage setting might cause real wages to be more or less responsive to unemployment (so that the effect on real rigidities would be ambiguous). Decentralization is likely to have a less ambiguous influence on the speed of adjustment of wages, however, since most of the explanations of nominal inertia provided in the literature rely on the presence of non-synchronized wage settlements across heterogeneous wage-setters, suggesting that inertia is positively related to the degree of disaggregation and non-synchronization. In so far as this is true, decentralization of wage bargaining would raise the extent of nominal rigidities;

(c) *Employment law reforms of the 1980s, which served to reduce the institutional power of trade unions*;

(d) *Reductions in the value of unemployment benefits and other welfare payments relative to wages* (see Atkinson and Micklewright 1989);

(e) *Elimination of Wages Councils that set minimum wages.* Reforms (c)–(e) above each relate to changes in the strength of various 'wage-push' variables, hypothesized to raise real wage demands for a given level of unemployment. To the extent that strong unions, high unemployment benefits, and the existence of minimum wages cause real wages to be higher than otherwise, for a given level of unemployment, then these reforms serve to reduce the NAIRU and raise the non-inflationary level of output;

(f) *Training initiatives*;

(g) *Improvements in public employment services, including job information and brokerage services and the provision of facilities to enhance job placement for the unemployed.* Training initiatives serve to both raise the level of productivity of workers (raising output and real wages), and to improve the responsiveness of the real wage to unemployment (i.e. lower real rigidities) since this improves the possibility for re-employment for the unemployed. This is also the idea behind the initiatives in the public-employment service. It is worth noting, however, that the influence of the wage-push variables on the NAIRU is positively related to the extent of the real and nominal rigidities, and in so far as these initiatives are successful in reducing rigidities, they offset the effects of measures which reduce the NAIRU through their influence on wage-push variables.

This brief discussion suggests that many of the reforms introduced to improve labour-market flexibility may have had little direct impact on macroeconomic performance, while those reforms which might have had an effect may have worked in offsetting directions in some instances (especially since the elimination of real and nominal rigidities reduces the NAIRU but also worsens the terms of trade in any inflation/unemployment trade-off that might exist during periods of adjustment to the NAIRU). However, we have already noted that the UK labour market did appear to behave differently during the late 1980s, and if this was not due to labour-market reform, then this anomalous behaviour requires an alternative explanation. We have alluded to one possible explanation: that wage-setting and employment were simply responding to the prolonged period of high unemployment that had been experienced since the late 1970s. In the following section, we briefly consider the microfoundations of wage and employment determination to elaborate on the mechanisms (some obvious, some less so) through which high unemployment rates might have exerted such an influence.

THE EFFECT OF UNEMPLOYMENT ON WAGE AND EMPLOYMENT DETERMINATION

The model which we use to illustrate the effects of unemployment on wage and employment determination is based on a 'competing-claims' view of the labour market. This hypothesizes that aggregate real wages and employment arise from the maximization of a union utility function subject to a firm's labour demand constraint. In such models, union utility, u_{it}, might be described by a function of the form:

$$u_{it} = ([w_{it} - p_t] - [w_{it}^* - p_t])^\theta (n_{it} - n_{it}^*)^{(1-\theta)} \qquad (1)$$

where the 'it' subscript refers to industry i at time t, n_{it} is the (log) employment level, w_{it} is the (log) nominal wage, p_t is the (log) price level, w_{it}^* is the log of a fall-back nominal wage, and n_{it}^* is the log of the fall-back level of employment. Here unions derive utility from real wages and from employment relative to some fall-back levels, with θ indicating the relative weight given to wages and employment in their utility function. The union is assumed to set wage levels, and the employer the employment level (the so-called 'monopoly union' model). Assuming technology can be represented as:

$$Y_{it} = N_{it}^\alpha D_{it} \qquad (2)$$

where D_{it} is a measure of the terms which shift the demand for labour (including, for example, productivity or capital stock levels) and Y_{it} is output, then, taking a static framework for simplicity, equilibrium employment and real wages are given (in logs) by the following two equations:

$$n_{it} = c + \frac{1}{1 - \alpha} (w_{it} - p_t) + \frac{1}{1 - \alpha} d_{it} + \varepsilon_{1it} \qquad (3)$$

$$(w_{it} - p_t) = (w_{it}^* - p_t) + (1 - \alpha) \frac{\theta}{1 - \theta} (n_{it} - n_{it}^*) + \Lambda + \varepsilon_{2it} \qquad (4)$$

where c and Λ are constants. Equations (1) and (2) correspond to the firm's and wage-setters' decision rules and are the basic building blocks of a model of the supply side of the macroeconomy, abstracting from the dynamics.[7]

As we saw in the previous section, the key properties of the model revolve around the 'output responsiveness' of firms' and wage-setters' decision-making. From the above derivation, there seems little scope for explaining the apparent changes in supply-side behaviour through the relationship in (3).[8] This follows because the derivation shows that the association between prices and output (via employment levels) in firms' decisions is governed by the real wage elasticity of demand for labour. This elasticity, in turn, is related to production function characteristics, and we have not advanced any reasons for thinking that these characteristics should have changed during the 1980s. The situation on wage determination is different, however. The wage equation given by (4) is sufficiently general to provide the possibility of an explanation for the changes of the 1980s; output responsiveness in wage-setting clearly depends in (4) on the determinants of the fall-back wage and fall-back employment levels, and there are good reasons to believe that these might have changed over time.

(i) Measurement of n_{it}^*

There has been considerable interest focused on the determination of the fall-back level of employment, n_{it}^*, largely emanating from the insider-outsider models of hysteresis. In these models, the time-path of employment in an industry itself influences the fall-back level of employment against which bargaining takes place.[9] A means of modelling the fall-back level of employment is to set $n_{it}^* = n_{i,t-1}$, or, more generally, to write:

$$n_{it}^* = \sum_{j=1}^{q} a_j n_{i,t-j} \quad \text{where} \quad \sum_{j=1}^{q} a_j = 1.$$

for some $q > 0$. This captures the view that a union might value only *changes* in employment, and not the level itself, so that the union's fall-back position simply ratchets up or down in response to recent history.[10] An

---

[7] Equations (3) and (4) correspond to equations (A1) and (A2) of the model in the Appendix, and this discussion therefore provides some microfoundations for that model. The model is reviewed in more detail in Henry and Lee 1996.

[8] Although, as explained below, this is not so in a more dynamic setting.

[9] See, for example, Lindbeck and Snower 1988; Blanchard and Summers 1986; and the review in Nickell 1990.

[10] If $n_{it}^* = 0.99 n_{i,t-1}$, for example, then the union would be concerned with employment levels, but for protracted periods the union would behave very similarly to one which was concerned only with employment growth.

alternative measure of the fall-back level of employment is that it depends on its minimum recent value, i.e. $n_t^* = \min(n_{t-1}, \ldots, n_{t-p})$, for some (arbitrarily chosen $p > 1$). This also captures the view that the fall-back level of employment is history dependent, and again implies that the union is ultimately unconcerned about employment levels. Either of these two assumptions, if true, would provide an important explanation for real wages not responding to high unemployment levels except over a protracted period.

(ii) *Measurement of* w_{it}^*

In the competing claims model, the fall-back wage plays a central role in capturing the influences on sectoral wages which are external to the sector. For example, this is the route through which the 'alternative wage' (i.e. the wage available in alternative employment should a worker lose his or her current job) or unemployment benefits influence sectoral wage-setting. Moreover, this is the most explicit route through which the (aggregate) unemployment rate is believed to influence sectoral wage-setting: a rise in the unemployment rate increases the probability of remaining unemployed should a worker lose his current job, and hence lowers the fall-back position of the worker.

But this process is clearly very indirect, and provides a further possible explanation for high unemployment having an influence on wage-setting only over a protracted period. According to this, high unemployment only exerts a downwards influence on wage-setting where workers perceive the unemployed as competitors for work should they lose their current job; highly 'localized' unemployment (by region or occupation) will not provide this downward pressure, and generally speaking neither will the long-term unemployed. Typically the unemployed will be 'competing' for work at the lower end of the wage distribution, and consequently wage-setters at the upper end of the wage distribution feel this influence only as the effects gradually work their way up the distribution by reducing the alternative wage available to progressively higher-paid workers. This is not to deny that high unemployment will be associated with downward pressure on wages therefore, but suggests that the process may take place only over many years.

The discussion above shows also how the presence of high unemployment will be associated with widening wage dispersion, and this provides a further avenue through which high unemployment will exert downward influence on wages. For example, a reasonable assumption on the 'alternative wage' available to a worker is that it is equal to a wage randomly located lower in the distribution than the wage that the worker currently receives. In any sector, this alternative wage is clearly related to the average wage in the economy, but it will also depend on the distribution of wages (which may itself vary over time): for a given average wage, the alternative wage available to any worker falls as the distribution widens and the lower tail of the distribution moves further below his or her current wage. Hence, for example, Henry and Lee (1996a) show that if sectoral wages are distributed according to the logistic distribution, then the expected alternative wage, averaged over all sectors in the economy, $E[w_{it}^a]$ is given by

$$E[w_{it}^a] = e\ [w_{it}] - \frac{\sqrt{3}\pi}{6}\ S[w_{it}], \qquad (5)$$

where $E[w_{it}]$ is the mean value of the w_{it}, averaged over sectors, and $S[w_{it}]$ is the standard deviation of the w_{it} across sectors. The importance of equation (9) is that it shows that the average ('economy-wide') fall-back wage rises one-for-one with the average wage in the economy, but that it also falls if the dispersion of wages rises. In the light of this discussion, the widening of the wage distribution in the UK during the 1980s can be seen as one of the reasons why the labour market might superficially appear to be becoming more responsive; in fact, this could be reflecting a further indirect influence of unemployment on wage setting, as high unemployment raises the dispersion of wages, which tends to reduce wage pressure.

(iii) *The Effect of Unemployment on Employment Adjustment Costs*

The discussion above is based on a purely static model, but it is worth noting at this point that there would be further effects of high unemployment on the *dynamic* adjustment of the labour market. In particular, as unemployment rises in general, it will become easier for any firm to recruit labour because the pool of workers who are available and willing to work becomes larger. Further, since workers' bargaining power is reduced in these circumstances, a more rapid contraction of the work-force will be less costly to the firm as the likelihood of a strike is reduced. Hence, the costs of employment adjustment will be reduced. As noted already, although this does not provide an explanation for possible changes in the equilibrium output/employment levels, it suggests that the speed of adjustment of employment to shocks will be more rapid in the presence of high unemployment.

Ultimately it is an empirical issue as to whether wage-setting and/or employment determination were significantly affected by the reforms of the 1980s, or whether wages and employment levels are still being determined much as they have been in the past, and that the apparently anomalous behaviour of wages and employment in the 1980s was simply the reaction to the unprecedentedly high levels of unemployment experienced through the 1980s. In studying the workings of the labour market, it is therefore most important to focus on whether there is evidence of a change in the underlying behaviour or not. The rest of the chapter reviews such evidence.

It does not provide new empirical results on these issues; that would be a very considerable task. Instead, the rest of the chapter reports on a number of interrelated studies on these issues by the authors together with a number of co-researchers. The principal studies are given in Henry, Karanassou, and Shin 1996; Henry and Lee 1996a,b; and Lee and Pesaran 1993. Other studies referred to are Henry and Karanassou 1996; and Henry and Snower 1996.

A SUMMARY OF SOME EMPIRICAL RESULTS

Following the structure of the chapter so far, the work that we discuss below considers first some empirical evidence investigating the stability of wage and employment equations over time to evaluate evidence for improved 'flexibility', and then considers some of the evidence directly investigating the responsiveness of wage-setting to changes in output (or unemployment).

Evidence for Change in Wage and Employment Relationships

An obvious way to test for change in the behavioural relationships determining wages and employment is to estimate representative wage and employment equations over different sample periods, and compare these. Some of our recent research has followed this approach. In Henry and Karanassou (1996), for example, quarterly employment and wage equations have been estimated to test for possible breaks in the relationships over various time periods from 1988 onwards. A representative example from our work on employment is shown in Table 5.2(a). This equation for employment (LE), depends on output (LY), the product real wage (LW) the real oil price and a deterministic time trend (treated as a strongly exogenous variable).[11] A representative wage equation is shown in Table 5.2(b), where wages are explained simply in terms of unemployment (UR) and a competitiveness variable $(LCOMP)$, proxying terms of trade effects.

These equations are fairly successful according to standard econometric criteria, passing most of the tests comfortably and according with a priori views on the determinants of wages and employment. Hence, they can be used as a test bed for tests of the stability of the behavioural relationships over time. In Table 5.3 we summarize orthodox (Chow Predictive Failure) stability tests applied to these equations, estimated over alternative sample

---

[11] These estimates use the Auto Regressive Distributed Lag (ARDL) method for obtaining long-run relationships. (See Pesaran and Shin 1995.) This version was estimated by instrumental variables (IV) due to the presence of the current value of output and the real wage as independent variables in the employment equation.

Table 5.2. Employment and wage equations

(a) Employment equations

	Constant	LY	LW	ROILP	T	(p,q)
LE	0.13	0.81	−0.25	−0.001	−0.002	(2,0,0,0)
	(0.90)	(3.43)	(1.3)	(2.9)	(2.7)	

	Constant	ΔLE(−1)	ΔY	ΔLW	ΔROILP	ECM(−1)
ΔLE	0.13	0.55	0.05	−0.02	0.0	−0.06
	(2.7)	(7.4)	(3.0)	(1.3)	(2.95)	(4.45)

$R^2 = 0.56$, $\chi_1^2(4) = 3.9$, $\chi_2^2(1) = 0.9$, $\chi_3^2(2) = 8.6$, $\chi_4^2(1) = 1.2$, $\chi_5^2(5) = 9.9$, $LR = 22.4$ (20.9)

(b) Wage equations

	Constant	UR	LCOMP	(q,p)
LW	3.5	−0.95	−0.11	(1,0,1)
	(14.1)	(5.54)	(2.27)	

	Constant	ΔUR	ΔLCOMP	ECM(−1)
ΔLW	0.58	−0.16	0.07	−0.16
	(4.9)	(3.9)	(2.1)	(4.6)

$R = 0.33$, $\chi_1^2(4) = 12.3$, $\chi_2^2(1) = 0.5$, $\chi_3^2(2) = 0.5$, $\chi_4^2(1) = 0.0$, $\chi_5^2(1) = 0.03$, $LR = 69.4$ (27.1)

Notes: In determining the dimension of the ARDL (p,q), the Schwartz Bayesian information criterion is used throughout. $\chi_1^2()$ is a Lagrange multiplier test of residual correlation, $\chi_2^2()$ is the Ramsey RESET test, $\chi_3^2()$ is a test for normality of residuals, $\chi_4^2()$ a test for heteroscedasticity, and $\chi_5^2()$ is Sargan's test that the instruments are valid. $LR(.)$ is the likelihood ratio given by Johansen's trace statistic, that $r = 0$, where r is the number of cointegrating vectors, and where the value shown as the second number in the parenthesis is the 95 per cent critical value.

periods, starting with a sample period ending in 1988 (which we take as probably the earliest time an improvement might have occurred). According to these formal statistical tests, there is no evidence to reject the view that wage and employment determination is explained by the same econometric relationship throughout the whole period; i.e. there is no evidence of change in the behavioural relationships having taken place. A similar conclusion is drawn from alternative methods for investigating the stability of the relationships, using CUSUM, squared CUSUM, and recursive parameter estimates. Figures 5.4(a) and (b) document the CUSUM tests, for example, illustrating that there is no evidence of a change in the equation describing wage determination, although there is some marginal evidence of instability

Table 5.3. Structural stability tests

Sample	Wages	Employment
1960Q1–1988Q1	χ (26) = 18.4 (38.9)	χ^2 (26) = 21.4 (38.9)
		χ^2 (9) = 10.8 (16.9)
1960Q1–1990Q1	χ^2 (18) = 18.79 (28.9)	χ^2 (18) = 18.6 (28.9)
		χ^2 (9) = 15.3 (16.9)
1960Q1–1991Q1	χ^2 (14) = 14.2 (23.7)	χ^2 (14) = 13.4 (23.7)
		χ^2 (9) = 11.7 (16.9)
1960Q1–1992Q1	χ^2 (10) = 8.3 (18.3)	χ^2 (10) = 12.3 (18.3)
		χ^2 (9) = 12.1 (16.9)

Notes: Tests refer to Chow's second test. Where available, tests of parameter stability are also included.

in the employment equations over the most recent past according to this test.

The formal statistical test for stability generally shows that the employment and wage equations appear unchanged throughout the period. However, the results of the CUSUM test provides some weak indication of instability in the former towards the end of the sample period, a finding which corresponds to a general view that employment did decrease faster in the 1990s recession than might have been predicted on the basis of previous behaviour. To investigate this further, and in particular to consider the possibility that employment adjustment costs might depend on the unemployment rate, we have also considered an employment equation which incorporates dynamics that change over time. In this (non-linear) employment equation, the coefficients on the lagged dependent variables in the equation are themselves functions of the unemployment rate, so that employment changes can speed up or slow down as unemployment rates alter. Henry and Lee (1996b) estimate such equations for each of nine industrial sectors covering UK manufacturing. These can be summarized in the following 'averaged' relationship:[12]

$$LE_{it} = (1.27 - 2.41\,UR_t) * LE_{i,t-1} - (0.36 - 2.28\,UR_t) * LE_{i,t-2}$$
$$+ (1 - 1.27 + 0.36 + (2.41 - 2.28)UR_t) * [1.84 - 0.005T_t + 1.07LY_{it}$$
$$- 0.37LY_{i,t-1} - 0.49LW_{it} - 0.11LW_{i,t-1}]$$

[12] Each of the coefficients presented in the 'average' relationship is the simple average of the corresponding coefficients obtained in the nine industrial equations. The coefficient on LY_t is the average of the sum of the coefficients on current industrial and aggregate output in each of the industrial equations.

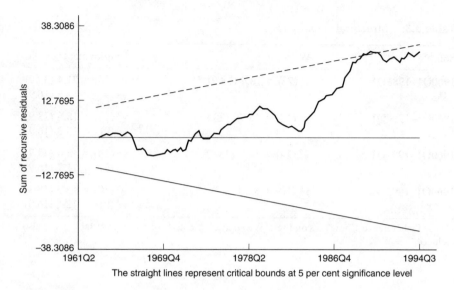

Fig. 5.4(a).   Plot of cumulative sum of recursive residuals (employment).
Source: Table 5.2(a).

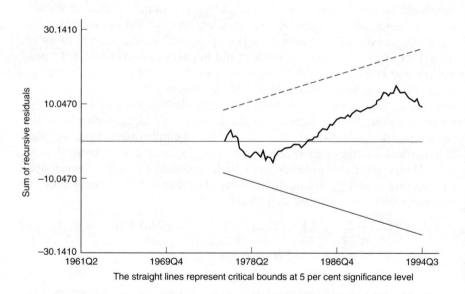

Fig. 5.4(b).   Plot of cumulative sum of recursive residuals (real wages).
Source: Table 5.2(b).

where notation is as before. The form of this equation ensures that the long-run elasticity of demand for labour, with respect to wages, output, and productivity, is unchanged. But the equation shows that the influence of the first lagged dependent variable falls as the unemployment rate rises, while the influence of the second lagged dependent variable rises. The overall effect is largely offsetting, although the sum of the effects is negative overall, and this is consistent with the view that adjustment does indeed speed up during periods of high unemployment. In some of the nine industries considered, the evidence of this effect was not strong, so that there is little evidence to suggest a statistically significant effect when the equations are taken together. On the other hand, the statistical significance of this unemployment effect *was* statistically significant at conventional levels in four out of nine industries. The fact that the effect is statistically significant in some, but not all, industries might explain the results obtained on the aggregate data discussed above which suggest only a marginal effect on employment dynamics.

In summary, therefore, the empirical findings summarized here indicate that the underlying behaviour of wage-setting and employment determination did not change dramatically over the late 1980s, although there might be evidence of changed dynamics in the employment equation. These latter changes are explicable in terms of the changing influence of the unemployment rate on employment adjustment costs, however, so that there is little statistical evidence to suggest that a behavioural change has resulted from labour-market reforms.

Wage-setting, Unemployment, and Wage Dispersion

Our contention has been that any apparent change in recent labour-market behaviour in the UK could be explained in terms of the reaction of firms and wage-setters to high unemployment, and without recourse to the effects of labour-market reform. We have seen some evidence to suggest that labour-demand behaviour might be influenced by the unemployment rate, and we now consider some empirical evidence on the effects of unemployment on wage-setting behaviour. The first results that we consider are those presented in Lee and Pesaran (1993) which provides estimated wage equations for each of sixteen industrial sectors based on annual data from 1954–90. The equations are based on the model given in (1)–(4), which can be transformed to give a wage equation of the form:

$$(w_{it} - p_t) = (1 - \theta)(w_{it}^* - p_t) + \theta(y_t - n_t) + (1 - \alpha)\theta(n_{it} - n_{it}^*) \qquad (6)$$

so that real wages in an industry are determined as a weighted average of the fall-back wage and industrial output per person productivity, plus a term involving $n_{it} - n_{it}^*$. This becomes a vehicle for investigating wage determination by (i) assuming that $n_{it}^* = n_{i,t-1}$ (i.e. the fall-back level of employment is simply last period's employment level);[13] (ii) assuming that the fall-back wage depends on the economy-wide average real wage, the unemployment rate (UR_t) and the unemployment benefit level (ρ_t); and (iii) allowing for dynamics by including a lagged dependent variable in the equation. The 'average' wage equation obtained by Lee and Pesaran across the sixteen industries was then:

$$LW_{it} = 2.89 + 0.41LW_{i,t-1} + 0.11(LY_{it} - LE_{it}) - 0.02\Delta LE_{it} -$$
$$0.01UR_t + 0.04\rho_t + 0.50LW_t$$

where LW_t is the (log) economy-wide real wage. As before, these coefficients represent simple averages of the industrial coefficients, although here this averaging conceals important behavioural differences. In particular, statistically significant effects of unemployment were found in just four of the sixteen sectors, but the (numerically) large coefficients on the unemployment variable were found in industries located at the bottom end of the wage distribution. This is an important finding in our judgement, since it provides empirical support for the view that high unemployment has a direct impact on wage dispersion.

Also, despite finding weak links between wage-setting and unemployment in any one industrial equation, these results imply a substantial effect of unemployment on aggregate real wages in the longer run. Note that, summing over the industrial sectors, the above industrial relationship provides an 'approximate' aggregate wage equation of the form:

$$LW_t \approx \frac{2.89}{1 - 0.50} + \frac{0.41}{1 - 0.50} LW_{t-1} + \frac{0.11}{1 - 0.50} (LY_t - LE_t) - \frac{0.02}{1 - 0.50} \Delta LE_t$$
$$- \frac{0.01}{1 - 0.50} UR_t + \frac{0.04}{1 - 0.50} \rho_t$$

$$\approx 5.78 + 0.81LW_{t-1} + 0.21(LY_{t-1} - LE_{t-1}) - 0.04\Delta LE_t$$
$$- 0.02UR_t + 0.08\rho_t$$

and the corresponding long-run relationship between wages and their determinants is given by

$$LW \approx 28.9 + 1.0(LY - LE) - 0.2\Delta LE - 0.1UR + 0.4\rho$$

These expressions represent approximations because the intersectoral interactions cannot be summed in precisely this way. But even though it is approximate, the equation conveys the important point that, when intersectoral comparisons are present, small impact effects observed at the sectoral level accumulate both at the aggregate level and across time. For

---

[13] See the discussion of the previous section on the implication of this assumption for unemployment hysteresis.

example, the small unemployment effect observed on impact in the sectoral equations is doubled in the aggregate equation. Moreover, the influence of the lagged dependent variable is also doubled in the aggregate equation, so that this aggregate equation possesses a high degree of inertia. As a result, the *long-run* effect of any of the determinants of wages can be numerically large, although it accumulates only slowly over time. Hence, in the equations above, the long-run unemployment effect is more than five times larger than its effect on impact, with a long-run elasticity estimated to be around -0.15 (indicating that a 1 per cent rise in unemployment causes real wages to fall by 0.15 per cent). However, given the inertia implicit in this system of equations, only 25 per cent of the effect of a change in unemployment would be felt over the first two years, and it takes five years for 50 per cent of the ultimate effect of the rise in unemployment to be exerted on wages and nine years for 75 per cent of the effect to be felt. The empirical evidence suggests that high unemployment can be expected to exert downward pressure on wages, therefore, but only very slowly over time, taking almost a decade for the large part of adjustment to a shock to occur.[14]

The final piece of applied work that we wish to note here is that provided in Henry and Lee (1996). Here, wage and employment equations are estimated together in a system using the 'Structural VAR' modelling framework described in detail in Pesaran and Shin (1996). This modelling framework allows for complicated dynamics in the underlying model, but more importantly estimates long-run relationships subject to plausible economic restrictions. In this chapter, annual aggregate data over the period 1954–91 is used to investigate the model set out in (2), (3) and (4). The estimated model is:

$$LE_t = -0.50LW_t - 0.68LA_t + LK$$
$$LW_t = LW_t^a + 2.75(LE_t - LE_t^*) + 0.16LA_t - 0.10UR_t - 0.01\rho_t$$

where LA_t and LK_t are measures of (log) technical progress and (log) capital stock, used to capture the demand shift terms (denoted d_t in the earlier model descriptions). LE^* is measured by the minimum level of employment experienced over the previous two years, and LW_t^a is measured as in (5).

The restrictions imposed on the model are acceptable (using a likelihood ratio test), and the model described in (2)–(5) appears to provide a reasonable description of the wage- and employment-setting processes in the UK. In particular, these equations pick up, as before, the downward influence of unemployment on wages, with an elasticity in the region of -0.1. Moreover, this model also captures the (downward) effect of (widening) wage dispersion, which is now implicitly included in the measure of LW_t^a. In so far as rising unemployment does result in widening wage dispersion, then, this

[14] See Henry and Snower 1996 for a similar point on the extent of persistence in the UK labour market.

empirical work suggests that this provides a further route through which, in the long run, high unemployment will exert downward influence on wages.

In summary, the evidence we have reviewed suggests that the high unemployment rates of the 1980s would be likely to exert significant downward pressure on real wages, both through the 'standard' route (of reducing re-employment opportunities, and hence agents' fall-back wages), and through the less standard route of widening wage dispersion (obtained as the unemployment rates exert influence primarily on those at the lower end of the wage distribution).[15] There is strong evidence that these effects show up only gradually as they accumulate across sectors and over time. It is therefore entirely plausible that any apparent improvement in wage responsiveness experienced in the UK towards the end of the 1980s/early 1990s resulted as the accumulated response to the unemployment experiences of the previous decade rather than the contemporaneous response to changes brought about by labour-market reforms implemented at that time.

CONCLUSIONS: THE VIEW FROM THE OTHER SIDE

Following this review of our own, rather negative, findings on the effectiveness of the recent labour-market reforms, what of the optimists? We comment briefly on two examples of the optimistic camp next, concluding that they do not persuade us that labour-market reforms have had the beneficial effects that these studies identify.

(i) *OECD*

The principal feature to which the OECD draw attention in their *Annual Survey for the UK* (1995) is that the recent response of unemployment to the changes in output appears very different from that in the last recession. However, as the OECD themselves point out in their comments on the apparent shortening of the lag between changes in output and changes in unemployment, the factor which seems to be mainly responsible for this is the large change in participation rates documented above. While we have noted that there is some evidence employment did decrease faster in the 1990s recession than would be predicted on the basis of previous behaviour, we have argued that there is little evidence of changes in either of the equations explaining employment or wage determination. Our reading of the OECD's evidence is that the improved responsiveness of unemployment to

---

[15] Our interpretation of the effect of dispersion has similarities with the views expressed in the literature on the effect of lengthening unemployment duration on the unemployment effect on wage-setting; see, for example, Barrell *et al.* 1995.

activity is based on the substantial changes observed in participation, and it is difficult to regard these as the primary objective of the labour-market reforms of the 1980s.

(ii) *Minford (1994)*

Minford's argument that there has been a substantial change in the natural rate since the early 1980s, due to the reforming process, is based on the Liverpool model for wages, prices, and unemployment. This incorporates the following reduced form for unemployment (Minford p. 141):

$$ln\ U = 11.2\ UNR - 5.3\ ln\ (1 + BOSS) + 5.0\ ln\ (BEN/(1 + TAXL)) +$$
$$\quad (7.0) \qquad (4.0) \qquad\qquad\qquad (3.9)$$
$$\quad 0.023\ TIME + 7.41\ (1 + VAT) - 2.72\ ln\ WT + const + prody\ dummies$$
$$\quad (0.03) \qquad\quad (4.7) \qquad\qquad (2.13)$$

where U is unemployment, UNR the unionization rate, $BOSS$ the employer's tax rate, BEN the real value of unemployment benefits, $TAXL$ the employee's tax rate, VAT indirect tax rate, WT is World Trade, and standard errors are in parentheses.

On the basis of this equation, Minford estimates that the natural rate fell dramatically from 1983 onwards, from over 12 per cent to just over 2 per cent. In a decomposition of the effects of the determinants of unemployment provided by the author, the principal explanations for this fall are the estimated effect of unionization on unemployment (see the coefficient on UNR in the equation above) and the change in the unionization rate over the period since 1983. However, while it is this estimate which appears to lead the author to argue that supply-side reforms have lowered the natural rate so dramatically, the unionization variable is clearly insignificant in the wage equation reported by Minford (p. 140). The major single factor accounting for the 'fall' in the natural rate does not seem to be a statistically significant determinant of real wages—and hence unemployment—on the author's estimates, therefore. This is not surprising. Henry and Snower (1996) argue that one important drawback to the argument that high levels of actual unemployment are due to a high natural (or NAIRU) rate, is that the main variables advanced by natural-rate theorists as the 'explanation' of this worsening natural rate—real benefits and unionization—were stable or fell over much of the 1980s. Their movements do not appear to help in accounting for the medium-term changes in unemployment over the 1970s and 1980s therefore.

In summary, we remain unpersuaded that any major improvement has occurred in the UK labour market following the reforms of the 1980s. Where does this leave the possibilities for job creation through growth? The issues may be highlighted using two of the recent EU White Paper scenarios.

(See European Commission 1993, ch. 1.) The two scenarios—which are EU-wide—postulate growth and productivity assumptions as follows:

(1) *Modest Growth, High Employment Intensity*: This assumes growth at potential of about 2 per cent p.a., with a gap between output and employment growth of 0.5 per cent p.a. This latter is what the White Paper refers to as 'employment intensity of output', although it is evidently nothing other than an assumption about the growth of average labour productivity (output per head). Arithmetically this case corresponds to a 'US' case of low productivity and low-wage growth: during the period 1973–90, productivity and wage growth averaged just 0.4 and 0.4 per cent p.a. respectively in the USA, while the economy grew by 2.3 per cent p.a.

(2) *High Growth, Modest Changes in Employment Intensity*: This scenario is for 3 per cent growth in GDP coupled with growth in employment intensity below the historical average at 1–1.5 per cent.

Scenario 2, which appears the preferred case in the White Paper, illustrates our concerns fairly simply. The question which a scenario of this sort immediately poses is 'Would growth at this rate simply lead to inflation?' The answer we submit, on the basis of the empirical work reviewed earlier, is that it would. To see this, note that output gaps in the UK for 1995 are estimated at (minus) 4.2 per cent.[16] If growth in potential output is assumed to be 2 per cent p.a., on the high growth assumption the output gap goes to zero by 1998, and by normal reckoning inflation should be expected to rise at, or before, this date. But if labour productivity falls from 2 to 1–1.5 per cent, as assumed in this scenario, then total factor productivity falls by between 0.7 and 0.35 p.p. (assuming for simplicity that labour share is 0.7). This brings forward the timing of full capacity utilization by at least a year, and hence the onset of higher inflation.

It is true that the scenario assumes that real wage growth falls to 0.5 per cent p.a.[17] In this event, inflationary pressures at given levels of unemployment (or more generally, capacity utilization) would clearly be lower than suggested by historical experience. But the White Paper does not show how, nor does it have specific policy recommendations which would enable, this *decoupling* of real wages from productivity to take place. The empirical results we have reviewed also suggest that the co-movements in real wages and productivity have not changed noticeably in the UK, so it is hard to justify such an assumption. In addition, lower productivity growth *per se* would be inflationary not simply through squeezed output gaps, but also because lower productivity would imply worsened competitiveness,

[16] This estimate is taken from IMF (1994), *World Economic Outlook*, 43.
[17] See p. 60, where employment is assumed to increase by 2 per cent, and the real wage bill by 2–2.5 per cent implying a fall in the average real wage, 0.5 per cent.

decreased net trade, and downward pressure on nominal effective exchange rates.

The message from this short review is, we suggest, that it will be difficult to promote substantial employment growth without re-igniting inflationary pressures. As any future government, Labour or Conservative, will have the aim of constraining inflation, there will clearly be a policy dilemma in the medium term. It is not the task of the present chapter to describe how this dilemma may be resolved, or even if it can. Rather, we have concentrated on the narrower question of whether a supply-side improvement centred on the labour market has occurred as a result of the reforms that have been implemented. As we noted earlier, some commentators take an optimistic view on this, and see high medium-term growth without inflation as a possibility. (See, for example, Bootle 1996 which is devoted to exploring issues which arise from the low inflation world he envisages.) According to the results of our research, however, such concerns are premature and rather more imagination *still* needs to be shown in developing supply-side policies which will enable the UK to achieve growth without increasing inflation.

APPENDIX

In this Appendix, we describe a stylized model of the macroeconomy to help clarify those aspects of the supply side of the macroeconomy which are important in defining 'labour-market flexibility' and which might affect macroeconomic performance. The model consists of the following four stylized relationships:[18]

$$\theta(L)n_t = -\pi_1 - \lambda(L)(w_t^e - p_t) + \psi d_t \qquad (A1)$$

$$\delta(L)w_t = \pi_2 + \mu(L)p_t^e - \phi(L)u_t + \pi_3 z_t \qquad (A2)$$

$$y_t = \alpha n_t + d_t \qquad (A3)$$

$$y_t = m_t + v_t - p_t \qquad (A4)$$

where n_t is the (log) employment level, w_t is the (log) nominal wage, p_t is the (log) price level, d_t is a measure of the terms which shift the demand for labour (including, for example, productivity or capital stock levels), u_t is the unemployment rate (approximately equal to $l_t - n_t$, where l_t is the (log) labour force), z_t represents wage-shift variables, y_t is (log) output, m_t is planned nominal expenditure, v_t is unplanned nominal expenditure, and the expressions $\theta(L)$, $\lambda(L)$, $\delta(L)$, $\mu(L)$, and $\phi(L)$ are polynomials in the lag operator L.[19] The 'e' superscript indicates that expectations are formed on the variable.

---

[18] The following is closely related to the more comprehensive survey of the literature on unemployment determination provided by Nickell (1990).

[19] For example, we write $\theta(L) = \theta_0 + \theta_1 L + \theta_2 L^2 + \theta_3 L^3 + \ldots$, and $\theta(L)x_t = \theta_0 x_t + \theta_1 x_{t-1} + \theta_2 x_{t-2} + \theta_3 x_{t-3} + \ldots$

Equations (A1)–(A3) provide a simplified model of the supply side of the macro-economy, incorporating an expression based on firms' decision-making in (A1), an expression based on wage-setters' decisions in (A2), and an expression describing production technology in (A3). Equation (A4) is then a simplified representation of the demand side of the economy. This stylized model makes explicit the nature of the dynamic processes operating on the supply side of the economy, and hence facil-itates discussion about what improved labour-market flexibility means. In the model, we have stripped the dynamics down to the bare essentials as follows: (i) In making their decisions, firms face costs of adjusting employment levels and hence lagged employment levels are included in equation (A1). For example, it is fre-quently assumed that firms incur costs when employment levels are changed (e.g. through hiring and firing costs) and that additional costs are incurred when employ-ment levels are changed at a relatively high rate (e.g. through training costs or indus-trial disputes).[20] Profit maximization in the face of such costs would generate a relationship between current employment and lagged employment levels as firms attempt to smooth the changes and the rate of change of employment in the face of changes in its determinants; (ii) Assuming that wage-setters are concerned with real wages, other things being equal, wages and prices should move in line in the long run so that $\mu(1) = \delta(1)$. However, in general, nominal inertia will exist, and might be substantial,[21] so that lagged values of nominal wages and prices enter into wage-setters' decisions; (iii) Current and lagged unemployment rates influence real wage levels through the lag polynomial $\phi(L)$. Given the indirect impact of unemployment on wage-setting, the higher order terms in this lag polynomial may be large (relative to the low-order terms) indicating that unemployment rates exert a downward influ-ence on real wages only after a considerable time. Moreover, if $\phi(L)$ has a unit root, so that $\Sigma_{s=0} \phi_s = 0$, then we can write $\phi(L) u_t = \phi^*(L) \Delta u_t$, for an alternative lag polynomial $\phi^*(L)$, and real wage-setting is influenced by current and lagged *changes* in unemployment only. This possibility is raised in the literature on unemployment hysteresis.

We can substitute (A3) into (A1) and (A2), noting that $u_t = l_t - n_t$, and rearrange to write (A1) and (A2) as follows:

$$p_t = \frac{\pi_1}{\lambda(L)} + w_t^e - \left[\frac{\psi}{\lambda(L)} + \frac{1}{\alpha} \frac{\theta(L)}{\lambda(L)} \right] d_t + \frac{1}{\alpha} \frac{\theta(L)}{\lambda(L)} y_t, \qquad (A1')$$

$$w_t = \frac{\pi_2 + \pi_3 z_t}{\delta(L)} + \frac{\mu(L)}{\delta(L)} p_t^e - \frac{\phi(L)}{\delta(L)} l_t - \frac{1}{\alpha} \frac{\phi(L)}{\delta(L)} d_t + \frac{1}{\alpha} \frac{\phi(L)}{\delta(L)} y_t. \qquad (A2')$$

In (A1'), based on firms' decision-making, prices depend on *inter alia* expected wages and the level of activity in the economy (through y_t) while in (A2'), based on wage-setters' decisions, wages depend on expected prices and, again, the economy's level of activity. The key expressions of the model are

$$a(L) = \frac{1}{\alpha} \frac{\theta(L)}{\lambda(L)}, \ b(L) = \frac{1}{\alpha} \frac{\phi(L)}{\delta(L)}, \text{ and } c(L) = \frac{\mu(L)}{\delta(L)}.$$

[20] See, for example, Burgess 1993.
[21] Due to the presence of desynchronized, staggered wage contracts, for example. (See Taylor 1980, *inter alia*.)

The long-run responsiveness of prices to cyclic activity is given by $a(1) = \Sigma_{j=1,\infty}a(j)$, and the long-run responsiveness of wages to cyclic activity is measured by $b(1)$. Note that the speed of adjustment of prices to changes in y_t are determined by the parameters of the lag polynomial $\theta(L)$, but that the overall effect is determined by $\theta(1)/\lambda(1)$, the long-run wage elasticity in the labour demand equation in (A1). Note also that the responsiveness of wages to the cycle depends on the lag polynomial $\phi(L)$, which captures the influence of current and lagged unemployment rates on real wage in (A2). If there is a unit root in $\phi(L)$, as suggested in the hysteresis literature, then $b(1) = 0$.

The values of $a(1)$ and $b(1)$ provide measures of the size of *real* wage and price rigidities (with higher values of $a(1)$ and $b(1)$ signifying lower real rigidities). *Nominal* rigidities are only found in the wage equation in this model,[22] and $c(L)$ captures the extent of these nominal rigidities. In the long run, wages and prices will move in line (i.e. $c(1) = 1$), but the presence of any impediments to instantaneous adjustment of wages (through the existence of desynchronized, staggered wage contracts, for example) will mean that higher-order terms in the lag polynomial $c(L)$ may be large, indicating protracted nominal adjustments.

Now, assuming expectations are formed rationally, the model in (A1)–(A4) can be solved to obtain the following expressions for y_t and price and wage surprises:

$$y_t = \bar{y}_t + \left[\frac{1 - c(L)}{1 - c(L) + a(L) + b(L)}\right] m_t + \left[\frac{1}{1 + a(L) + 2b(L)}\right] v_t \tag{A5}$$

and

$$(p_t - c(L)p_t^e) + (w_t - w_t^e) = (a(L) + b(L))\left[y_t - \left[\frac{a(L) + b(L)}{(1 - c(L) + a(L) + b(L)}\right]\bar{y}_t\right], \tag{A6}$$

where

$$\bar{y}_t = \frac{-\left[\frac{\pi_1}{\lambda(L)} + \frac{\pi_2 + \pi_3 z_t}{\delta(L)}\right] + \left[\frac{\psi}{\lambda(L)} + a(L) + b(L)\right]d_t + \frac{\phi(L)}{\delta(L)}l_t}{1 - c(L) + a(L) + b(L)z}.$$

In the long run, when $c(L) = 1$, expression (A6) shows that price and wage expectations are consistent with their actual levels at $y_t = \bar{y}_t$. Expressions (A5) therefore illustrates the significance of real and nominal rigidities in determining this level of output (and the corresponding level of unemployment, often termed the 'NAIRU'). Four points are worth noting. *First*, in the long run when $c(1) = 1$, a once-and-for-all increase in planned expenditures will leave output unaffected. Further, in these circumstances, if unplanned expenditures are zero on average, the non-inflationary level of output depends primarily on the price-wage markup (π_1), the wage-shift variables (z_t), and the demand shift variables (d_t). Moreover, the relative importance of these variables depends on the long-run 'output responsiveness' of price and wage-setting; i.e. on the parameters $a(1)$ and $b(1)$. Hence, output levels increase as 'output responsiveness' grows, because the importance of the (positive) term involv-

[22] Although it would of course be possible to incorporate corresponding nominal inertia in the expression for firms' decision rules also.

ing d_t rises and that of the (negative) term involving π_1 and z_t falls. *Secondly*, despite the fact that agents form expectations rationally, the presence of real and nominal rigidities in this model means that a perfectly anticipated continual expansion of planned expenditure (at a constant rate of g per annum, say) would cause output to be above its natural rate, with the extent of this higher-output level depending on the rate of increase in planned expenditure.[23,24] *Thirdly*, in the presence of even low levels of nominal inertia (so that $c(L)$ is near unity), once-and-for-all increases in planned expenditures can have effects on output for protracted periods (with no consequences for inflation in the long term) if unemployment levels exert an influence on wages over a long period or if the costs of adjustment in the labour-demand equation are (relatively) high.[25] And *fourthly*, the long-run effect of unplanned expenditures on output are also related (inversely) to $a(1)$ and $b(1)$, so that output stability (around the non-inflationary level) is improved through increased output responsiveness in prices and wages.

In terms of the model given in (A1)–(A4), we note that: (i) measures to reduce hiring and firing reduce the value of $\theta(1)$, but are likely to be offset by changes in $\lambda(1)$ to leave the long-run real-wage elasticity in (A1), and hence $a(1)$, unchanged; (ii) decentralization in wage bargaining will have an ambiguous effect on $\phi(1)$, and hence $b(1)$, but is likely to raise the value of $\delta(1)$, reducing $b(1)$, and to extend $c(L)$; (iii) measures which lower z_t serve to raise $\bar{y}_t$, but increases in real and nominal rigidities reduce the influence of z_t in the determination of $\bar{y}_t$; and (iv) measures to improve training or the employment service raise d_t, and hence $\bar{y}_t$, and also raise $\phi(1)$, and therefore $b(1)$.

REFERENCES

Atkinson, A. and Micklewright (1989), 'Turning the Screw: Benefits for the Unemployed 1979–1988' in A. Dilnot and I. Walker (eds.), *The Economics of Social Security* (Oxford: Oxford University Press).

Barrell, R. (1994) (ed.), *The UK Labour Market* (Cambridge: Cambridge University Press).

[23] For example, $(1 - c(L))/(1 - c(L)+a(L) + b(L))$ can be rewritten as $1 - d(L)$, for some lag polynomial $d(L)$. Now, assume that $d(L) = dL + d(1-d)L^2 + d(1-d)^2L^3 + \ldots$, which has the desired property that $d(1) = 1$. In these circumstances, if planned expenditure grows at a constant rate g (i.e. $m_t = m_{t-1} + g$), then $(1 - d(L))m_t = g/d$.

[24] Of course, this is valid only while firms' and wage-setters' decisions are reflected by the equations given in (A1) and (A2). If expenditure was continually rising, then it is unlikely that (A1) and (A2) would continue to hold, as decisions would be based not only on expected contemporaneous values of wages and prices, but also on expected *future* values.

[25] For example, even if $\phi(L)/\delta(L) = 1$, but $\theta(L) = 1 - 0.9L$ (indicating that employment adjustment costs are high in (1)), then $1/(a(L)+b(L)) = \alpha\lambda (1 + 0.9L + 0.9^2L^2 + \ldots)$ and output is substantially influenced by m_t lagged over a considerable period.

—— Morgan, J., and Pain, N. (1994), 'Employment Inequality and Flexibility', mimeo, NIESR, London.

Bean, C. (1994), 'European Unemployment: A Survey', *Journal of Economic Literature,* 32/2 (June), 572–691.

Bootle, R. (1996), *The Death of Inflation* (London: Nicholas Brearley).

Brown, W. and Wadhwani, S. (1990), 'The Economic Effects of Industrial Relations Legislation Since 1979', NIESR, London.

Burgess, S. (1993), 'Non-Linear Dynamics in a Structural Model of Employment', in M. H. Pesaran and S. Potter (eds.), *Non-Linear Dynamics, Chaos and Econometrics* (Chichester: Wiley).

Calmfors and Driffell, J. (1988), 'Centralisation of Wage Bargaining and Macroeconomic Performance', *Economic Policy,* 6 (April), 13–61.

Coulton, B. and Cromb, R. (1994), 'The UK NAIRU', Government Economic Service Working Paper No. 124, HM Treasury.

European Commission (1993), *Growth, Competitiveness, Employment: The Challenges and Ways Forward into the 21st Century* (Brussels: Commission of the European Communities).

Freeman, R. (1988), 'Labour Market Institutions and Economic Performance', *Economic Policy* (Apr.), 63–80.

—— (1995), 'Doing It Right? The USA Labour Market Response to the 1980s/1990s', *Centre for Economic Performance,* DP no. 231 (March).

Henry, S. G. B., and Lee, K. C. (1996a), 'Identification and Estimation of Wage and Employment Equations: An Application of the Structural VAR Modelling Approach', mimeo, DAE, University of Cambridge.

—— —— (1996b), Employment Determination in the UK Manufacturing Sector in the Presence of Variable Adjustment Costs: A Disaggregated Analysis', mimeo, University of Leicester.

—— and Snower, D. (1996), 'The Dynamics of European Unemployment', mimeo, IMF.

—— Karanassou, M., and Shin, Y. (1996), 'An Econometric Analysis of the UK Labour Market', mimeo, DAE, University of Cambridge.

International Monetary Fund (1994), *World Economic Outlook* (Washington, DC: IMF), 43.

Layard, R., Nickell, S., and Jackman, R. (1991), *Unemployment: Macroeconomic Performance and the Labour Market* (Oxford: Oxford University Press).

—— —— —— (1994), *The Unemployment Crisis* (Oxford: Oxford University Press).

Lee, K. C. and Pesaran, M. H. (1993), 'The Role of Sectoral Interactions in Wage Determination in the UK', *Economic Journal,* 103: 21–55.

Lindbeck, S. and Snower, D. (1988), *The Insider-Outsider Theory of Employment and Unemployment* (Cambridge, Mass.: MIT Press).

Metcalf, D. (1994), 'Transformation of Britain Industrial Relation? Institutions, Conduct and Outcomes 1980–1990' in Barrell (ed.) *UK Labour Market.*

Minford, P. (1994), 'Deregulation and Unemployment: The UK Experience', *Swedish Economic Policy Review* 1/1–2: 115–41.

Nickell, S. (1990), 'Unemployment: A Survey', *Economic Journal,* 100: 391–439.

OECD (1995), *UK Annual Survey* (Paris: OECD).

Pesaran, H. M. and Shin, Y. (1995*a*), 'An Autoregressive Distributed Lag Modelling Approach to Co-integration Analysis', DAE Discussion Paper No. 9514, University of Cambridge.

—— —— (1995*b*), 'Long Run Structural Modelling', DAE Working Paper No. 9419, University of Cambridge.

Taylor, J. (1980), 'Aggregate Dynamics and Staggered Contracts', *Journal of Political Economy*, 88/1: 1–23.

6. Inflation, Economic Performance, and Employment Rights

Simon Deakin and Keith Ewing

INTRODUCTION

This chapter examines the system of labour law which would be required to underpin an economic strategy aimed at containing inflation and enhancing competitiveness, without having resort to mass, long-term unemployment as an instrument of labour discipline. In addition to there being a good case from the point of view of social justice for the enactment of more effective legal protection for workers, a strong economic case exists for regulation aimed at promoting co-operation between management and labour and enhancing competitiveness by placing incentives on both firms and individuals to invest in labour quality. The basic elements of such a labour law system in Britain would include legal guarantees of work-force representation at the level of the firm, the existence of representative institutions at sector level to regulate working conditions, and the enactment of a comprehensive labour code designed to ensure respect for the basic rights at work of the worker. Particularly important here is the issue of collective bargaining at multi-employer level, which can operate as a mechanism for reducing inflationary pressures.

Multi-employer bargaining has been in rapid decline in Britain since the mid-1980s as it has in other systems which have experimented with labour-market deregulation, most notably the USA (where it has never been very strong), New Zealand and, to a lesser extent, Australia. Yet this experience has not been universally shared. Most member states of the European Union retain effective forms of collective bargaining at sector or industry level, thereby ensuring that basic labour standards in such areas as pay, working time, job security, and occupational health and safety are widely observed. At the level of the EU itself, the development of transnational collective bargaining, once thought impossible, is now closer to becoming a reality as a result of the process of *social dialogue* which was encouraged by the Maastricht Treaty. These developments suggest that with an appropriate regulatory framework, we may see the re-emergence in Britain of institutions which can serve as mechanisms for setting, implementing, and monitoring labour standards.

LABOUR LAW, COLLECTIVE BARGAINING, AND DEREGULATION

During the period of neo-liberal ascendancy which has lasted in Britain since 1979, labour law has seemed to become, at times, an arm of economic policy. The removal of 'rigidities' in the labour market through 'deregulation' was meant to contribute to the reduction of inflationary pressures and to the promotion of a competitive economy. Although other rights-based justifications for changes in labour law were made at this time—such as the protection of consumers, non-union members, and others against 'abuses' of power by trade unions (see Fredman, 1989)—economic considerations have always been prominent. Successive administrations have broadly followed a strategy most clearly laid out in the 1985 White Paper, *Employment: The Challenge for the Nation*. This formally rejected the idea that unemployment was caused by deficient demand, and identified instead the labour market as the 'weak link in the economy'. A three-pronged approach to economic policy was laid out, consisting of control of the money supply; the creation of jobs through deregulation of the labour market; and, in exceptional circumstances only, government intervention to assist the long-term and youth unemployed through active labour-market policy (Department of Employment 1985).

Of these three, labour market deregulation has been the policy most consistently pursued during the period since 1979 as a whole. Monetary policy has seen significant shifts of emphasis and has failed, in general, to conform to the theoretical postulates laid out by its advocates in the 1970s and early 1980s, while active labour market policy has waxed and waned according to the state of the economy and pressures to reduce public expenditure. By contrast, the process of labour market deregulation has intensified with the adoption of a succession of Acts of Parliament cutting back on both collective and individual employment rights. Employment relations have also been affected by government policies aimed at promoting competition in the markets for products and services. Redundancies, restructuring, and changes to terms and conditions have followed on the introduction of price regulation in the privatized utilities, the imposition of competitive tendering of services on local government and the NHS, and introduction of internal 'quasi markets' in the public health and education sectors. While these measures stop a certain way short of removing public regulation altogether from the labour market, their effect has been to isolate the United Kingdom within the European Union and to place it on a par with such systems as

New Zealand and the USA (Deakin 1992), although not, significantly, the industrializing countries of East Asia, which by comparison are highly regulated (see Deery and Mitchell 1993).

Although frequently used, the term 'deregulation' is potentially misleading here, at least if it is taken to imply a reduced role for the state: 'contrary to all appearances, the 'activist' state is by no means dismissed', since 'far from simply rejecting all interference, the state is assigned the task of setting the elementary conditions for a functioning market' (Simitis 1987: 128). The continuing presence of the state is clearest, perhaps, in those areas where competition policy has given rise to vast new fields of substantive regulation and administrative discretion which are only incompletely controlled by principles of public law and democratic accountability, as is the case with the regulatory bodies charged with overseeing competition in the utilities and in the NHS internal market.

It is also the case with the labour market, where the state now assumes the role not just of dismantling those legally binding labour standards which are the product of an earlier era, but of intervening to prevent the adoption, implementation, and monitoring of standards by collective organizations outside the state. A good example of this is to be found in the conditions regulating compulsory competitive tendering: legislation denies local authorities the contractual power—which they would otherwise have—to insist that external contractors observe basic employment conditions, such as commonly accepted rates of pay, or even to monitor contractors' adherence to remaining legislative standards in such fields as health and safety and equality of treatment.[1] More generally, legislation now plays an important role in restricting the activities of organizations of workers, in particular where collective economic pressure is brought to bear in support of standards operating at an inter-firm or market level. Restrictions over the collective right or freedom to take industrial action without liability at common law, and controls over the internal governance of trade unions, reached unprecedented levels in the 1980s (Davies and Freedland 1994). Thus, whatever the case might be in other systems for talking about a system of labour law 'without the state' (Arthurs 1996), in the United Kingdom the state remains an active player, using the law and associated regulatory mechanisms to reshape the labour market.

---

[1] The principal legislation here is the Local Government Act, 1988, as amended.

COLLECTIVE BARGAINING DECLINE AND DECENTRALIZATION[2]

(a) *General Trends*

The government's position on labour relations has played an important role in helping to undermine collective institutions (for an assessment of the various influences see Deakin 1992). The period since 1979 has been characterized by a declining coverage and decentralization of collective bargaining, with only a minority of British workers now covered by agreements. The *decline in collective bargaining coverage* has in fact been one of the most significant developments in the last seventeen years, and appears to be without parallel in any of the other OECD countries, a recent survey concluding that 'the decline in collective bargaining has been most pronounced in Great Britain' (OECD 1994: 185). Collective bargaining coverage in Britain has fallen from an estimated 70 per cent in 1980 to an estimated 47 per cent in 1990 and the position is in fact worse when we take into account that at least another 11 or 12 per cent of workers were formerly covered by Wages Council orders, pushing joint regulation up to in excess of 80 per cent, perhaps as high as 85 per cent (Milner 1995). On this basis, coverage has in fact fallen to an estimated 47 per cent from an estimated 80–85 per cent since 1980. But not only is our decline the sharpest, we are as a result among the OECD countries with the lowest levels of collective bargaining coverage. To put the matter in perspective, in 1994 coverage in Australia stood at 80 per cent, Finland 95 per cent, France 92 per cent, and Germany 90 per cent.

Related to this is the *decentralization of collective bargaining*, now extending from the private sector into the public sector as well. This has seen the break-up of national or sectoral bargaining arrangements (with only 1 in 10 workers in the private sector now thought to be covered by multi-employer bargaining arrangements) and a greater emphasis on enterprise-based bargaining. One reason why this is important is that collective bargaining decentralization is sometimes associated with low levels of coverage, with a recent OECD study pointing out that '[c]ountries characterised by single-employer bargaining tend to have lower coverage rates compared with countries where bargaining is conducted at higher levels and where employer organisations and union federations are strong' (OECD 1994: 168). Although decentralization is also a feature of bargaining developments in other countries, 'there has been great variation between countries in the nature and extent of employers' flexibility initiatives' (Ferner and Hyman 1995: p. xxi). But few countries it seems have gone as far as we have, and

---

[2] This section draws heavily on IER (1996), and in particular on work contributed by Phil James of Middlesex University to whom we are most grateful for permission to use it here.

even as late as 1994 the OECD survey could record that 'in a majority of OECD countries the sectoral level has remained the principal arena for wage determination' (OECD 1994: 186).

(b) *The Reasons for Decentralization*

The decline in sector-level bargaining, which has been developing since 1945, has taken two forms. First, as already indicated, there has been the complete abandonment in many sectors of multi-employer agreements, a trend which has gathered pace since 1979. In parts of the private sector this trend away from multi-employer bargaining has since 1979 coincided, to some extent, with another. This is the tendency for employers to create more devolved and decentralized arrangements organized on the individual workplace, division, or business unit. Where this has occurred, however, the employers concerned nevertheless retain considerable central control over pay settlements. But even where multi-employer bargaining has remained, a second symptom of decentralization has been the reduction in the regulatory effect of agreements, most notably through a movement towards the specification of 'minimum' rather than 'actual' pay rates.

This twofold process of decentralization has been influenced by a variety of factors. Notable among them have been a desire on the part of employers to bring their bargaining and human resource strategies into line with more devolved management structures; a wish to link pay more closely to rewards; a desire to develop locally more flexible working patterns; and in the public sector, political initiatives and pressures designed to create less centralized institutional structures, introduce greater competition and allow pay to better reflect local labour-market and operational conditions. Such developments have influenced both the level at which bargaining takes place and the content of the agreements concluded. Where multi-employer bargaining has been dismantled or where larger employers have withdrawn from it, initiatives have often been taken substantially to revise grading systems and working patterns, and introduce a variety of incentive pay arrangements, both within and between different parts of the business. The same is true, although probably to a lesser degree, where single-employer arrangements have been decentralized.

(c) *The Equivocal Benefits of Decentralization*

These changes may be of financial benefit to the employers concerned in terms of contributing to increased labour flexibility and productivity, greater employee commitment, and reduced unit labour costs. However the changes may not always have beneficial consequences in the longer run. In particular, the decentralization of bargaining may:

- reduce the power of unions and hence enable employers to worsen terms and conditions of employment and to compete more through low labour costs rather than more efficient capital investment;
- by leading to a multiplication in the number of 'pay decision points', create the potential for an inflationary pay spiral in tight labour-market conditions; and
- in the case of the decentralization of single-employer bargaining arrangements, act, as part of a more general devolution of human-resource management, to reinforce the already *ad hoc* and short-term nature of human resource management within many UK-based organizations.

Nor can the desirability of decentralization be assessed purely on the ground of the financial benefits to particular companies. The issue also raises important questions about the quality and standards of living of workers and families. Two related points arise here. The devolution of bargaining structures, by creating more isolated and smaller bargaining units, creates a greater potential for trade union derecognition and may make membership loss more likely to arise as a result of member disillusionment and direct employer pressure. Secondly, as already pointed out, the abolition of multi-employer arrangements acts to reduce the degree of union regulation in the labour market, because such agreements have always tended also to affect pay and conditions in both non-union and non-affiliated organizations. Indeed as the OECD study points out, the density of collective bargaining coverage is likely to be significantly lower in countries with decentralized bargaining systems.

LABOUR STANDARDS AND ECONOMIC PERFORMANCE: COMPARATIVE EVIDENCE

The undermining of collective institutions has been accompanied by an increase in labour-market inequality in Britain, as it has in the USA and New Zealand. It is often argued that such inequality is the price to be paid for a more efficient labour market. As evidence for this, in the 1980s and 1990s the USA has enjoyed a much faster rate of job creation than the more highly regulated EU systems. On the face of it, the higher employment rate of the USA lends some plausibility to the hypothesis of a trade-off between wage equality and the rate of employment growth: 'maybe the United States "paid" for employment creation through low or declining wages, while Europe "paid" for high or rising wages with sluggish growth of employment' (Freeman 1994: 14). A similar point is sometimes made with regard to the UK, although evidence for a significant job-creation effect arising from deregulation is confined to the brief period of the Lawson boom from

1986 to 1989 (Deakin and Wilkinson 1996). Evidence for a positive employment effect in New Zealand in the wake of the Employment Contracts Act 1991 is even more elusive (Anderson, Brosnan, and Walsh 1995).

Closer study has shown that the major cause of job growth in the USA since the early 1980s has been population growth (Houseman 1995). In the USA, there was a large increase in the working-age population, which the US economy was able to absorb, leading to dramatic headline increases in jobs and a less dramatic, if still significant, growth in employment participation rates. The converse of the United States' superior jobs record, however, is its relatively poor record on wage growth and on productivity. In the USA, working hours have been extended and average wages have fallen in real terms since the early 1970s, and labour productivity has grown more slowly than in France, Germany, or the UK. US GDP per head has also declined relative to the larger EC economies in the same period (Deakin and Wilkinson 1994). The OECD, among others, has noted the 'poor quality' of jobs created in the USA in the 1980s (OECD 1993: 30; see also Loveman and Tilly 1988; Freeman 1993). The downside for the US economy, then, is not simply its reduced capacity to generate good jobs: it is also felt in terms of reduced efficiency in the use of labour and, ultimately, in a reduction in its capacity to generate wealth.

When economic performance is measured in terms of labour productivity and real-wage growth, not only do the European economies fare better than the USA, but within Western Europe it is those systems with the most intensive forms of labour regulation—above all, Germany and France—which do best of all. Buchele and Christiansen's recent econometric study of the G7 countries found that 'productivity and real-wage growth from the early 1970s to the late 1980s are, indeed, positively related to workers' rights . . . we invariably find that in countries where worker rights are strongest, labour productivity and real-wage growth are highest' (Buchele and Christiansen 1995: 419). These findings require the use of indices of the strength of labour standards across countries which involve, inevitably, some degree of subjective judgement. However, the results 'at the very least ought to caution European policy-makers about the potential negative consequences for productivity and real-wage growth of attempts to reduce unemployment by wholesale deregulation and dismantling of worker rights' (Buchele and Christiansen 1995: 419).

The European Commission's *White Paper on Social Policy*, published in 1994, reflects the dilemma facing policy-makers in the EU. On the one hand, the Commission insisted that it was not seeking a 'dilution of the European model of social protection' (European Commission 1994: 10). At the same time, the White Paper identified the issue of the employment rate as the 'key' to improved social and economic cohesion, and advocated an employment policy in which 'as well as supporting high-productivity jobs, the

Union maximises its ability to generate and sustain jobs at other levels, particularly in the unskilled, semi-skilled and personal and local services fields' (European Commission 1994: 10). This statement may be read as implying a greater stress on labour-market flexibility, particularly when coupled with the admittedly rather ambiguous suggestion that 'the need to alter fundamentally, and update, the structure of incentives which influence the labour market is still not adequately recognized' (European Commission 1994: 11) One option which the Commission has been considering is the partial removal of employment protection for certain forms of employment, designed to make it more attractive for employers to hire workers on lower pay or in certain forms of employment, such as part-time or fixed-term contract employment; another is the use of targeted reductions in social-security contributions and other forms of social charges, similarly designed to subsidize employment creation.

The first of these options, the creation of unskilled and semi-skilled jobs alongside higher-productivity jobs through partial deregulation, appears to be based on a contradiction. How will economic competitiveness be maintained in those sectors which become heavily reliant on low-wage, low-productivity employment? While it might once have been possible for parts of the public sector or for sectors such as retailing and distribution, which have been insulated from international competition, to perform this function, it seems doubtful that they can continue to do so in the future, given the shrinkage of the public sector and the opening up of a wider range of services to international competitive pressures as economic integration increases. These sectors, in just the same way as manufacturing, are under constant and increasing pressure to improve their labour-productivity rates. More generally, there is a danger that measures aimed at subsidizing low-paid and low-skilled employment will create a 'disincentive to upgrade the productive system if this would involve the labour losing its subsidy . . . the economy may be diverted towards those low-skill, low-investment sectors that are subsidised by the policy' (Michie and Wilkinson 1995: 148).

Nor is it necessarily clear that much progress would be made by cutting charges on employment in the form of taxes and social-security contributions. At first sight, it would seem that social-security contributions, in particular, represent a substantial charge on employment in virtually all EU countries. Employers' contributions are on average over 30 per cent of wages in Italy, over 25 per cent in Belgium, between 20 and 24 per cent in Spain and between 15 and 20 per cent in the Netherlands, Germany, Greece, Portugal, and France; the average for the EU is 19 per cent. To this must be added employees' contributions (which are in effect met by employers as a proportion of payroll costs) and employees' income tax, at an EU average of 10 and 13 per cent of wages respectively. Not only is the overall level of charges high by contrast to the USA and Japan, but there are considerable differences between member states. However, as the European Commission has pointed out, 'there is no simple, causal relationship between the level of social contributions and the total cost of labour' in any given member state (European Commission 1993*b*: 87). In systems with relatively low mandatory contributions—such as the United Kingdom and, above all, Denmark, where employers' contributions are on average only 3 per cent of wages—contractual payments by the employer tend to be more important, by way of compensation, or wages themselves have to rise in order to enable employees to make their own contributions. It is sometimes suggested that the element of statutory compulsion in some systems introduces unnecessary rigidity and inhibits flexibility in hiring during periods of low demand in the business cycle (Emerson 1988). However, the employment record of systems with very low mandatory charges, such as Denmark, is no better than those of systems in which uniform contribution rates are set by law.

One option might be to reduce the impact of regulation and taxation on a selective basis, for example by excluding certain forms of low-paid employment from the scope of statutory social-security contributions. Together with partial exemptions from employment-protection legislation for part-time and temporary work, this technique has been quite widely adopted within member states since the early 1980s. The German Employment Promotion Act of 1986 (renewed in 1992) removed restrictions on fixed-term hirings in the case of new recruits and apprentices completing their training. In each case, the employer was permitted to offer a fixed-term contract of up to eighteen months, after which the worker had to be offered a permanent employment if he or she was to be retained. The measure also allowed newly established firms, and firms employing fewer than twenty employees, to make use of fixed-term contracts of up to two years (Mückenberger 1992). In France there has been a series of measures aimed at promoting labour flexibility, in particular by encouraging self-employment and part-time work through rebates on social security contributions (Supiot, Lorvellec, and Kerbouc'h 1992; Lyon-Caen, Pélissier, and Supiot 1993: 117), and similar legislation promoting fixed-term employment has been in operation in Spain since 1984 (Ojeda Aviles 1992; Auvergnon and Gil y Gil 1994).

Yet the outcome of these initiatives has been at best unclear, and possibly even counter-productive. Studies suggest that one effect of the German Employment Promotion Act has been to encourage employers to dismiss workers during downturns in the business cycle, and that overall the impact of the Act on job creation has been minimal and possibly slightly negative (Büchtemann 1993). There is doubt as to whether part-time jobs of the kind subsidized by the Act constitute 'bridges' into regular employment or, more likely, 'traps' from which it is difficult to find a good job (Büchtemann and Quack 1989). In Spain, over 90 per cent of new hirings now take the form of fixed-term employment in one of its subsidized forms (Recio 1993). Overall, these forms of intervention suffer from the familiar 'deadweight' and 'displacement' effects which have dogged many more direct forms of labour-market subsidy: either employers would have created the jobs in any event, or the new jobs displace other workers from more regular employment.

Whereas in the mainland European systems the focus of deregulation policies has been on part-time and temporary work, in the USA and Britain it is often full-time employment which is associated with very low pay and poor working conditions, as a result of the general decline in institutional wage determination in those systems. Yet even in the USA, with its generally superior record on employment, there are limits to what deregulation can achieve: 'the fact that less skilled and low-paid American men had relatively poor employment prospects despite falling real wages shows that the American problem goes beyond a simple trade-off analysis' (Card and Freeman 1994: 233). In Britain, most of the recent employment growth is accounted for by forms of self-employment at very low rates of pay and by part-time work below the minimum threshold at which social-security contributions become payable (Joseph Rowntree Foundation 1993: 53).

The policy choice facing the European systems is, then, a complex one. It is not a simple question of a trade-off between job creation and social protection; nor a matter of sacrificing the rights of 'insiders' in an effort to re-integrate excluded groups into employment. All the signs are that the wholesale removal of labour standards would have a harmful effect on economic performance, as well as further undermining the financing of the welfare state. But equally, there is no guarantee that high labour standards which promote high productivity will provide, of themselves, a solution to the problem of unemployment. With inflation kept in check by restrictive macroeconomic policies, and by the impact of the EMU convergence criteria on taxation and public expenditure decisions, the mainland European systems can produce only 'jobless growth'.

DEVELOPMENTS IN EUROPEAN COMMUNITY SOCIAL POLICY

To break this log-jam in labour-market policy, a potentially important idea which is emerging within the European debate is that of 'social policy as a productive factor',[3] or 'the creation of an original social model combining competitiveness and social cohesion' (European Commission 1996: 5). This

---

[3] Speech of President of the Commission, Jacques Santer, to the European Social Forum, Brussels, 28 Mar. 1996: 'une nouvelle approche de l'emploi et de la politique social comme facteur productif, au cœur de notre projet politique'.

implies that social policy should form part of an integrated strategy for sustainable employment growth. Two aspects of this process may be emphasized here: the modernization of labour standards and the role played by social dialogue between representatives of management and labour at European level.

(a) *The Modernization of Labour Standards*

This approach sees labour-market regulation as a necessary aspect of the efficient use of labour and places greater stress in the elaboration of policy on the collective benefits which flow from social regulation, as opposed to the near-exclusive focus on the costs of regulations to individual firms and enterprises which tends to prevail at present. Examples of such benefits include the reduction of absenteeism and of the costs of illness and injury which are brought about by health and safety legislation; the reduction of turnover and search costs which are brought about by the regulation of dismissals; and the raising of skills levels through public provision of training.

It follows that the aim of regulatory policy with regard to the labour market should be to achieve an appropriate balance between co-operation and competition, rather than always seeking to maximize the intensity of competition as such. The former approach is based on the understanding that the competitiveness of firms and industries depends to a large extent on the effectiveness of the linkages between the different elements involved in the process of production—between labour and management, and between firms at different points in the chain of supply. Co-operative relations, based on a long-term orientation and on the fostering of mutual trust between the parties, require a certain degree of control over 'destructive' competition, in the sense of competition based on price alone as opposed to competition based on the quality of products and services (Deakin and Wilkinson 1996). In seeking to regulate against destructive competition, labour standards should be put in place in order to provide incentives for *competition based on quality*, on the understanding that this is the best long-term basis for the competitiveness of the EU economies.

There is also a growing recognition that labour standards generate collective economic benefits in so far as they strengthen social cohesion and reduce inequality. The direct costs of inequality include the additional burden on public expenditure which arises from extra health-care costs, and from social-security programmes which support the unemployed and top-up the wages of the low-paid. Less directly, inequality threatens the social fabric in a variety of ways; in this context, there should be a recognition that social policy can bring about broader benefits, or reduced costs, in terms of enhanced social stability, reductions in levels of crime, and improvement in health care. The issue, from this point of view, is no longer whether regulation is necessary, but what form it should take. Individual measures would be carefully assessed for their wider economic and social effects, but deregulation *as such* would not be the goal. Notwithstanding the criticisms which employers and others have levelled against particular regulations, both at EU level and within member states, it is significant that the *UNICE Regulatory Report* of 1995 suggested that rather than always seeking less regulation, companies more frequently would like to see 'targeted changes to improve the quality and harmonisation of regulations . . . and their enforcement' (UNICE 1995: 39).

(b) *Social Dialogue*

Provision is made for social dialogue in the Agreement on Social Policy of the Maastricht Treaty, which imposes a duty on the Commission to promote the consultation of management and labour at Community level and to take measures to facilitate their dialogue. To this end the Commission is required to consult the social partners 'on the possible direction of Community action' as well as on the content of any proposed Community action. It is also provided, however, that where management and labour so desire, 'the dialogue between them at Community level may lead to contractual relations, including agreements'. Agreements concluded in this way may be implemented in one of two ways, 'either in accordance with the procedures and practices specific to management and labour and the Member States' or in some cases 'at the joint request of the signatory parties, by a Council decision on a proposal from the Commission'. The latter method of enforcement can be used only in respect of matters which are covered by Article 2 of the Agreement, which include health and safety, working conditions, equality between men and women, and protection from dismissal. A Declaration appended to the Agreement expressly provides, however, that there is no obligation on member states to apply the agreements directly or to work out rules for their transpositions.

At the time of writing one agreement has been made under this procedure though it has not yet been implemented. This is the Framework Agreement on Parental Leave which provides for three months' parental leave (for each parent) following the birth or adoption of a child, the right of workers to return to their job after parental leave, and time off work for urgent family reasons. The agreement leaves much of the detail to be implemented by legislation and/or collective bargaining, but in the case of Britain, however, it is clear that these decisions would have to be taken by Parliament which in the absence of an adequate collective bargaining infrastructure will be the principal vehicle for the implementation of this and other instruments made under this procedure, which at the time of writing does not of course apply to the United Kingdom. Many will regard it as paradoxical that we should be bound to rely mainly on legislation (primary or secondary) to implement the fruits of the collective bargaining process.

It is thus possible under Community law not only for standards to be established by collective bargaining, but also for standards to be implemented by collective bargaining. This is true of several instruments including, for example, the Working Time Directive[4] which lays down minimum standards in terms of minimum daily rest periods, rest breaks, weekly rest periods, maximum weekly working time, and annual leave. The Directive provides that it may be implemented either by laws or by agreement between the two sides of industry. It also provides for the possible derogation from standards 'by means of collective agreements or agreements concluded between the two sides of industry at national or regional level or, in conformity with the rules laid down by them, by means of collective agreements'. That is to say '[d]erogations at enterprise level are to be shaped by framework agreements at national or regional level' (Bercusson 1994: 47). In member states where there is no statutory system for collective bargaining at national or regional level, derogations may also be allowed by collective agreements concluded between the two sides of industry 'at the appropriate collective level'.

We are not suggesting that the absence of sector level bargaining arrangements in Britain would make it impracticable to implement this or other EC directives. It is clearly possible for legislation to be the primary vehicle for the carriage of directives into domestic law in the usual way and for derogations to be made at enterprise level by collective agreements, this being the appropriate collective level in this country for concluding such agreements. But although this would be feasible, and indeed inevitable unless there are reforms to the bargaining machinery, the effect would be to impose a heavy load on legislation. It would also encourage the adoption and application of the barest of minimum standards, and it would be a wasted opportunity for the social partners in each sector to take responsibility for the transposition of these obligations in their own industry in a manner which more accurately reflects the needs and experience of employers and workers in the sector in question. Transposition in this way is not necessarily secured at the expense of flexibility within enterprises for it is clearly contemplated that the possibility for further derogations can be devolved by the terms of a sectoral agreement to individual enterprises.

[4] Directive 93/104 EC.

REFORM OF COLLECTIVE BARGAINING IN BRITAIN: REBUILDING FROM BELOW

There are two broad approaches which can be adopted to the rebuilding of an institutional framework for the joint regulation of working conditions in Britain. The first involves using legislation to encourage the growth of trade union recognition at the level of the enterprise or firm. The TUC proposes that a union with 50 per cent membership in the defined bargaining unit should be entitled automatically to negotiating rights (TUC 1995). Below that, a union which can demonstrate majority support in a bargaining unit by those participating in a survey or ballot, to be conducted by a proposed new Representation Agency, will also be entitled to negotiating rights. Below that a union with lower levels of support, but with at least 10 per cent membership, will be entitled to general consultation rights which would apply to matters other than the mandatory issues prescribed by EC law (notably collective redundancies and transfers of undertakings); and in workplaces where there is no union support of this level the employer would be required to establish what is in effect a standing works council (unlike the *ad hoc* measures which the government is proposing to permit), referred to as 'elections as a fall-back' (EFB) in which unions would have a right to nominate candidates, and with which consultations would take place on the European issues.

These are interesting and important proposals, although there are a number of problems which have to be addressed, some more significant than others. The first is the fact that the extensive discretion vested in this Representation Agency may mean that we are in danger of returning to the battlegrounds of the 1970s when ACAS was severely undermined by judicial review proceedings, at a time when judicial review as we know it today was in its infancy (Ewing 1995). There is the possibility of problems arising in terms of how surveys are conducted; of determining the scope and extent of the bargaining unit; and of deciding who is entitled to vote at the election. Secondly it is not clear what is to happen to these elections as a fall-back procedure if the union should subsequently acquire consultation rights about the same issues in its own right by securing 10 per cent support from the work-force. If the union candidates win a majority of the places in the election, it is proposed that the union should be granted general consultation rights and the EFB will not then be established. But if the EFB is established first and the union then acquires general consultation rights, is the EFB to be wound up (and 90 per cent non-union members disenfranchised), or is the employer to consult with both about the same issues?

The other part of the strategy involves promoting minimum standards agreements across industry, 'which will provide a floor of minimum standards at work for all employees' (TUC 1996*b*). A recent example is provided by the reported initiative of the TUC to seek meetings with the leading employers' organizations (the CBI, the Institute of Directors, the Institute of Management, and the British Chambers of Commerce) with a view to setting minimum standards at work in order to prevent good employers being undercut by the bad, and to explore ways by which employers and trade unions can implement standards agreed at European level. In the case of the latter this was said to include the making of agreements on matters such as parental leave and working time, with the law operating as a safety net. It is proposed that the agreements should deal with training and education, job security, and the 'adoption of a minimum floor under wages that would be a powerful incentive to develop the careers of the low paid and also the performance of the firms for which they work'.[5] This is self-evidently also an important initiative which provides clear evidence of the importance of multi-employer measures as a means of promoting social justice in the workplace on the one hand and transposing European standards on the other.

It remains to be seen how far voluntary initiatives of this kind can be taken and it may not be insignificant that at least one of the employers' organizations mentioned is reported as having responded in a sceptical vein. The problem is that agreements of this kind are likely to be concluded by those employers who least need to have them in the sense that it is they who are already unionized and are already paying decent wages and observing more than adequate standards. There is thus the question of how any minimum-standards agreement; of this kind could be introduced into sectors where they are most likely to be needed but most likely to be resisted, and, where they are introduced, how they could be extended to employers who have no wish to be bound by their terms. At least in the latter case it would be impossible to contemplate the extension of agreements without some form of legal intervention in the form of the procedures once contained in Schedule 11 of the Employment Protection Act, 1975. This provided a procedure whereby a trade union could make a claim to require employers paying less than the going rate to observe terms and conditions settled by collective bargaining, or failing which, 'the general level' of terms and conditions.

These proposals are not free from difficulty (Ewing 1996), and although potentially valuable may not be enough to ensure the coverage of collective bargaining across large sectors of the economy. The mechanism suggested may not be enough on its own because it requires trade unions to devote a great deal of resources to organizational activity, at a time when resources are stretched. It may be insufficient, secondly, because it requires the

---

[5] *Financial Times,* 29 Feb. 1996. For an earlier initiative by the Transport and General Workers' Union, see the *Record,* Aug. 1995, p. 1.

investment of considerable resources for what may be little influence, namely the right once 10 per cent of the work-force is signed up into membership to no more than general consultation rights, which may be little more than an annual meeting in some cases. And it may be insufficient, thirdly, because it will almost certainly lead to employer resistance and to wasteful and damaging litigation in the courts which will inevitably have some impact in drawing the teeth of the legislation. All of this is not to deny the merits of the TUC's approach, which seeks 'to combine the best features of voluntarism with the establishment of a wider range of legal rights' (TUC 1996*b*: 12). But we do suggest that if the economic goal is to raise standards effectively and comprehensively, the proposed strategy may need to be complemented by other initiatives.

THE RESTORATION OF SECTORAL REGULATION OF WORKING CONDITIONS[6]

It remains to be seen how far the TUC strategy will extend the frontiers of collective bargaining and help the unions to march into new territory, though we should not underestimate the flexibility and subtlety of these proposals as a strategy for the extension of collective bargaining. As a package it ought to be able to meet the problems presented by the majority-rule requirement of the US legislation and overcome the problems in the United States where a union has to demonstrate 50 per cent support for certification in a 'death or glory' election. It is of the greatest significance that under the TUC proposals a union with 10 per cent membership will be entitled to general consultation rights, not just on what one might refer to as the European issues of redundancy and business transfers, but more generally to include 'management proposals involving significant changes in employment numbers or working conditions'. Admittedly it is not clear how far this will go, but it is nevertheless a crucial measure which will reward unions for support and give them encouragement to build up membership to secure full recognition rights thereby giving workers the right to have their terms and conditions covered by a collective agreement.

But although arrangements of this kind will undoubtedly help trade unions, we should also be realistic about what these proposals can be expected to deliver. If we return to the OECD survey we are reminded of the fact that countries characterized by single-employer bargaining tend to have lower rates of coverage of collective agreements. More specifically the survey points out that collective bargaining coverage in the United States is 18 per cent, Japan 23 per cent, and Canada 38 per cent, all countries not

---

[6] This section draws heavily on Ewing (1996), and IER (1996).

only dominated by establishment-based bargaining, but also countries with a legal framework for trade union recognition which is geared towards single-employer bargaining. It is true that the TUC proposals are predictably more union-friendly than the legal regimes operating in the USA or Canada. But it remains the case that under these proposals a union will need majority support in the bargaining unit to negotiate on pay, unless the employer agrees to collective bargaining on a voluntary basis. It may well be that we will simply have to become accustomed to lower levels of bargaining coverage and a diluted form of trade union representation, unless this particular strategy is combined with others which seek actively to take the initiative at the sectoral level to encourage multi-employer regulation of working conditions.

(a) *The Low-Pay Strategy*

One possible area which has potential for development is the low-pay strategy proposed by the Labour Party. Although the precise details are uncertain, this involved at one stage the creation of a tripartite Low Pay Commission with responsibility for fixing a statutory minimum wage. Proposals published at the time of writing suggest that the Commission will be tripartite in composition, its members presumably appointed by the Secretary of State, and suggest also that its recommendations, for example, on the level of the minimum wage, will not necessarily be binding on the government. It is unclear whether the Commission will be asked to set a single flat rate of universal application, or whether it will be empowered or indeed required to set sectoral, occupational, or geographical variations. It is also unclear whether it will be empowered to deal with matters other than pay. Is it possible, for example, to regulate pay without regulating in some way the question of working time? Questions will also arise as to the legal status and enforcement of the Commission's recommended minimum, though if adopted by the government any recommendation could presumably be implemented by way of statutory instrument and constitute an enforceable minimum below which no one would be permitted to fall.

Although not conceived to do so, the low-pay strategy is capable of metamorphosing into something much more ambitious and much more comprehensive in order to deal with the problem of declining collective bargaining coverage and in order to relieve the state of its responsibility of direct regulation of working conditions through legislation. There are thus two opportunities provided by this strategy. The first relates to the issues which the Low Pay Commission is asked to deal with. As already suggested these need not necessarily be confined to pay, for even if the Commission is to concentrate its efforts on the low paid, there is no evidence to suggest that pay is the only matter for which the vulnerable need standards to be regulated by a body such as the Low Pay Commission. Obvious candidates for inclusion would be working time and parental leave. The second opportunity relates to the possibility that this Commission could perform these tasks through what might be called sectoral chambers or councils so that rather than having a flat rate or common term for every worker in the country, there are sectoral variations which are sensitive to the needs of each particular industry or sector. If this approach were adopted it would be possible to build up the sectoral chambers or councils slowly with the emphasis initially on those sectors where there is no effective collective bargaining.

(b) *Rebuilding National Bargaining*

A second possible initiative would be to consider the restoration of multi-employer collective bargaining. This might take the form of encouraging such arrangements to be re-established in all parts of the private sector. A variation of this, which could perhaps be combined with other strategies, is to require national bargaining to be conducted in selected industries, notably the privatized utilities. Yet despite the social benefits, despite the fact that it happens elsewhere, and despite the importance of collective bargaining as a method of workplace regulation, it would be very ambitious to seek to reassert the primary role of sectoral bargaining in this way. In the first place it would require a commitment to reconstruction as great as that demonstrated in 1917, but without the spectre of Communism haunting Europe to drive the engine of reform. Secondly, it would mean setting up sectoral wages councils or statutory joint industrial councils in every industry, at a time when organization on the employers' side appears to have weakened if not disintegrated. Thirdly, it would mean confronting rather than appeasing the resistance of employers at a time when there is no ideological stomach for such a fight and no obvious political capital to be gained in picking one.

These problems indicate that a determined effort to reassert the primacy of sectoral bargaining in Britain would be a great deal to contemplate by voluntary means alone. Even with a strong political commitment, it is open to question whether it could be done without the support and co-operation of employers, and there is no evidence of any enthusiasm on their part for such structures. Indeed the opposite appears to be the case, with William Brown pointing out for example that '[e]mployers' determination to remain with single-employer bargaining if they are to have any sort of bargaining is strongly implied by their rejection of existing forms of employer collaboration' (Brown 1993: 198). Further evidence of employer resistance to the idea was indicated some time ago by the CBI (1991) which was clearly of the view that it would be unrealistic to turn back the tide given the trend towards decentralization in the 1980s. Despite the admitted advantages of a highly centralized system of pay bargaining, they thought it more sensible, and in keeping with current practices and institutions, to enhance wage flexibility by moving more rapidly towards decentralization in pay determination, taking advantage in the process of the weakened market power of trade unions.

(c) *A Radical Option: Sectoral Employment Commissions*

There are thus a number of steps which could be contemplated with a view to re-establishing sectoral determination of working conditions. There are also a number of problems standing in the way of any such initiative. A more radical approach still, perhaps more accurately reflecting the urgency of the current situation, is to build on all of the initiatives and options canvassed in this chapter in order to construct more directly by legislation the conditions in which sectoral regulation may take place. We have in mind here the possibility of sectoral bodies being established by statute (Sectoral Employment Commissions?) both empowered and obliged to regulate the working conditions in the sector in question. Indeed the jurisdiction of such bodies (bipartite in composition) could be extended also to include the transposition of EC directives, training arrangements for the sector in question, and pension provision for those engaged in the sector. But in addition to the type of problems already discussed in relation to the other options canvassed (which are likely to be compounded in relation to this particular option), there are more practical difficulties likely to arise here and which would have to be faced before an initiative of this kind could be contemplated.

First and most obviously the economy would need to be divided into a number of sectors for this purpose, a huge administrative task particularly when the economy does not neatly divide into identifiable sectors. Quite apart from the mechanics of the operation who would be its engineer? Secondly there is the question of who would sit on these commissions and what would happen if employers refused to participate: would the procedure be mandatory or consensual? Thirdly there is the question of the functions and duties of these Commissions and what would happen if they were unable to reach an agreement on any particular matter: who would resolve any disagreements between the parties? Fourthly there is the question of how any such initiative would relate to existing collective bargaining structures and procedures: would such a Commission be established where there was adequate coverage of collective agreements? Fifthly, there is the question of the status of any agreement which is made, and the related question of to whom it would apply: would it apply to everyone in the sector in question, or only to union members or only to workers of employers in some way engaged in the process? And finally there is the question of flexibility:

would employers and workers be bound by a rigid framework when their own local needs called for a different set of arrangements?[7]

CONCLUSION

We have argued for the need to rebuild in the United Kingdom the institutional framework for the joint regulation of working conditions. This could be done in one of two ways, either by encouraging enterprise-based initiatives and their extension outwards and upwards; or by indirect or direct forms of institution building at sectoral level. Although the public-policy agenda and debate is currently dominated by the former strategy, in our view this may not be an adequate response on its own in light of the goals which are to be realized. For a number of reasons which we explain this strategy is much less efficient than the latter and is much too unpredictable in terms of whether it could create a comprehensive framework of institutions for the joint regulation of working conditions. This is not to deny that such a strategy has a role to play, but it is to suggest that it needs to be complemented by one based more consciously on the building of institutions at the sectoral level. While we are conscious of the political and practical difficulties surrounding the adoption of a 'top-down' strategy, we are equally conscious of the fact that the practical difficulties are not incapable of resolution if there is the political will to overcome them.

REFERENCES

Anderson, G., Brosnan, P., and Walsh, P. (1995), 'Flexibility, Casualisation and Externalisation in the New Zealand Workforce', *Journal of Industrial Relations*, 36: 491–518.

Auvergnon, P. and Gil y Gil, J.-L. (1994), 'La Réforme du Droit du Travail en Espagne', *Droit Social*, 199–208.

Arthurs, H. (1996), 'Labour Law without the State', *University of Toronto Law Journal*, 46: 1–45.

Bercusson, B. (1994), *Working Time in Britain: Towards a European Model*. Part 1: *The European Union Directive* (London: IER).

Buchele, R. and Christiansen, J. (1995), 'Productivity, Real Wages and Worker Rights: A Cross-national Comparison', *Labour*, 8: 405–22.

Büchtemann, C. (1990), 'More Jobs through Less Employment Protection? Evidence for West Germany', *Labour*, 3: 23–56.

---

[7] These issues are considered more fully in IER (1996).

—— and Quack, S. (1989), ' "Bridges" or "Traps"? Non-standard Employment in the Federal Republic of Germany', in Rodgers and Rodgers (eds.), *Precarious Jobs*.

Card, D. and Freeman, R. (1994), 'Small Differences that Matter: Canada vs. the United States', in Freeman (ed.), *Working under Different Rules*.

CBI (1991), *UK Inflation Performance* (London: CBI).

Castro, A., Méhaut, P., and Rubery, J. (1992) (eds.), *International Integration and the Organisation of Labour Markets* (London: Academic Press).

Davies, P. and Freedland, M. (1994), *Labour Legislation and Public Policy* (Oxford: Clarendon Press).

Deakin, S. (1992), 'Labour Law and Industrial Relations', in Michie (ed.), *The Economic Legacy*.

—— and Morris, G. (1995), *Labour Law* (London: Butterworth).

—— and Wilkinson, F. (1994), 'Rights vs. Efficiency? The Economic Case for Transnational Labour Standards', *Industrial Law Journal*, 23: 289–310.

—— —— (1996), *Labour standards—Essential to Social and Economic Progress* (London: IER).

Deery, S. and Mitchell, R. (1993) (eds.), *Labour Law and Industrial Relations in Asia* (Melbourne: Longman, Cheshire).

Emerson, M. (1988), 'Regulation or Deregulation of the Labour Market: Policy Régimes for the Recruitment and Dismissal of Employees in Industrialised Countries', *European Economic Review*, 32: 775–817.

European Commission (1993a), *Employment in Europe 1993* (Luxemburg: OOPEC).

—— (1993b), *Social Protection in Europe* (Luxemburg: OOPEC).

—— (1994), *European Social Policy: A Way Forward for the Union. A White Paper*, COM (94) 333 (Luxemburg: OOPEC).

—— (1996b), *For a Europe of Civic and Social Rights*, Final Report by the Comité des Sages chaired by Maria de Lourdes Pintasilgo (Brussels: Commission of the European Communities).

Evans, S., Goodman, J., and Hargreaves, L. (1985), *Unfair Dismissal Law and Employment Practice in the 1980s*, Research Paper No. 53 (London: Department of Employment).

Ewing, K. (1995), 'Democratic Socialism and Labour Law', *Industrial Law Journal*, 24: 103–32.

—— (1996), 'Rights at the Workplace: An Agenda for Labour Law', in McColgan (ed.), *The Future of Labour Law*.

Ferner, A. and Hyman, R. (1995), *Industrial Relations in the New Europe* (Oxford: Blackwell).

Fredman, S. (1992), 'The New Rights: Labour Law and Ideology in the Thatcher Years', *Oxford Journal of Legal Studies*, 12: 24–44.

Freeman, R. (1994), 'How Labor Fares in Advanced Economies', in Freeman (ed.), *Working under Different Rules* (New York: NBER/Russell Sage Foundation).

Houseman, S. (1995), 'Job Growth and the Quality of Jobs in the US Economy', *Labour*, 8: S93–S124.

Institute of Employment Rights (IER) (1996), *Working Life: A New Perspective on Labour Law* (London: IER).

Joseph Rowntree Foundation (1995), *Inquiry into Income and Wealth*: ii (York: Joseph Rowntree Foundation).

Loveman, G. and Tilly, C. (1988), 'Good Jobs or Bad Jobs? Evaluating the American Job Creation Experience', *International Labour Review*, 127: 593–611.

Lyon-Caen, G., Pélissier, J., and Supiot, A. (1994), *Droit du Travail*, 17th edn. (Paris: Dalloz).

McColgan, A. (1996) (ed.), *The Future of Labour Law* (London: Mansell).

Michie, J. (1992) (ed.), *The Economic Legacy: 1979–1992* (London: Academic Press).

—— and Grieve Smith, J. (1994) (eds.), *Unemployment in Europe* (London: Academic Press).

—— and Wilkinson, F. (1994), 'The Growth of Unemployment in the 1980s', in Michie and Grieve Smith (eds.), *Unemployment in Europe*.

—— —— (1995), 'Wages, Government Policy and Unemployment', *Review of Political Economy*, 7: 133–49.

Milner, S. (1995), 'The Coverage of Collective Pay-setting Institutions in Britain', *British Journal of Industrial Relations*, 33: 69–91.

Mückenberger, U. (1992), 'Federal Republic of Germany', in Veneziani (ed.), *Law, Collective Bargaining and Labour Flexibility*.

OECD (1993), *The OECD Jobs Study—Facts, Strategies, Analysis* (Paris: OECD).

—— (1994), *Employment Outlook* (Paris: OECD).

Ojeda-Aviles, M. (1992), 'Spain', in Veneziani (ed.), *Law, Collective Bargaining and Labour Flexibility*.

Recio, A. (1992), 'Labour Market Segmentation in Spain', in Castro, Méhaut, and Rubery (eds.), *International Integration*.

Rodgers, G. and Rodgers, J. (1989) (eds.), *Precarious Jobs in Labour Market Regulation* (Geneva: International Institute for Labour Studies).

Sengenberger, W. (1994), 'Labour Standards: An Institutional Framework for Restructuring and Development', in Sengenberger and Campbell, *Creating Economic Opportunities*.

—— and Campbell, D. (1994), *Creating Economic Opportunities: The Role of Labour Standards in Industrial Restructuring* (Geneva: International Institute for Labour Studies).

Simitis, S. (1987), 'Juridification of Labor Relations', in Teubner (ed.), *Juridification*.

Supiot, A., Lorvellec, S., and Kerbouc'h, J. (1992), 'France', in Veneziani (ed.), *Law, Collective Bargaining and Labour Flexibility*.

Teubner, G. (1987) (ed.), *Juridification of Social Spheres* (Berlin: Walter de Gruyter).

TUC (1995a), *Your Voice at Work. The TUC Proposals for Rights to Representation at Work* (London: TUC).

—— (1995b), *Rebuilding Job Security* (London: TUC).

UNICE (1995), *Releasing Europe's Potential Through Targeted Regulatory Reform. The UNICE Regulatory Report 1995* (Brussels: Union of Industrial and Employers' Confederations of Europe).

Veneziani, B. (1992) (ed.) *Law, Collective Bargaining and Labour Flexibility in EC Countries* (Rome: ASAP).

Part III

Pay and Employment Strategies

7. Is There a Pay Problem?

Peter Robinson

INTRODUCTION

Over the period from Spring 1993 to Winter 1995–6 employment in the British economy rose by over 700,000 and unemployment, as measured by the Labour Force Survey fell by over 600,000. This represented a fall in the ILO unemployment rate from 10.4 per cent to 8.3 per cent. Over the same period the rate of growth in average earnings in the whole economy showed no signs of any acceleration. Contrary to more pessimistic expectations, a steady recovery in Britain in the mid-1990s resulted in no upward pressure on wage inflation.

Does this represent substantive evidence that the trade-off between unemployment and inflation has improved since the 1980s as a result of the Conservative government's supply-side reforms? This is the interpretation offered by a range of observers. The unemployment rate consistent with stable inflation—the natural or equilibrium or non-accelerating inflation rate of unemployment—has fallen because of a range of policies designed to make the labour market more 'flexible' and to secure other improvements in the functioning of the supply side of the British economy.

At one extreme a consistent supporter of those supply-side reforms, Patrick Minford, has long argued that the policies pursued in the 1980s have lowered the natural rate of unemployment (NRU) to 3.5 per cent or less and that only perversely tight monetary policy has prevented the British economy from benefiting from a significantly lower actual rate of unemployment. At the other extreme a range of 'inflation pessimists' believed that the UK economy in early 1996 was already at or close to the NRU and that further substantial supply-side reforms would be needed before unemployment could return to anything like its pre-1979 levels. These commentators see accelerating inflation lurking not too far around every corner.

This range of opinion over the scope for further falls in unemployment without renewed inflationary pressure is largely unaltered from the late 1980s. The range of estimates for the NRU in the mid-1990s was very close to the range of estimates being offered at the end of the last decade. Any agreement amongst economists over the scale of the underlying constraints facing the British economy remains as remote as ever.

The purpose of this chapter is to explore the terms of the debate amongst economists over the nature of the trade-off between unemployment and

inflation. At the heart of the argument presented is the concern that economists may have misread the lessons from the experience of the boom of
the late 1980s. At this time a sharp fall in unemployment produced some
upward creep in wage inflation. However, a mythology seems to have developed that this experience proves that any sustained reduction in unemployment below some quite high level is bound to lead to accelerating inflation.

This chapter argues that the UK's experience since the early 1980s suggests that there is an asymmetry in the inflation process, but one which is
the exact opposite of that usually described. Very significant increases in
unemployment are required to reduce wage inflation, but equally significant
reductions in unemployment do not lead to the same upward shift in wage
inflation. The slope of the Phillips Curve is very different depending on
whether the economy is facing disinflation or expansion, as represented in
a stylized fashion in Figure 7.1. If this is a correct description of the dynamics of the trade-off between unemployment and inflation (in the absence of
external shocks) then it allows one to be more sanguine about the prospects
for further falls in unemployment without the re-emergence of any significant inflationary threat.

The first part of the chapter looks at the data on the nature and extent
of Britain's 'pay problem'. The second part looks at the debate in the mid-
1990s amongst economists over the scope for further falls in unemployment
without the re-emergence of inflationary pressure. It presents a range of estimates for the NRU for this period and compares them with estimates for
the NRU which informed the debate over unemployment in the 1980s.

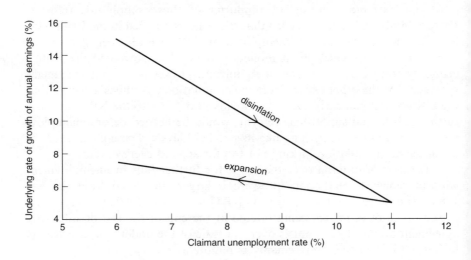

Fig. 7.1. The Phillips Curve: a 'stylized' representation of the asymmetry.

The third part looks back at the experience of stagflation and disinflation in the 1970s, 1980s and early 1990s and asks to what extent economists have learned the right lessons from these episodes. Finally, some conclusions for macro- and microeconomic policy are outlined.

THE PARAMETERS OF BRITAIN'S 'PAY PROBLEM'

The British economy has suffered from two episodes when wage inflation has risen above an annual rate of 20 per cent. These episodes coincided with the two oil shocks in the mid- and late 1970s. The more modest increase in wage inflation in the late 1980s by contrast was not associated with any adverse external shock. A recession has followed each of these episodes, a rather modest one in the mid-1970s, the most severe post-war recession in the early 1980s and an almost as severe recession in the early 1990s. The last two recessions were very clearly policy-induced as the authorities deliberately deflated the economy in order to subdue inflation. It is these two recessions and the subsequent recoveries which are the focus for this chapter.

Figure 7.2 shows the nature of the relationship between unemployment and wage inflation over the period 1981–96. By 1981 inflation was already tumbling as unemployment soared. By 1983 the underlying rate of wage inflation had plateaued out at an annual rate of around 7.5 per cent, a rate which was to persist over the next three years. The unemployment rate had by this time increased to over 10 per cent and continued to creep up to a post-war high of 11 per cent by early 1986.

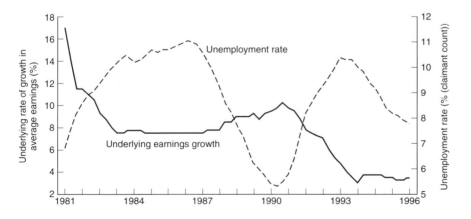

Fig. 7.2.   Average-earnings growth and unemployment in Britain, 1981–1996.
Source: Office for National Statistics.

Between 1986 and 1990 the rate of growth in output and employment accelerated and claimant unemployment halved from 11 per cent to nearly 5 per cent. Wage inflation began to creep up in 1987 when unemployment rapidly fell below 10 per cent. Wage inflation peaked at an annual rate of just over 10 per cent in 1990 just after the economy slid back into recession and unemployment began to increase again. By 1993 the claimant unemployment rate had risen back to over 10 per cent and wage inflation had fallen to just 4 per cent. Between 1993 and early 1996 claimant unemployment declined by over three-quarters of a million but wage inflation actually fell back slightly. Just as the experience of the late 1980s led to considerable pessimism about the nature of the trade-off between unemployment and inflation, so the subdued rate of wage inflation in the recovery of the mid-1990s has lead to a degree of optimism that the nature of that trade-off has improved.

The data in Figure 7.2 refer to nominal earnings growth. Figure 7.3 shows the movement in real-earnings growth, as represented by the gap between the line showing the growth in nominal earnings and the line showing the trend in the British government's target measure for consumer price inflation, the RPI minus mortgage-interest payments. In the mid-1980s real earnings grew very strongly, at an average annual rate of over 3 per cent between 1983 and 1989. With the onset of the recession in 1990 the growth in real earnings fell to an annual rate of 1.5 per cent between 1990 and 1992. Annual real-wage growth averaged less than 1 per cent over the period of the recovery from 1993 to 1995. By contrast between 1983 and 1985 real-wage growth was an average 2 percentage points faster. So nominal-

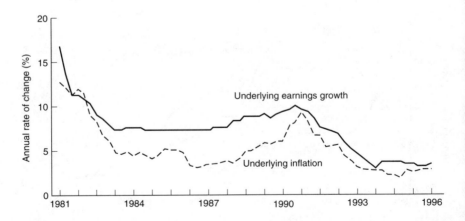

Fig. 7.3. Average-earnings growth and underlying inflation in Britain, 1981–1996. *Source*: Office for National Statistics.

earnings restraint in the mid-1990s has been matched by real-earnings restraint.

The restraint in real take-home pay in the mid-1990s has been even more significant. 1995 was the first year since 1982 that average real take-home pay (as measured by average earnings deflated by the tax and prices index) actually fell (Fig. 7.4). In the period 1983 to 1989 average real take-home pay rose at an annual rate of around 4 per cent, with the rate of increase accelerating to nearly 6 per cent between 1986 and 1988. In 1992, at the trough of the recession, people in work saw gains in average take-home pay of over 3 per cent. In sharp contrast in each year of the recovery after 1992 the rate of growth in real take-home pay decelerated as a result of subdued growth in average earnings and increases in taxation designed to reduce the budget deficit.

Fig. 7.4 presents striking evidence as to why the economic recovery in Britain in the early to mid-1990s was associated with the lack of a 'feel-good factor'. In sharp contrast to the mid-1980s, the growth in average real take-home pay has been very subdued. Instead of increases in real take-home pay of 4, 5, or 6 per cent per annum, people in work have seen gains of just 1 or 2 per cent and in 1995 a fall in real take-home pay. The recovery has brought about a steady improvement in employment opportunities and a fall in unemployment, but little perceived gain for the majority in work who do not experience unemployment.

Aside from the restraint in nominal and real earnings and in real take-home pay, another piece of evidence comes from the declining share of

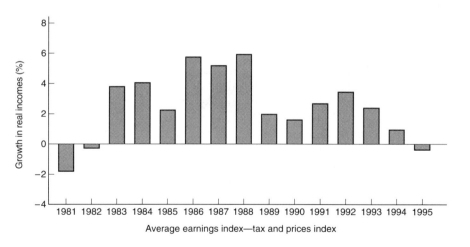

Fig. 7.4. The growth in real take-home pay for those in work, 1981–1995.
Source: Office for National Statistics.

income from employment in GDP (Fig. 7.5). This figure presents a slightly longer time-series so as to illustrate the sharp increase in the share of employment income in GDP following the first oil shock. However, the share of employment income fell very sharply after 1975 during the period of the Social Contract, so that by 1977 it had fallen back to its 1973 level. Both subsequent cycles have seen an increase in the share of employment income during the recession followed by a fall in the recovery, with this cyclical pattern occurring around a steady downward trend in the share of employment income in GDP.

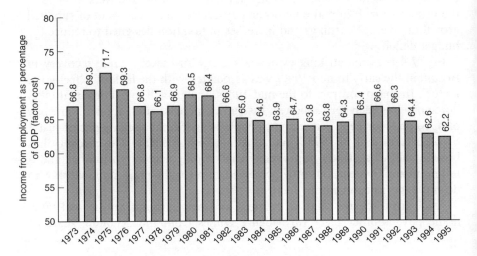

Fig. 7.5.   The share of income from employment in GDP.
Source: Office for National Statistics.

Between 1992 and 1995 the share of income from employment in GDP fell by 4 percentage points. However, this fall is similar to the fall of around 4 percentage points in the share of employment income which took place between 1981 and 1984, and is less sharp than the fall which occurred between 1975 and 1978 when the share of employment income fell by nearly 6 percentage points. So the decline in the share of income from employment from the trough of the early 1990s recession is not out of line with the experience of recoveries from previous cyclical troughs.[1]

Rather what is clear from Figure 7.5 is the trend decline in the share of income from employment in GDP from its unprecedented spike in 1975 following the first oil shock. In the mid-1970s and into the early 1980s the

[1] If the share of income from self-employment is added to income from employment the fall in labour's share in the early 1990s is sharper than the fall in the early 1980s, but not as sharp as the fall in the mid-1970s.

'excessive' share of labour in GDP and the associated 'depressed' share of profits were often the focus for concern and were held to be part of the explanation for the growth in unemployment following the two oil shocks. However, the trend decline in the share of income from employment in GDP from 1975 removes this explanation as a source of any real concern. By the mid-1990s the share of employment income had fallen to levels lower than in the 1960s and the share of gross trading profits had recovered to the levels of the 1960s.

The subdued rate of growth of nominal and real earnings in the mid-1990s despite a modest fall in unemployment appears to stand in stark contrast to the inflationary problems which apparently accompanied the sharp fall in unemployment in the late 1980s. How far has this lead to a re-appraisal of the constraints facing the British economy?

PESSIMISTS AND OPTIMISTS: ESTIMATES OF THE INFLATION CONSTRAINT

Many economists subscribe to a model of the labour market which is based around the concept of the existence of a level of unemployment which is consistent with stable inflation—the natural, equilibrium, or non-accelerating inflation rate of unemployment. If unemployment is above this level, inflation will be on a downward path and with a given rate of growth in nominal demand, real demand will increase and unemployment will fall until the natural rate is reached. If unemployment is below the NRU, inflation will accelerate, real demand will be squeezed and unemployment will rise. More precisely the proposed relationship is between the level of unemployment and the rate of wage inflation, making it clear that it is the labour market which is the primary focus for analysis.

In addition many economists have argued that the speed of adjustment of unemployment to the natural rate might have consequences for inflation. If unemployment falls too fast this might generate inflationary pressure even if unemployment is above the natural rate, as a result of short-term bottle-necks arising due to constraints relating to shortages of capital or skilled labour.

Related to this is the concept of hysteresis. A rise in the actual rate of unemployment might in turn lead to an increase in the NRU, at least in the short run. This is because the recession might lead to the scrapping of capacity and the unemployed might lose skills or motivation. This could make it more likely that any significant recovery might run into capacity or skilled-labour shortages which in turn might cause upward pressure on prices and pay. However, the corollary of this is that the recovery will even-tually lead to an expansion of capacity and the unemployed who find jobs will recover their motivation and develop their skills. So the short-run NRU will fall back again.

The natural rate itself can only be reduced through supply-side reforms designed to overcome the structural problems in the labour or product markets which are held to be responsible for the adverse trade-off between unemployment and inflation.

This model of analysis has dominated policy-making in Britain since the mid-1970s and seemed to carry with it straightforward policy prescriptions. Macroeconomic policy should aim to keep the growth in nominal demand steady, allowing unemployment to fall gradually to its natural rate if unemployment is above the NRU. At the same time microeconomic reforms have to be instituted to eliminate the structural problems which lead to a high natural rate in the first place. The common list of such structural problems includes excessive trade union power or other institutional features of the labour market such as minimum-wage regulations which hold pay above market-clearing levels, over-generous unemployment benefits, lack of skills or motivation amongst the unemployed, high levels of taxation, and from a different perspective a lack of effective capacity due to low levels of investment.

Unfortunately the clarity of this formal analysis is rather spoilt by the enormous range of estimates for the NRU which economists have in practice come up with. Table 7.1 presents a range of estimates for the NRU in Britain in the mid-1990s drawn from six of the seven original members of the Treasury's panel of independent forecasters. The range of estimates neatly illustrates the division of opinion between the pessimists and optimists in relation to Britain's medium-term prospects.

The clarity of the economic debate is also spoilt by the tendency to conduct the discussion in terms of estimates of the 'output gap' rather than estimates of the NRU. This is because the 'output gap' sounds like a technical and neutral term which does not carry with it the emotive connotations of the term the natural rate of unemployment. In fact the two concepts are intimately linked. Depending on the value of the 'Okun coefficient' linking the growth rate in output to the change in unemployment, one can directly infer from any estimate of the output gap what the associated level of the NRU

Table 7.1. Estimates of the natural rate of unemployment in Britain in the mid-1990s (as percentage of the labour-force (claimant count))

Minford	Sentance	Congdon	Currie	Brittan	Davies
3.5	4–6	6–7	6.5–7.5	7–8	7–8

Sources: The Panel of Independent Forecasters, Nov. 1995 Report, HM Treasury; Sentance 1995.

is. Saying that the output gap is 4 per cent, with an Okun coefficient of 2, is equivalent to saying that the actual rate of unemployment is 2 percentage points above the NRU. So when economists remark that they think that the output gap is close to being eliminated, it is equivalent to saying that unemployment is close to the natural rate.

At one extreme in Table 7.1 is Minford's estimate that the NRU in Britain has now fallen to just 3.5 per cent of the work-force or less, or about the one million mark. In the late 1970s Minford argued that the high NRU in Britain at that time was a consequence of excessive trade union power, over-generous unemployment benefits, and high levels of taxation. As in the 1980s all of these structural problems are seen to have been effectively tackled by government supply-side reforms, Minford has argued consistently for many years that unemployment could continue to fall without any acceleration in inflation provided that monetary policy was relaxed sufficiently. The upward blip in inflation in the late 1980s is put down to an excessively rapid decline in unemployment running into short-term capacity constraints.

At the other extreme are the inflation pessimists (Davies and Brittan) who in 1995–6 were still concerned that the NRU was in the range of 7–8 per cent. At the end of 1995 claimant unemployment fell below 8 per cent so that the actual rate of unemployment was not far from the estimated natural rate. However, it is worth noting that in 1993 these two economists plus a third (Currie) were talking about a natural rate of 9 or 10 or even 11 per cent. They expected inflation to begin accelerating soon after any fall in unemployment from its cyclical peak.

These are the 'line in the sand' economists. As unemployment fell towards 10 per cent there were warnings that inflation might rise. Unemployment fell below 10 per cent and nothing happened. As unemployment fell towards 9 per cent there were warnings that inflation might rise. Unemployment fell below 9 per cent and nothing happened. As unemployment fell toward 8 per cent there were warnings that inflation might rise. In late 1995 unemployment fell below 8 per cent and nothing happened. By early 1996 the 'line in the sand' had been redrawn at between 7 and 8 per cent.

These economists have been deeply sceptical that any of the government's supply-side reforms have succeeded in significantly lowering the natural rate. As an *ad hoc* response to the fall in unemployment without any sign of accelerating inflation there may have subsequently been an acceptance of at least partial success on the part of the structural reforms of the 1980s.

Other economists (for example Barrell *et al.* 1995) have consistently stuck to 7–8 per cent as their best estimate of the NRU and so in 1996 were also waiting with bated breath to see if wage inflation would indeed accelerate if unemployment fell through this barrier. One economist (Nickell 1996) actually believes that the NRU in the early to mid-1990s was higher than in the late 1970s.

A fifth member of the original panel (Congdon) has held views similar to those of Minford over the necessity for and the success of Conservative supply-side reforms in the 1980s. However, his estimate of the NRU is significantly higher than Minford's.

A former panel member (Sentance) holds the view that the NRU probably never rose as sharply in the 1970s as others have claimed, but that some supply-side reforms have helped to bring it down. However, the main feature of his analysis is that a series of inflationary shocks and the subsequent sharp disinflations have appeared to deliver an adverse trade-off between unemployment and inflation. However, with these shocks out of the way there is no reason why unemployment could not decline at a modest and steady rate to levels significantly lower than were experienced in the 1980s and early 1990s.

The final original panel member (Godley) has specifically rejected the natural rate hypothesis as a framework for analysis, a reminder that this orthodox approach is not universally accepted. In common with some other traditional Keynesians he sees Britain's economy as facing a fundamental balance of payments constraint. Ironically those who take this view are therefore even more pessimistic about the future path of unemployment than are those who believe in the NRU. They come to the same conclusions about the inability of any significant increase in aggregate demand to in itself bring about a sustained reduction in unemployment, not because the increase in demand might reduce unemployment below the NRU and result in accelerating inflation, but because the increase in aggregate demand would quickly lead to an unsustainable increase in the current account deficit.

So one feature of the debate over unemployment in Britain is that the most clear advocate of the natural-rate hypothesis is the most sanguine about the scope for further significant falls in unemployment, while an economist who rejects the natural-rate hypothesis is the most pessimistic.

Official bodies such as the Bank of England and the OECD tend, unsurprisingly, to be cautious about estimates of the NRU and therefore the scope for monetary policy to reduce unemployment. The OECD has revised down its estimate of the NRU in Britain to under 7 per cent (OECD 1996). The Bank of England concluded that the unemployment rate in Britain in early 1996 (at 7.9 per cent) was above the NRU on the unobjectionable grounds that the rate of growth in average earnings was still stable. However, over the period from 1993 the Bank was consistently worried about the re-emergence of wage inflation. The UK Treasury makes no comment about the level of the NRU, consistent with its position that it makes no specific comment about the prospects for unemployment at all.

The six estimates of the NRU derived from the six original members of the Treasury's panel of independent forecasters, plus the OECD's estimate and the estimates of Barrell *et al.* (1995) and Nickell (1996), give an average estimate for the NRU in the mid-1990s in Britain of 6.7 per cent, with a range from 3.5 to 8.9 per cent (Table 7.2). These estimates are placed alongside estimates of the NRU covering the period from 1969–73 to 1988–90.

Table 7.2. Estimates of the natural rate of unemployment in Britain over the period 1969–1973 to 1996 (as percentage of the labour-force (claimant count))

	1969–73	1974–80	1981–7	1988–90	1995–6
NRU: range	1.6–5.6	4.5–7.3	5.2–9.9	3.5–8.1	3.5–8.9
NRU: average	2.9	5.7	7.0	6.1	6.7
Actual rate of unemployment (average)	2.5	3.8	10.1	6.8	8.2
Number of estimates	11	13	15	5	9

Sources: The Panel of Independent Forecasters, Nov. 1995 Report, HMTreasury; Cromb 1994; Barrell, Pain, and Young 1995; Nickell 1996.

It is striking that the average and the range of estimates for the NRU in the mid-1990s is almost identical to the average and the range of estimates in the late 1980s. The fact that the estimates of the NRU for the mid-1990s are no different from those arrived at during the Lawson boom seems to signal that there is still no consensus that the government's structural reforms have in fact improved the trade-off between unemployment and inflation.

Another striking feature of the table is that estimates of the NRU seem suspiciously pro-cyclical. Estimates of the NRU appear to go up when actual unemployment rates rise and then fall again when actual unemployment falls. Robert Solow used to joke that the NRU simply followed the path of the actual rate of unemployment. The forecasters appear to have embodied this joke in their models.

The average mid-1990s estimate of the NRU is little different from the average estimate from the early to mid-1980s, when pessimism over the performance of the British economy was at its height. The mid-1990s estimate is still higher than the average estimate of the NRU for the late 1970s. The late 1970s were the time of 'rampant' trade union power, 'overgenerous' welfare payments, and 'excessive' taxation and regulation. Despite a raft of supply-side reforms since 1979 only one economist (Minford) clearly believes that the sustainable rate of unemployment is lower than that inherited by the Conservative government in 1979. Excluding this economist, the consensus view appears to be that we do still have a 'pay problem' in that at some point further falls in unemployment will lead to accelerating wage inflation and subsequently to a tightening of monetary policy which will bring this fall in unemployment to a halt when unemployment is still at an uncomfortably high level.

What exactly underlies this pessimism?

MISREADING THE LESSONS OF HISTORY?

The British economy responded very badly to the inflationary supply-side shocks of the 1970s. The resultant wage–price spiral in Britain was more severe than in most other industrial counties and after the second oil shock required a deep recession to suppress. Given this it is clear why by the early 1980s most estimates of the NRU were quite high, reflecting the experience that whatever the precise structural problems identified in the British economy, it had proved especially vulnerable to the impact of external shocks. It is not hard to see why the case for fundamental structural reforms was advanced at that time.

In the early 1980s significant increases in unemployment appeared to be required to bring down inflation. Between 1981 and 1983 an increase of 2 percentage points in unemployment was required to shave 4 percentage points off the rate of increase in average earnings. This gives a 'sacrifice ratio' of 0.5, that is to say an extra 0.5 per cent on the unemployment rate was required to reduce wage inflation by 1 per cent.

In the early 1990s the process of disinflation was just as painful. Between 1991 and 1993 an increase of 2 percentage points in unemployment was required to shave 4 percentage points off the rate of increase in average earnings. So the sacrifice ratio was unaltered at 0.5. There was no sign that any increase in labour-market 'flexibility' had made the process of reducing inflation any less costly in the early 1990s when compared with the early 1980s.

This then is the second reason for pessimism over whether the trade-off between unemployment and inflation has really improved. During periods of disinflation the costs in terms of higher unemployment of achieving a given reduction in wage inflation do not appear to have diminished despite all the supply side-reforms.

However, what really appears to condition the views of the inflation 'pessimists' is their interpretation of the expansion of the late 1980s when wage inflation began to increase as unemployment fell below 10 per cent. It was this early apparent increase in wage inflation which led to the belief of the 'line in the sand' economists that the recovery in employment from 1993 would quickly lead once again to upward pressure on wage inflation as unemployment fell below 10 per cent.

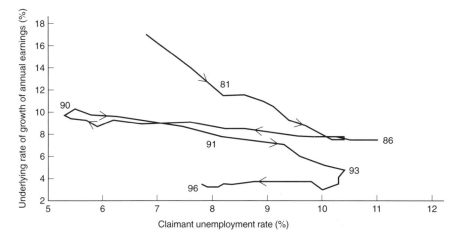

Fig. 7.6. The Phillips Curve: average-earnings growth and unemployment, 1981–1996.

Source: Office for National Statistics.

Figure 7.6 graphs the same data which was used to construct Figure 7.2, but this time plots a Phillips Curve. One can confirm from comparing the slope of the Phillips Curve between 1981 and 1983 with the slope between 1991 and 1993 that the experience of disinflation in these two periods was similar in terms of the cost of higher unemployment.

However, the Phillips Curve also illustrates a striking asymmetry. After 1986 when unemployment began falling, a reduction in the unemployment rate of nearly 6 percentage points added less than 3 percentage points to wage inflation. This gives a 'gain ratio' of 2, that is to say a fall of 2 per cent in the unemployment rate was required before wage inflation increased by 1 percentage point. The fall in unemployment required to produce a given increase in wage inflation was significantly greater than the rise in unemployment required to produce a given reduction in wage inflation. This is illustrated graphically by noting the very shallow slope of the Phillips Curve between 1986 and 1990. It is much flatter than the slope of the curve during periods of disinflation. Over the period 1993–6 the Phillips Curve is basically flat as the reduction in unemployment brought about no increase in wage inflation at all.

These observations are striking because of the widely held assumption of both academics and most importantly Central Bankers that the asymmetry in the inflation process is precisely the opposite way round (Bean 1994). That is to say the view which dominates the minds of policy-makers is that the extra unemployment required to secure a given reduction in wage inflation is greater than the fall in unemployment which might be achieved at the expense of a given increase in wage inflation. In other words the 'sacrifice ratio' is greater than the 'gain' ratio. British experience over the period 1981–96 suggests that this is not true.

This finding is important because the commonly held view over the nature of the asymmetry in the inflation process is used as another justification for Central Bank caution. If any reduction in wage inflation required a bigger increase in unemployment than the fall in unemployment which might be secured when growth is encouraged and some increase in wage inflation tolerated, then this counsels caution about tolerating any upward creep in inflation at all. This is likely to lead to a rapid, but perhaps unnecessary, tightening of monetary policy at any sign of *any* increase in wage inflation.

The underlying rate of growth in whole-economy productivity in the British economy over the last complete economic cycle (1979–90) was 1.9 per cent. So real-wage growth of around 2 per cent per annum would be consistent with a constant share of income from employment in GDP. Growth in average earnings of around 4.5 per cent would be consistent with a target for underlying inflation of 2.5 per cent. With average earnings growth running at around 3.5 per cent at the beginning of 1996, some modest upward creep in wage inflation could be tolerated without placing the British government's inflation target at risk.

It is not clear that the lessons of the late 1980s have been correctly learned. The rapid fall in unemployment between 1986 and 1990 produced only a modest upward creep in wage inflation. During the first six months of 1990 there was little evidence that unemployment (then below 6 per cent) was below the NRU. If this had been the case the forecasters would have been projecting either a rapid acceleration of inflation or a sharp increase in unemployment to contain wage inflation (Jackman 1992). In fact none of the forecasters were predicting this and other labour-market indicators, such as the level of vacancies, were not providing conclusive evidence that the labour market was in a state of excess demand. The sharp blip in headline inflation in 1990 had much to do with increases in mortgage rates and indirect taxes feeding directly into retail prices, which serves as a reminder that inflation can increase temporarily due to factors which are nothing to do with the labour market.

The upward creep in inflation in the late 1980s may have been a response to too rapid an adjustment to the NRU. Between 1986 and 1990 the expansion in demand and the fall in unemployment was faster than would have advocated by an unreconstructed Keynesian. Capacity constraints and skill shortages did lead to some inflationary pressure even though unemployment was almost certainly still significantly above its natural rate. A more steady, balanced recovery in employment would have placed fewer strains on an economy battered by earlier recessions. Arguably such a steady recovery is precisely what the British economy experienced between 1993 and 1996 and this explains why there was no real additional inflationary pressure at all at this time.

This interpretation is close to that offered by Sentance (1995). He offers a range for the NRU of between 4 and 6 per cent. The lower end of that range is not far from Minford's estimate of 3.5 per cent. However, Minford's view is that significant supply-side reforms have reduced the NRU which was very high in the late 1970s as a result of a range of structural rigidities. The view of Sentance and this author is that if the NRU is a useful concept then it serves as a counsel of caution against over-ambitious demand management which seeks to push unemployment down too far and above all too fast. The NRU may not have risen as far as is commonly believed in the 1970s, and some supply-side reforms have contributed to a lower NRU.

Further gradual reductions in unemployment need not put intolerable upward pressure on wage inflation. At exactly what point unemployment would fall to a level where significant inflationary pressure might re-emerge is unclear, but the British economy seems unlikely to reach that level at any time in the next few years.

POLICY IN A NON-INFLATIONARY ENVIRONMENT

The fact that estimates of the NRU and therefore of the threat of a re-emergence of a pay problem vary so widely means that whatever its theoretical attractions, the concept cannot readily be used to guide macroeconomic policy. This needs saying because many of the 'line in the sand' economists invest so much authority in their estimates of the NRU and use them to offer advice on the correct stance of monetary policy. They would always counsel excessive caution on the Central Bank, arguing that monetary policy should be tightened to prevent unemployment falling below their current estimates of the NRU.

With estimates of the NRU varying so widely and all too often seeming to follow with a lag the actual rate of unemployment, it would seem dangerous to take too seriously the idea of basing monetary-policy decisions on any one specific estimate of the NRU.

Clearly what is required is a macroeconomic policy robust to different estimates of the NRU, to different formulations of what determines the NRU and adjustment towards it, and indeed to different theoretical frameworks. A target for nominal demand or GDP might fit the bill. With underlying productivity growth at around 2 per cent per annum and with some modest growth in the labour-force, growth in real output of around 3 per cent a year would allow unemployment to fall gradually towards the NRU, whatever level the NRU is at. With an underlying inflation target of 2.5 per cent, this would suggest a target for the rate of growth of nominal demand of around 5.5 per cent a year, set within a target range of perhaps 5–7 per cent.

The analysis presented here in relation to the favourable asymmetry in the trade-off between inflation and unemployment as between periods of disinflation and periods of expansion, does suggest a more relaxed attitude to any modest upward creep in wage inflation. There is already room for manœuvre with respect to an inflation target of 2.5 per cent, which would be consistent with average earnings growth of around 4.5 per cent. Any modest overshoot would require less of an increase in unemployment to achieve any given reduction in wage inflation than the gain in the form of lower unemployment which might be associated with any given increase in wage inflation. This is why the band around the central target for the growth in nominal demand could lean in the upward direction from that central target.

A moderate and balanced expansion of aggregate demand and output would allow for a slow move towards whatever the underlying NRU is. One role of supply-side policy is to ease that slow adjustment to the NRU and to share out the employment gains across all households.

What could possibly disturb such a benign scenario? All that has been said so far only holds in the absence of further external shocks with inflationary implications. There is no way of knowing, because there has not been an external inflationary shock since 1979, whether the British economy is less prone to a re-emergent wage/price spiral now than it was in the 1970s. There is every reason to fear that it is just as prone. And once significant inflation does take hold as the result of an external shock the costs of disinflation are likely to be as severe as they were in the early 1980s and again in the early 1990s. In other words the new labour-market regime in the UK has yet to be really tested.

This suggests that Britain's labour market may face an incipient pay problem in that it is no better placed to deal with inflationary shocks now that it has ever been. In addition Sentance makes it clear that his belief that unemployment might not be able to fall below 4–6 per cent is based on the view that in the context of the British labour market a 'reserve army' of the unemployed is required to restrain wage inflation at anything approaching full employment. This raises the question as to whether in the immediate post-war period in Britain and in other European countries there existed a set of institutions and, more importantly, values which led to a process of pay determination which obviated the need for such a 'reserve army'.

The development of a system of co-ordinated pay bargaining therefore remains on the agenda, to prevent a destructive pay/price spiral which might result from any significant external inflationary shock, and to reconstruct the system of pay determination which arguably helped to maintain full employment in the immediate post-war period. The rest of the 1990s might offer a breathing space to discuss the case for such a system, precisely because its development is likely to prove easier while conditions are relatively benign than in the context of a crisis.

REFERENCES

Bean, C. (1994), 'The Role of Demand Management Policies in Reducing Unemployment', Discussion Paper No. 222, Centre for Economic Performance, London School of Economics.

Barrell, R., Pain, N., and Young, G. (1995), 'Structural Differences in European Labour Markets', in R. Barrell (ed.), *The UK Labour Market: Comparative Aspects and Institutional Developments* (National Institute of Economic and Social Research/Cambridge University Press).

Cromb, R. (1994), 'The UK NAIRU', Government Economic Service Discussion Paper No. 124.

Jackman, R. (1992), 'An Economy of Unemployment?', in E. Mclaughlin (ed.), *Understanding Unemployment: New Perspectives on Active Labour Market Policies* (London: Routledge).

Nickell, S. (1996), 'Can Unemployment in the UK be Reduced?', in D. Halpern, S. Wood, S. White, and G. Cameron (eds.), *Options for Britain: A Strategic Policy Review* (Aldershot: Dartmouth).

OECD (1996), *Economic Survey: United Kingdom, 1996* (Paris: OECD).

Sentance, A. (1995), 'Are We Entering a New Golden Age of Economic Growth?', *London Business School Economic Outlook* (November).

8.   Economic Policy, Accumulation, and Productivity

Geoff Harcourt

We live in an increasingly competitive environment, nationally and internationally, both with regard to industrial and commercial capital, and to
financial capital. One consequence of attempts to cope with this situation
has been the emergence of sustained mass unemployment in the advanced
capitalist economies. Yet inflation still remains stubbornly persistent in
most countries and there has also been a decline in the rate of growth of
productivity in some of them. We have witnessed as well instability in major
markets—those for foreign exchange, labour, property, and financial
assets—and great variability in the rate of accumulation around unsatisfac-
tory average levels in many industries and in economies as wholes.

In this chapter I want to examine the interrelationships between these
phenomena in order to try to reveal their causes and to suggest in broad
outline some policy proposals through which to tackle their unacceptable
effects. Though I have the UK most in mind, the analysis, I hope, does
apply to the workings of advanced capitalist economies. The cures suggested are part of a larger scheme of interrelated policies which I have outlined elsewhere (see Harcourt 1995, chs. 1–3; Grieve Smith *et al.* 1996).

I

I start by setting out antecedents and obligations. I only met the late Wilfred
Salter a few times but, as it happens, I had something to do with virtually
everything he wrote. In particular, I wrote the review article of his classic,
Productivity and Technical Change (1960) for the *Economic Record* (Harcourt
1962; 1982, ch. 9). His work on productivity and technical change was the
major inspiration for several of my papers in the 1960s and 1970s. So when
I started to think about themes for the present chapter, I naturally returned
to his 1960 book and its splendid sequel which is buried in a 1965 IEA vol-

I am most grateful to, but in no way implicate, Willy Brown, Andrew Glyn, John Grieve
Smith, Bryan Hopkin, Brian Reddaway, Bob Rowthorn, and John Wells for their comments
on a draft of this chapter. I would also like to thank, with the same proviso, the participants
in the Post Keynesian Economics Study Group, 9.2.1996, and in the conference of the volume
in Robinson College on Wednesday, 15 May, 1996 for their comments.

ume edited by Austin Robinson. I came away from the 1960 book refreshed by his crystal clear analysis of the relationship between demand, prices, and investment in new techniques at the margins of the existing stocks of capital goods. I was also struck anew by the crucial relevance of his major policy conclusions and by how just about all current policies in most capitalist countries, and especially in this benighted country, are in effect the exact opposite of what Salter proposed. In particular, the current fetish for what are euphemistically called flexible labour markets and for their supposed roles in setting real wages and allocating labour, itself cruelly and unnecessarily vastly underemployed, flies in the face of common sense, good economic analysis, and policy recommendations, that is to say, of analysis of the sort which masters such as Wilfred Salter consistently supplied.

Other sources of inspirations for the chapter are, first, Michal Kalecki's 1943 classic 'The Political Aspects of Full Employment', especially the crucial distinction which he made there between the political economy of *attaining* full employment, on the one hand, and of *sustaining* it, on the other. The distinction is central to the argument of the present chapter. Secondly, and this is a sad one, because it comes so soon after the death of James Meade just before Christmas 1995, is the 1957 Meade-Russell paper which is a classic in the Australian literature. Meade wrote it with my other Australian mentor, the late Eric Russell, who was my closest friend at Adelaide. Any understanding of how the Australian economy works must start from this paper, but the analysis is not confined to my native land. It concerns the process of income distribution between capitalists and wage-earners in a small open economy in which the principal exports are from the primary sector and are subject to price fluctuations on world markets (see Harcourt 1977; 1982, ch. 21 for an account of the origins and contents of the paper).

Building on this paper both Eric and Wilfred gave sage advice to the then ACTU advocate, Bob Hawke, for the late 1950s Basic Wage Case concerning the principles which should guide the setting by the Arbitration Commission of the Basic Wage and, in effect, the rate of increase of the average money-wage in Australia as a whole. Salter provided the statistical data, conceptual analysis and argument, Russell, the theoretical argument and statement of principles.[1] Between them they not only influenced greatly the setting of the Basic Wage through the 1950s and 1960s but they also sowed the seeds for the principles behind the various Accords which were crucial planks of the policy of the Hawke-Keating ALP government of 1983–96. The fact that the Accords were relatively successful for a number of years, both in reducing inflation and in being associated with rising employment, no doubt makes me more sanguine about the feasibility and

---

[1] Eric subsequently published his principal arguments for such a policy for Australia in *Australian Economic Papers* in 1965.

effectiveness of incomes policies than many UK economists and commentators.

There is, finally, James Meade's last book, published only a few months before he died, *Full Employment Regained?* (1995).

II

Having set out inspirations, antecedents, and aims, I now outline the arguments and, in a general way, the package deal of policies which follow from the political and economic analysis. Basically, the aim is to provide a set of policies which allow sustained full employment with agreeable rates of inflation and more satisfactory rates of growth of GDP and productivity. A necessary corollary of achieving these is to raise the overall level of accumulation.

We may start by reminding ourselves of Salter's analysis. The problem he set himself to explain was why, in situations in which technical progress is steadily occurring, old machines of an inferior vintage are to be found operating alongside new best-practice techniques in most industries, a problem which was never clearly stated nor satisfactorily solved either in classical analysis (including Marx) or by neoclassical analysis, and especially not by Marshall. In fact, we may read into both sources that in the final long-period position,[2] if it were ever reached, we would only find operating machines incorporating current best-practice techniques. The capital/labour and capital/output ratios associated with these machines would have been determined by the expected movements in long-period prices and wages at the beginning of the analysis (and period). The state of knowledge—the capital/labour and capital/output ratios of the array of best-practice techniques—is summed up conveniently in terms of either a family of isoquants or, if there are constant returns to scale, a unique isoquant of various associations of inputs per unit of output.

Salter's crucial contribution was to show that if we suppose that technical progress in each industry is steady but discrete (and if, for the moment, we abstract from the effects of the cycle), investment in the current best-practice techniques chosen in the existing situation will, in competitive conditions, be pushed to the point where the prices established for the output which these machines and the accumulated vintages from past bursts of accumulation help to produce allow only the normal rate of profit to be received on the best-practice techniques. That is to say, *total* long-period costs including normal profits are just covered by the prices set and sales receipts received. The sales receipts associated with the outputs of previous vintages which are still operating and contributing to the current supply

---

[2] It is an equilibrium of long-period supply and demand in the neoclassical case.

only have to cover their existing *variable* costs in order to remain operating—'Bygones are bygones'. Of course, all but the marginal vintages will do better than this. Machines are retired and, sometimes, scrapped only when their quasi-rents are less than zero. In this way the benefits of technical progress are embodied in the stocks of capital goods and passed on to consumers in lower prices, yet some older vintages are able to exist side by side with the new improved ones.

Both at the level of each industry and, even more, at the level of the economy as a whole, the levels and rates of increase of wages are crucial to the process. (Wage movements may legitimately be regarded as exogenous at the level of the firm or even of the industry in many cases, but are obviously endogenously determined at the level of the economy as a whole.) They are among the principal determinants of variable costs, both directly and indirectly, and therefore of which machines remain in operation and of how far investment in new machines may go before prices reach levels where only normal profits are received so that accumulation comes temporarily to a halt: temporarily, because technical progress is a continuing process so that new sets of best-practice techniques become available over time and the accumulation and retiring/scrapping processes start up anew. (Of course, this is an artificial way of putting it, first, because individual industries are not synchronized by time and period so that, *overall*, accumulation and embodiment are continuous; and, secondly, because we have made the simplifying assumption that technical advances occur at discrete intervals in order to make the analysis of output, accumulation, and price-setting tractable. We have also concentrated on the volume of accumulation determined by wage movements, keeping at the back of our heads the effect of relative prices on the choice of the best-practice techniques (see Harcourt 1968; 1982, ch. 11; Harcourt and Kenyon 1976; 1982, ch. 8).

The analysis is essentially Marshallian in spirit but overcomes the vagueness and misleading inferences of Marshall's own long-period analysis (but see Dennis Robertson's defence of the master (1956), that there were two concepts of the long period in Marshall, one abstract, theoretical, the other more attuned to real life). Moreover, Salter (1960: 90–3) shows that if we have imperfectly competitive or even oligopolistic market structures, much the same processes tend to occur though the forces driving decision-makers to instal and retire may be neither as strong nor as persistent as in the competitive situation. This view was first set out by Marx though not as explicitly nor as convincingly. Salter considers either profit-maximization or strategic behaviour in the non-perfectly competitive situations. We consider later the implications of some of the mark-up theories which link the profit margin and price-setting to investment requirements.[3]

---

[3] Brian Reddaway has pointed out to me that both Salter and I are 'assuming away' a host of problems which spring from the presence of imperfect competition, especially the

III

For the purposes of the present chapter, it is the systemic implications of these industry processes which are most relevant. (Salter extended his analysis to the system as a whole in Salter 1965.) From what we have argued so far, if we are interested in overall growth of output as a whole and of output per head,[4] the most favourable conditions for achieving high rates of growth in both is that declining industries and expanding industries do so quickly. For this to occur, the last thing we want is a flexible labour market for its proponents tell us that the money-wages of labour should reflect the respective levels and rates of change of productivity in their particular industries.[5] But this means money-wages *for the same sorts of labour* will be low and the rates of increase low in the declining industries, so that they linger on, their existing vintages still profitable to keep operating, *ceteris paribus*. By contrast, the industries that should be expanding rapidly have the required accumulation process held back by high money-wages based on the capacity to pay! The outcome is certainly a lower level of productivity in the economy overall and probably a lower rate of increase of productivity overall, than would be the situation if the levels and advances of money-wages were to follow the more efficient and equitable course for which we argue below.[6]

In brief, the guiding principle should be that money-wages are adjusted for changes in the cost-of-living and effective productivity—the overall change in productivity adjusted for any permanent change in the terms of trade. Thus Salter drew these basic policy conclusions from his analysis (see Salter 1960: 153–4) which may be summarized as follows:

(a) government economic policy should be directed towards creating a flexible economy which enables an easy transference of resources

---

implications of non-homogeneous commodities. I do rather feebly try to tackle this later in the chapter. He added that 'uncertainty is largely responsible for non-investment and retention of old models'. I can only respond by saying that if the analysis of this chapter is correct and if the package deal of policies proposed were to be implemented, the environment so created might well reduce the effects of uncertainty and allow higher rates of accumulation to occur.

[4] Not only are they desirable in themselves, they are also the necessary prerequisite for obtaining and sustaining full employment and of having some chance of implementing an incomes policy which is consistent with an overall rate of inflation that maintains the competitiveness of the economies concerned.

[5] Bryan Hopkin has challenged me to quote chapter and verse for this. It does seem to me to be the implications of the arguments currently in the public domain for the virtues of flexible labour markets and that economists of a Chicago bent would be inclined to provide an analytical rationale in terms of competitive marginal-productivity theory.

[6] Bryan Hopkin has pointed out a potential *non sequitur* here: it is low-productivity industries which should go, high-productivity ones which should grow and they are not necessarily synonymous with declining and expanding industries respectively. Salter does obliquely cover himself on this point (see Salter 1960: 153).

from declining, high-cost and high-price industries to expanding, low-cost and low-price ones;

(b) wages policy should be national in scope rather than related to the circumstances of particular industries. Relating earnings to the 'capacity to pay' of particular industries tends to bolster declining industries and hamper expanding, progressive ones. It delays the introduction of new techniques and has a harmful effect on overall economic growth; and

(c) a high rate of gross investment is necessary to allow the structure of production to change quickly and, given the structure of demand, increase the output and productivity of those industries where technical advances are most rapid.

IV

In Salter's book the level and rate of growth of aggregate demand were external to each industry. But when discussing pay policy and full employment, this cannot remain so. It is here that Kalecki's distinction, mentioned above, becomes vitally relevant. While business people are happy (or at least, used to be!) for some government activity to be taken to lift an economy out of a deep slump which has reduced their profits and dimmed their animal spirits, they are not at all happy with the social and political conditions which emerge when full employment is reached and then sustained, despite the obvious advantage which high demand brings them. The sack ceases to be effective as a regulator of work effort and wage changes, since the balance of political, social, and economic power tends increasingly to pass from capital to labour. Yet if animal spirits are to be revived and maintained, the maintenance of something akin to sustained full employment is necessary—witness, for example, the experience of the Golden Age of Capitalism. But unless continual and persistent action is taken about pay policy, the situation will be increasingly threatened by cumulative inflationary pressures associated especially with the setting of money-wages. For though real wages are an ultimate determinant of the standard of living and increases in it, in a monetary production economy, i.e. our world as we know it, the wage bargain may only be made in monetary terms, as Keynes taught us long ago.

So we must be able to implement an incomes policy, despite the fact that each employer would like to be free of the inconvenience which the policy brings to him or her. The policy must include as one of its features, increases which are consistent with the control of inflationary pressures, as determined by our international situation, yet which also allow the great potential benefits of the Salter processes to be realized in the growth of productivity associated with operating at full employment output levels. Such a position will, of course, be favourable for the support of the animal spirits necessary to allow the accumulation processes identified by Salter to be implemented. All this coming together will reward the economic communities for agreeing to money-income restraints, so allowing everyone to share fairly and fully in the rising prosperity—a virtuous, cumulative, reinforcing process will have been created.

V

An obvious implication of Salter's analysis is that the guiding principle of wage setting should be that, *ceteris paribus*, money-wages change by amounts dictated by changes in the cost-of-living and effective productivity. This guiding principle is just as well as efficient. At the level of the economy as a whole capital and labour are complements and so jointly contribute to the rise in overall productivity. It is just, therefore, that all citizens should share in the benefits that flow from this. Including the change in the cost-of-living insures people who are unable to protect themselves against a decline in their real incomes from sustained inflation, thus removing a major cause of anxiety and insecurity and, incidentally, making it easier for people generally to agree to money-income restraint in an overall package policy deal.[7] This deal nevertheless will not be easy to secure because it has to pay some heed to past ruptures of established relativities, the need to match job opportunities with some (limited) financial incentives and the need to have a floor to the level of money-wages (and other incomes) in a minimum wage, for reasons which are related to the efficiency-wage hypothesis.[8]

As to the main guide line, while it may be *relatively* easy to get agreement on what constitutes the cost-of-living index and its increases—certainly that is something which trade union, employer, and government representatives could profitably get together on—a real problem of principle may arise in the measurement of effective productivity changes in a world dominated by floating exchange rates. Why? Because with floating exchange rates and

[7] The confident tone of this argument probably reflects Australian experience where we have had many periods in which cost-of-living adjustments have been an integral part of national wage cases and/or automatic. Bryan Hopkin is deeply sceptical, calling the proposals the 'principle of hope over experience' in the light of UK experiments in the post-war period; but he is in favour of incomes policy in principle.

[8] Willy Brown has pointed out that there are serious social problems for some regions as well, in that even if there were to be full employment, children may have to move from regions dominated by declining industries in which their parents were initially employed. This could be offset, to some extent anyway, by encouraging investment in new industries to go to the regions containing these communities.

deregulated financial markets, we have a classic case of markets where stocks dominate flows and speculative influences dominate real economic factors in the setting of both day-to-day market prices and the average of prices over the medium to longer term. This state of affairs is compounded when we take into consideration that in a dynamic world economy in which the Salter processes are of very unequal strength as between different countries and regions, the notion that there exists an underlying set of stable long-period equilibrium exchange rates, only awaiting to be found by market forces, is, to say the least, problematic.

It follows that the idea of effective productivity—domestic productivity adjusted for changes in the terms of trade—is an elusive concept in theory and certainly in practice as far as agreed-upon estimation is concerned. Yet some rough agreement, some compromise, would need to be found between interested groups. No doubt the institutions set up to tackle the problem of ruptured relativities could also be expected to make reviews and periodic adjustments for the effects of revisions of estimates of effective productivity as well. Clearly this requires people of good will—are there any left?—but all consensus and sensible and, ultimately, efficient policy-making requires this anyway.[9]

We mentioned earlier that Salter processes are at their most effective when competitive market structures, or something akin to them, may be assumed to be present. But much effort has been devoted in Post-Keynesian circles (and others, of course) to describing non-competitive (or imperfectly competitive) market structures and their implications for pricing and the investment decision. We mention Ball (1964), Eichner (1976), Wood (1975), Harcourt and Kenyon (1976; 1982, ch. 8), Coutts, Godley, and Nordhaus (1978), Kaldor (1986), as obvious examples. Much of this work is microeconomic in character and the systemic effects have at best only been sketched. Nevertheless, there are some disquieting aspects that need to be thought about.[10] Before doing so, let me conjecture that with the increase in international competitiveness of the last two decades, both in goods and in services, especially financial services, the world economy *may* be closer to the competitive model, albeit a ruthless jungle, red in tooth and claw, than it was when the writings referred to above were first developed. If so, our minds may be put more at ease on that score anyway,

The most disquieting microeconomic result is an implication of the work

---

[9] John Wells has kindly pointed out to me that *Economic Trends* carries estimates of the terms of trade by quarters from 1970 on and has drawn my attention to an annual series of UK GDP per capita in real terms adjusted for the terms of trade from 1950 on. Bryan Hopkin reckons I have over-emphasized the difficulties (this reflects the fierce debates on this issue in Australia in the 1960s) and that some rough approximation could well be agreed to.

[10] At this point Brian Reddaway made a typically down-to-earth comment: 'The fact that commodities are not homogeneous and have varying amounts of services attached to them is particularly awkward for the would-be producers of elegant analysis.'

202 GEOFF HARCOURT

which I did with Peter Kenyon. There, we argued that prices in oligopolistic industries characterized by large price-leaders are set by profit margins designed to raise the internal funds needed to finance investment and that there was a process of mutual determination involved. It follows that margins would be greater, the greater was the investment that was planned, *ceteris paribus*. But investment would be less, the higher were the margins and therefore the prices set, because this would allow older vintages to remain in operation that much longer, thereby reducing the shortfall in expected output which new investment would be needed to cater for. In microeconomic terms at least this is a drawback on accumulation, productivity growth and attaining and sustaining full employment. Moreover, the higher price levels, *ceteris paribus*, may make the control of inflation more difficult. I am not sure that these arguments go through at the level of the system as a whole, but at the very least, they need to be explored.

VI

Let me conclude: by relating the nature of Salter processes to their policy implications for incomes policy we have identified interrelationships which promise a virtuous, cumulative performance of higher growth and higher employment, a performance which has some possibility of being sustained, if reasonable skill is shown over macroeconomic policies (notably demand management). For the policy measures promise to create an environment where animal spirits may be more consistently robust, even dynamic, and the resulting potential rise in the standard of living rewards the community for acquiescing in a policy of money-income restraint. I do not wish to overstress the cosy side of the story. There are deep-seated structural problems present in many advanced industrialized countries, not least the UK, so that bottlenecks and balance of payment constraints are only too real and often bite. Moreover, while it may be possible to create favourable climates for business people there is no guarantee that they will necessarily do their thing or do it properly—this was certainly the experience of Australia during many years of the Accord when the level and composition of investment were far from what was needed. It may be that governments can give some general pointers by the use of broadly based investment-incentive schemes, as I suggest in Harcourt (1995: 38, n. 3). But whatever misgivings we may have,[11] what is proposed is surely more efficient and more just than the pre-

---

[11] Andrew Glyn has drawn my attention to Rudolf Meidner's 1993 paper on 'Why did the Swedish Model Fail?'. The economic analysis is similar to that of this chapter and some salutary lessons from history are documented; but see Rowthorn (1992), the conclusions of which made me more optimistic about the possible success of the policies proposed in this chapter.

sent hotch-potch of non-policy and one-sided attacks on the standard of living and employment opportunities of wage-earners.

REFERENCES

Ball, R. J. (1964), *Inflation and the Theory of Money* (London: Allen and Unwin).

Coutts, Kenneth, Godley, Wynne, and Nordhaus, William (1978), *Industrial Pricing in the United Kingdom*, DAE Monograph 26 (Cambridge: Cambridge University Press).

Eichner, A. S. (1976), *The Megacorp and Oligopoly* (Cambridge: Cambridge University Press).

Grieve Smith, John *et al.* (1996), 'Full Employment Without Inflation: A Strategy For Pay' (London: Employment Policy Institute).

Harcourt, G. C. (1962), 'Review Article of W. E. G. Salter, *Productivity and Technical Change* (1960)', *Economic Record*, 38: 388–94, repr. in Harcourt 1982: 129–37.

—— (1968), 'Investment-Decision Criteria, Investment Incentives and the Choice of Technique', *Economic Journal*, 78: 77–95, repr. in Harcourt 1982: 146–67.

—— (1977), 'Eric Russell, 1921–77: A Great Australian Political Economist', the 1977 Newcastle Lecture in Political Economy, repr. in Harcourt 1982: 331–45.

—— (1982), *The Social Science Imperialists: Selected Essays*, ed. Prue Kerr (London: Routledge and Kegan Paul).

—— (1995), *Capitalism, Socialism and Post-Keynesianism: Selected Essays of G. C. Harcourt* (Aldershot: Edward Elgar).

—— and Peter Kenyon (1976), 'Pricing and the Investment Decision', *Kyklos*, 29: 449–77, repr. in Harcourt 1982: 104–26.

Kaldor, N. (1986), *Economics without Equilibrium: The Okun Memorial Lectures at Yale University* (Cardiff: University College, Cardiff Press).

Kalecki, M. (1943), 'Political Aspects of Full Employment', *Political Quarterly*, repr. in Kalecki 1971: 138–45.

—— (1971), *Selected Essays on the Dynamics of the Capitalist Economy 1933–1970* (Cambridge: Cambridge University Press).

Meade, J. E. (1995), *Full Employment Regained? An Agathotopian Dream*, DAE Occasional Paper 61 (Cambridge: Cambridge University Press).

—— and Russell, E. A. (1957), 'Wage Rates, The Cost of Living and the Balance of Payments', *Economic Record*, 33: 23–8.

Meidner, Rudolf (1993), 'Why did the Swedish Model Fail?', in Miliband and Panitch (eds.), *Real Problems*, 211–28.

Miliband, Ralph and Panitch, Leo (eds.), (1993) *Real Problems False Solutions: Socialist Register 1993* (London: Merlin Press).

Pekkarinen, Jukka, Pohjola, Matti, and Rowthorn, Bob (eds.), (1992) *Social Corporatism: A Superior Economic System?* (Oxford: Clarendon Press).

Robertson, D. H. (1956), *Economic Commentaries* (London: Staples Press).

Robinson, E. A. G. (ed.), (1965) *Problems in Economic Development: Proceedings of a Conference held by the International Economic Association* (London: Macmillan).

Rowthorn, Bob (1992), 'Corporatism and Labour Market Performance', in Pekkarinen, Pohjola, and Rowthorn (eds.), *Social Corporatism*, 82–131.

Russell, E. A. (1965), 'Wages Policy in Australia', *Australian Economic Papers*, 4: 1–26.

Salter, W. E. G. (1960), *Productivity and Technical Change*, 2nd edn. with addendum by W. B. Reddaway, 1966 (Cambridge: Cambridge University Press).

—— (1965), 'Productivity Growth and Accumulation as Historical Processes', in Robinson (ed.), *Problems in Economic Development*, 266 91.

Wood, A. (1975), *A Theory of Profits* (Cambridge: Cambridge University Press).

9.   Devising a Strategy for Pay

John Grieve Smith

At the beginning of the 1980s, an observer of the British economic-policy debate might have been forgiven for believing that it was largely a technical tussle between 'Keynesians' and 'monetarists' about the respective roles of fiscal and monetary policy. But a decade and a half later, the conflict between those who supported the post-war Keynesian consensus and those who sought to overthrow it can be seen to be much more fundamental. For as Beveridge and others clearly foresaw, the maintenance of full employment after the war went hand-in-hand with a revolution in the structure of society. In his 1944 *Report on Full Employment in a Free Society* Beveridge maintained that 'the labour market should always be a seller's market rather than a buyer's market. From this, on the view of society underlying this Report—that society exists for the individual—there is a decisive reason of principle . . . A person who cannot sell his labour is in effect told he is of no use.'[1] Such a change in the balance of power within society would have pervasive effects on the distribution of income and the bargaining power of the trade unions. Beveridge warned of 'a real danger that sectional wage bargaining, pursued without regard to its effects upon prices, may lead to a vicious spiral of inflation'.[2] As a consequence he maintained that 'so long as freedom of collective bargaining is maintained, the primary responsibility of preventing a full employment policy coming to grief . . . will rest on those who conduct the bargaining on behalf of labour'.[3]

Beveridge was right in foreseeing that pay restraint would come to be a key requirement for avoiding full employment leading to inflation and for the first twenty-five years after the war it did so. From 1946 to 1970 prices in the UK rose on average by 3.6 per cent a year and unemployment only exceeded 2.5 per cent in 1970. Moreover in this period we successfully surmounted the first of the post-war shocks in 1950–1 when import prices rose by 50 per cent. The system only broke down in the 1970s when successive governments were unable to secure or maintain the consensus with the unions needed to avoid an accelerated wage/price spiral. At one key point the unions came to the government's rescue when in 1975 Jack Jones, leader of the Transport and General Workers' Union was the initiator of the successful pay policy limiting all increases to £6 per week. But public opinion was more heavily influenced by the miners' strike in 1974 which brought

---

[1] Beveridge (1944) para. 5.   [2] Ibid., para. 284.   [3] Ibid., para. 288.

down the Heath Government and the public-sector strike in the 1978–9
'Winter of Discontent' which brought down the Callaghan Government.
The seed had been sown for a counter-revolution in economic policy which,
whatever its theoretical economic trappings, would tackle inflation by
reducing the bargaining power of labour and in so doing fundamentally
alter the post-war social balance. The rise in unemployment due to the
deflationary macroeconomic policies followed throughout most of the 1980s,
together with the changes in trade-union law and deregulation of the labour
market eventually achieved this end.

The question we face today is not a technical one about detailed ways of
changing the economy, but a fundamental social and political choice: do we
accept the continuance of unemployment at something like recent levels as
a 'price worth paying' for regulating inflation or we are prepared to try
again to tackle the pay-bargaining problem by consent rather than brute
force. The dire effect of present policies in terms of inequality, poverty, and
insecurity are discussed in other chapters. But for those in government the
unspoken attraction is that ministers are not involved in continual negotiations with unions and employers about pay or subject to the political haz-
ards of pay policies coming to grief. (They may still, however, be subject to
damaging disputes in the public sectors.)

There are then, of course, those portions of society who have benefited
directly from the Thatcher revolution, the more highly paid, or the middle
classes looking for cheap domestic help. But as economic insecurity has
spread widely through society, the new regime has become less popular. A
1992 survey showed that half of men and over 40 per cent of women in
employment had witnessed a reduction in numbers employed at their workplace in the previous two years.[4] Some managers may have been pleased at
the restoration of their 'right to manage' but since (for all save a small
minority) making people redundant is by far the hardest and most unpleasant aspect of management, it is doubtful whether the average manager
can be said to have gained. Certainly his or her job has become a lot more
insecure.

The alternative of creating the conditions for restoring and maintaining
full employment without inflation would require fundamental changes, not
least in the approach to pay bargaining. A stronger demand for labour
would tilt the balance of power between employers and employed back
towards the latter and strengthen the bargaining power of the unions. It
would then be necessary once again to ensure that this bargaining power
was used responsibly and not in an inflationary manner. Indeed the required
change in approach to pay bargaining needs to take place before we can
make any substantial progress towards full employment.

[4] White (1996).

GETTING THERE

The only previous occasion on which the British economy has moved from mass unemployment to full employment was at the outbreak of the last war when unemployment fell from 13 per cent in 1938 to 2 per cent in 1941. That experience holds little guidance for our immediate problems. The difficulty today is that of raising aggregate demand without an acceleration in inflation. To achieve this we have not only to deal with the problem of pay bargaining, we also need to rebuild our industrial capacity which has become attuned to the economy operating at consistently high levels of unemployment. The National Institute, for example, described the economy at the start of 1995, when unemployment stood at 2.5 million, as running 'close to normal capacity utilisation'.[5] In returning to full employment the objective we now have to achieve is to ensure that industrial capacity builds up in line with the rise in demand—while the rate of increase in demand remains above trend—a problem discussed in the previous book in this series, *Creating Industrial Capacity*.[6]

In some industries, particularly in the service field, 'capacity' can be built up quite quickly; at the other extreme in capital-intensive industries, like steel, it is a slow process with a lead-time of three or four years. In the first category the mere fact of higher demand will tend to lead to capacity increases. (Andrew Sentance and Rebecca Emerson give an interesting but optimistic assessment of this process in their recent report, *Manufacturing Capacity and Investment: Is there a Constraint?*)[7] But in the latter category the key factor is firms' assessment of the future course of the economy and demand for their products (together with a corresponding assessment of export markets). In between these extremes, expectations of future growth will also be a major factor in deciding about investment in new capacity.

Any government aiming to reduce unemployment substantially therefore has to convince industry both that it is in earnest and also that it will not be thrown off course by the re-emergence of faster inflation or exchange-rate crises, both of which are to some extent interlinked. It therefore needs a convincing strategy for reducing unemployment embodying a new approach to pay bargaining and inflation. A major difficulty here is the need to achieve a new consensus on these issues, at least with key employers' representatives and union leaders—a Labour government would be unlikely to receive any overt support from the political opposition. One of the great tragedies of the period of the post-war consensus was that even though both Conservative and Labour governments followed largely similar incomes policies when in power, they bitterly criticized them when in opposition and

---

[5] N.I. Economic Review No. 151.   [6] Michie and Grieve Smith (1996).
[7] Published by the Foundation for Manufacturing and Industry in September 1995.

abolished their predecessors' institutions as soon as they came into power—what Michael Stewart has called the 'Jekyll and Hyde' syndrome.[8]

But, it may be said, why bother about pay policy now, just when every-thing seems to be going fine, and wage increases are quite moderate despite the fall in unemployment? First, it is the general belief that at some point in the process of reducing unemployment, the increased strength of labour is likely to lead to a higher level of wage demands. At what point this may come it is difficult to say. At the optimistic end of the spectrum (for example the OECD and Patrick Minford) it is suggested that it will not be until unemployment is down to 1.5 million. The Treasury and the Bank of England clearly believe the crunch would come much sooner.[9] Secondly, the time to start is now *before* the system comes under pressure—and agreement becomes that much harder. Thirdly, one clear lesson from the past is that the real test is to be able to contain inflation in the face of an external shock in the form of a major increase in import prices which means an inevitable reduction in real wages. The longer any new system had operated success-fully and real wages had been seen to increase, the better the chance of maintaining an industrial consensus in the face of adverse circumstances.

Starting at a time when wage claims and the rate of inflation are at acceptable levels should mean that the 'momentum effect' will favour the policy—i.e. basing claims on the rate of inflation since the last settlement will be consistent with the agreed policy. The critical problems arise when pay policies are introduced in order to help slow down inflation and workers are expected to accept settlements which fail to compensate for the previous rise in the cost of living.

PRINCIPLES

In seeking a general agreement on guidelines for pay negotiators, one gen-eral principle should be paramount—differing rates of growth of productiv-ity in different sectors of the economy should be reflected in changes in relative prices rather than relative pay. This should be clear both to those who are ardent believers in a free labour market and those who are not. On market principles, people with the same skills (and in the same location) would expect to get the same pay whichever sector they were working in. On grounds of equity, if wages were to be related to productivity growth in dif-ferent sectors, those with little scope for increasing their productivity, like nurses and teachers (or indeed academics and journalists) would become progressively worse off relative to those in manufacturing. Over the course of time, the growth of productivity in different sectors reflects technical

---

[8] Stewart (1977).   [9] Evidence to Treasury Select Committee on the 1995 Budget.

advance and capital investment rather than any increased input of labour deserving exceptional awards. This is not to deny the need that as between individual plants or firms there will from time to time be circumstances where some special 'productivity deal' is justified. But whatever current fashion may suggest, it is misleading to think that in a well-run organization every change or innovation has to be linked to a change in pay and that employees have to be continually bribed to do of their best. On the contrary in a well-managed organization with good morale it is all part of the job.

The concept of a 'going rate' for wage increases in a particular annual wage-round thus remains an economically relevant one, as well as a fact of life. One element in the going rate is the increase in the cost of living since the last settlement. The other main element should be the overall increase in productivity across the economy. In other words in normal circumstances the going rate should be a prescription for a gradual increase in real wages without any acceleration in the rate of inflation. (In special circumstances, such as an import-price shock this principle may need to be modified.) In the simplest terms the core of any pay policy is to get general agreement between employers and unions on an appropriate going rate or norm.

INSTITUTIONAL REFORM

The basic idea behind any pay initiative is to inject into individual bargaining discussions the potential effects of any settlement on the economy as a whole in the form of inflation—effects which will in time have an impact on all employees and employers. This wider impact should be most easily seen the greater the coverage of any particular negotiation. Indeed Germany and Japan developed modes of successful non-inflationary bargaining which in effect relied on the responsibility of large-scale bargaining units, e.g. in Germany IG Metall and the engineering and steel employers set the pace in their annual negotiations. Since its membership amounts to more than one-third of all unionized workers in Germany it is well placed to play this role. But while the larger unions have held the key to successful policies in the UK, this has mainly been a reflection of the essential need to get their support through the TUC for pay policies put forward by the government. In this country the TUC clearly has an essential role to play as the body on the employees' side with the broad coverage to link the level of pay settlements with their macroeconomic consequences. On the employers' side the CBI has a similar task to perform, but its structure makes it more difficult for it to commit individual employers than for the TUC to commit individual unions.

The first question in launching any such policy is who should participate and how far should it be formalized. It has sometimes been suggested that the employers should take the lead and the government not be formally involved.[10] This seems the prescription least likely to command union support. Both unions and employers need to be equally involved from the start. But the government itself is also bound to be a major participant, partly as an employer and partly because of its general responsibility for economic policy. Any discussions on pay need to be set in the context of the government's own economic strategy—although there may also be scope for some input from an 'impartial' pay body or secretariat of some sort.

The choice is then between launching any initiative in a series of *ad hoc* meetings between the Government, the CBI, and the TUC or setting up a new forum not only to discuss pay, but also for any tripartite discussions on different aspects of economic policy. There seems a good case for setting up a new Economic Policy Council for this purpose, in effect a successor to the former National Economic Development Council (NEDC). It seems doubtful, however, whether it is necessary to have an independent secretariat or policy staff on the lines of the National Economic Development Office (NEDO). The new forum could be serviced by the Treasury, thus bringing the latter into closer contact with industry.

If the introduction of a new pay policy is to be part of a strategy for restoring full employment, then the initial task of the Council would be to discuss, and so far as possible agree, government proposals for such a strategy. This would both provide a setting for pay discussion and also highlight the key supply-side problems to be overcome. As mentioned above, the most important and difficult of these is the need to persuade firms to base their decisions about investment in new capacity on the assumption of a trend in demand and output consistent with a reduction in unemployment, rather than a continuation of existing conditions. There may also be potential shortages of certain skills, remedying which (in so far as they can be identified) should be top priority in any education and training programme. Other key topics to be covered in a 'Strategy for Full Employment' would be public-expenditure programmes, public revenue and the PSBR, and the outlook for the balance of payments. Whilst the basic strategy, in the sense of objectives and policies to achieve them, should not be constantly revised, any detailed projections and programmes should be renewed annually. Such a review might take the form of an extended annual Red Book (Financial and Budget Report).

NEW PROBLEMS

It is frequently suggested that the decentralization of pay bargaining and the decline in union membership in recent years rules out any effective over-

[10] Soskice (1990).

all incomes policy.[11] If this were so, two conclusions would follow. Either we should have to continue to rely on heavy unemployment to moderate wage claims, or changes in the present pattern of negotiations would have to be sought as part of any policy to restore full employment. It is important to remember, however, that it is not coincidental that the pattern of bargaining changed in this way at a time when the demand for labour was substantially weakened. It was to a large extent part of a deliberate shift in the balance of power against the trade unions. For example in many large companies (e.g. British Steel), the move to local pay bargaining was quite deliberately aimed at breaking the power of the national unions. The strengthening of the position of labour associated with a return to full employment is likely in itself to lead to yet further changes in the pattern of bargaining.

While, however, changes in the pattern of bargaining mean that any new pay policy will differ markedly from its predecessors, they by no means rule it out of court. In many respects the present bargaining structure makes a government's task easier. It is important here to distinguish between the political and economic efficacy of any policy. Attitudes to past policies are dominated by the associated political crises rather than any assessment of their economic impact—Heath lost a general election during the 1974 miners' strike; Callaghan lost an election after the 'Winter of Discontent'. Such disputes incidentally generally took place in the public sector and the government is still liable to be involved in politically damaging conflict of this kind as an employer even in the absence of any overall pay policy. But the fact that there are not so many major national agreements as there used to be eases the *political* difficulties of embarking on any new policy—and could be a major factor in persuading the politicians to have another go. The changes have all tended to lessen the danger of the government becoming involved in politically damaging pay disputes. As regards the potential *economic* efficacy of any new policy, it is extremely difficult to assess. In so far as a higher number of national agreements and greater trade-union involvement helped keep pay increases within or near to the official guidelines, recent changes make any policy more difficult to police. They have also made pay more sensitive to market forces, so that strengthening the demand for labour may have a greater effect on pay than it would in the past. On the other hand there is less danger of spectacular high settlements setting the pace in bending the guidelines. It must also be remembered that trade-union membership is not necessarily a reliable measure of the effect of union agreements in affecting increases. Many small organizations, with little or no union membership, for lack of any other starting point, take union rates or changes in union rates for guidance. On balance, the decline

[11] Brown (1994).

in the political risks of embarking on such a course seems relatively assured, but the statistical outcome in terms of overall wage movements more difficult to predict.

COVERAGE

An unresolved point throughout the post-war period has been whether, or how far, successive policies effectively applied outside the areas where pay was settled by formal collective bargaining. Policies which were fundamentally about moderating wage increases determined by formal collective-bargaining procedures were for reasons of equity extended so far as possible to cover all wages and salaries, and on occasion to dividends as well. Formal salary scales in the public sector and large firms, also generally followed the rules. Wages in smaller firms probably followed their big competitors. But self-employed workers remained outside the scope of all these policies. Any practical policy for the future will be limited to affecting negotiated rates and those that follow them. It will send out hopefully, powerful signals, but will not dictate pay increases throughout the economy. Nevertheless it seems improbable that any general pay agreement will be torpedoed by masses of small employers giving their employees higher pay increases than their larger competitors who are following the agreed guidelines. It still seems likely that, as in the past, any major attack will come from the big battalions rather than guerilla forces. The fact that the big battalions are now fewer and weaker should in that respect make any policy more secure.

MINIMUM WAGE

The introduction of a statutory minimum wage would have major implications for pay policy. If such a measure is to help the lowest paid without inflationary consequences, it is essential that the 'knock-on' effect on the wages of those already earning more than the prescribed minimum should be kept as low as possible. There will be some pressure to restore differentials but it should be containable. A high proportion of the lower-paid are working in the service sector (e.g. retail distribution, hotels, and catering) and increasing their pay is unlikely to stimulate significant pressure from better-paid workers in those sectors or elsewhere. Only a small proportion of low-paid workers are in manufacturing, where the knock-on effects might be expected to be greatest because the skilled workers are effectively unionized. But nevertheless an essential quid pro quo for the introduction of a minimum wage should be general agreement among the unions to accept the consequent increases for the lower-paid as exceptional and not as setting the pace for increases across the board.

Similar considerations apply to the annual updating of the minimum wage, particularly if the intention were to set it low to start with and then increase it relative to the average level of wages over say, a four-year period to promote gradual adjustment. In this case it would be essential to make this intention clear from the start and get general agreement on such an approach. Otherwise what might be substantial annual increases in the minimum wage in percentage terms might be cited as the going rate for settlements in general.

PUBLIC SECTOR

It is ironic that governments, who are totally opposed to any general policy for pay, have little hesitation in dictating stringent pay policies for the public sector. The fact is that no government can escape responsibility for public-sector pay either as a direct employer or as the provider of finance. Indeed (as noted earlier) many of the most sensational labour disputes have occurred in the public sector. If private-sector pay demands were to follow those in the public sector, this would represent an indirect form of pay policy, albeit set unilaterally by the government. But for the most part, it is the private sector that sets the pace and public-sector workers are perpetually trying to catch up. The one important exception to this is that the lowest-paid in the public-sector have done better than those in the private sector. One of the weaknesses of trying to settle public-sector pay without any overall pay policy, is that it often becomes entirely dominated by a desire to keep down public expenditure, and is held down until comparisons with the private sector make 'catching-up' increases necessary. This applies particularly in areas not covered by the Pay Review Bodies.

It is fallacious to base public-sector pay policy on the assumption that any real increase in pay can only be justified by improvements in productivity within that sector. The rate of growth of productivity in labour-intensive public services such as health or education is bound to lag behind the average rate of growth of productivity in the economy as a whole; and it is the latter which should, and will in the end, determine the general rate of increase of real wages. Trying to limit increases in *real* wages in health or education to improvements in productivity within these sectors is merely a recipe for ensuring that pay falls behind comparable rewards elsewhere— until sooner or later exceptional increases are given to catch up. Trying to limit increases in *money*-wages to improvements in public-sector productivity is even more unreasonable as long as some degree of inflation continues.

This problem is compounded if public-expenditure planning and control are based on similarly unrealistic assumptions about pay. In so far as public-sector workers then do manage to get the same increases as elsewhere without corresponding increases in their productivity, cash limits can only be met by cutting staff numbers and a deterioration in the standard of services—as has been happening in schools.

IMPLEMENTATION

The key question, and one with heavy political overtones, is what steps, if any, should be taken to ensure that individual settlements are compatible with the agreed policy. Any return to statutory enforcement is both undesirable in principle and politically out of the question. No long-term policy could depend on legal scrutiny of individual agreements with any industrial disputes which threatened to breach the guidelines leading to legal entanglements for all concerned. The problem is rather how best to institutionalize the pressure of public opinion and economic competition to get individual employers and unions to adhere to an essentially voluntary policy. In the past, even with a very high demand for labour, breakdowns have not in the main come through employers initially offering pay increases which breach the guidelines, but through the eventual settlements doing so in response to threatened or actual industrial action. (This goes for both the private and public sectors.) The first problem therefore is to keep union demands (or at least their expectations of the ultimate settlement) within the policy guidelines, and the second one is to develop better machinery for settling any residual disputes short of industrial action. The first problem is partly a political one of securing as wide agreement as possible on the union side, and partly an institutional one of the TUC's ability to get a potential minority to follow majority decisions.

The field where there may be most scope for institutional reform is in the use of conciliation and arbitration procedures to assist in arriving at adequate settlements. Such procedures would, however, have to take place against the background of the agreed policy, not in a void. The scope for improvement is most obvious in the public sector where there is a dichotomy between those sectors under central Pay Review Bodies and those where pay is settled by straightforward negotiations. There is a case for a neutral advisory body in some form to put together the facts (including comparisons with the private sector) and play a part in settling pay in those parts of the public sector at present not covered by the Review Bodies.

As regards the private sector, the first essential is to keep track of what is happening in the way of demands and settlements. The second, more difficult, question is to devise some form of institutional intervention which will both reduce the risks of major industrial disputes and of settlements breaching the guidelines. On both counts there is a case for setting up some institution, which was seen to be neutral as between unions and employers and would have an advisory function in the case of difficult negotiations—a 'Pay Advisory Commission'. The Commission should have powers to gather information on pay negotiations. It would in addition have the authority to make representations to both parties in any negotiations, and to give advice during any recourse to conciliation. The crucial question then remains: what happens if the parties cannot settle within the guidelines of the policy? Here the most obvious instrument would be to make greater use of arbitration, with the proviso that arbitrators would be bound to take into account the guidelines in the agreed national pay policy.

ARBITRATION

The practical unpopularity of pay policy in the past has been not so much with the policies themselves as the industrial disputes to which they are believed to have given rise. Certainly industrial disputes, particularly in public services and transport, are very unpopular and (whatever the rights and wrongs of individual disputes) have been a major factor in public support for anti-union legislation. It is thus in the long-term interests of the unions themselves to seek better ways of avoiding damaging disputes, and they have in the past frequently favoured the use of arbitration machinery. From the employers' point of view, greater use of arbitration, taking into account nationally agreed pay policies, should reduce the risk of their willingness to resist a strike being the last defence of any pay policy.

There remains the question of whether any element of compulsion should be introduced into either the resort to arbitration or adherence to its results. There is a case for proposing that the 'Pay Advisory Commission' or some similar body should have the power to refer any negotiation which seems likely to breach the guidelines to arbitration, at the request of either or both parties, or on its own initiative. This leaves the final and most difficult question: should the arbitration outcome be 'binding' on both parties? It is difficult to determine what sanctions could be applied if it were breached—but again the key to success is not legal compulsion but the power of public opinion.

OTHER FORMS OF PAY

There must in practice be some *de minimis* provision which limits the final arrangements to firms with more than a certain number of employees. In this sense, and the fact that self-employed workers (e.g. the building trades) are not covered, means that the coverage is not comprehensive. But in the past this has not been an issue because on the whole the people not covered at shop-floor level are not generally a source of envy. The position of managers etc. is trickier, particularly with the decline in formal pay scales. Most difficult, however, is the problem of the highly visible pay of directors and the magnitude of the increases they have been awarded. Compensation committees of non-executive board members have proved a largely ineffective method of dealing with this, because the concept of 'competitive salaries' is merely a way of making sure that as many directors as possible follow the leader upwards. A much more effective curb would be to involve employee representatives. The salaries paid to leading Town Hall staff or trade-union general secretaries suggest that the influence of such representatives would be moderating but not excessively so.

Finally there is the issue of prices, profits, and dividends. There can no longer be any question of imposing price controls as a quid pro quo for wage restraint. But on the other hand, where price regulation already exists in the case of the privatized utilities, the pricing policies followed should be seen to be reasonable, as should their dividends and directors' remuneration. Elsewhere in the private sector, competition (particularly international competition) would be the main instrument for influencing pricing; but the Monopolies and Mergers Commission might be specifically involved where prices or price increases seem inflammatory or unreasonable.

The division of profits between dividends and undistributed profits deserves further consideration on a number of counts. We have now moved into a situation where employees rather than shareholders take the risks: employees are sacked in a recession whereas dividends are maintained.[12] (In Japan and Germany it has been the other way round.) This tends to erode effective capacity in a recession and makes it harder to meet demand in the next upswing and hence a speedier return to deflationary policies and further closures and redundancies. We need to aim at establishing a norm where the firm strives to hold together its labour-force in a recession. Shareholders should either be prepared to see dividends fluctuate more over the business cycle, or preferably, accept a lower share of the profits (smoothed over the cycle) thus allowing greater reserves to be built up for investment purposes. Whether or not shareholders would lose in the long run by such policies, British industry and those who work in it would be clear gainers, and there seems little danger that such a change would lead to any shortage of risk capital.

---

[12] Grieve Smith (1996).

CONCLUSION

Both unions and employers have a great deal to gain from a successful pay agreement which would allow more expansionary policies to be pursued. The unions and their members would gain from lower unemployment and the improvement in conditions associated with a stronger demand for labour. Firms, particularly in manufacturing industry would gain from a more rapid increase in demand for their products with greater opportunities for investment and innovation. To achieve these long-term gains, however, they would each have to accept shorter-term limitations on their freedom of action. The unions would have to operate within the limits of a national pay agreement and not exploit their increased bargaining strength in an inflationary manner. Employers would have to revert to a more co-operative and less autocratic style of management—as indeed many of the most successful do already: the 'right to manage' should mean the right to lead not the right to dictate. The challenge to any government which is serious about reducing unemployment is to bring together the unions and employers in a constructive partnership to achieve a long-term solution to this problem.

REFERENCES

Beveridge, W. H. (1944), *Full Employment in a Free Society* (London: George Allen & Unwin).

Brown, W. (1994), 'Incomes Policy in Britain: Lessons from Experience' in R. Dore *et al.* (eds.), *The Return to Incomes Policy* (London: Pinter).

Grieve Smith, J. (1996), 'Rebuilding Industrial Capacity', in J. Michie and J. Grieve Smith (eds.), *Creating Industrial Capacity* (Oxford: Oxford University Press).

House of Commons Treasury Committee (1996), *Third Report, The 1995 Budget* (London: HMSO).

Michie, J. and Grieve Smith, J. (1996) (eds.), *Creating Industrial Capacity* (Oxford: Oxford University Press).

National Institute Economic Review No. 151.

Sentance, A. and Emerson, R. (1995), *Manufacturing and Investment: Is There A Constraint?* (London: Foundation for Manufacturing and Industry).

Soskice, D. (1990), 'Wage Determination: The Changing Role of Institutions in Advanced Industrialized Countries', *Oxford Review of Economic Policy*, 6/4.

Stewart, M. (1977), *The Jekyll and Hyde Years: Politics and Economic Policy Since 1964* (London: Dent).

White, M. (1996), 'The Labour Market and Risk', in P. Meadows (ed.), *Work Out—Or Work In?* (York: Joseph Rowntree Foundation).

Part IV

Policies for Full Employment

10. Paying for Job Creation

Andrew Glyn

This chapter discusses how expansionary programmes should be financed. First, the distributional implications of a range of job-creation policies are reviewed and the budgetary cost of these noted. The limitations on increased borrowing are then considered. The relatively low tax burden in the UK, and how it has been kept down since 1979 is reported. Finally it is argued that a higher share of taxation is inevitable if public services are to be improved, the trend towards greater inequality stemmed, and high employment levels restored.

ALTERNATIVE POLICIES AND DISTRIBUTIVE OUTCOMES

Policies for job creation vary along a number of dimensions. Table 10.1 provides a summary account of a range of policies, concentrating on their distributional implications. Comparing labour-market deregulation and an expansion of public expenditure, policies with perhaps the most divergent distributional effects, highlights what is at stake.

Labour market deregulation (Table 10.1, column 1) aims at generating jobs through forcing down pay at the bottom end of the labour market through changes in the benefit system, employment security provisions, minimum wages, and so forth. The extent of the impact on jobs is quite problematic (row 2), depending on the relevant elasticities (Boltho and Glyn 1995), but it is clear that most would be created in private services (row 1) and would be filled by less-qualified workers (row 4). This would reduce joblessness where it is most prevalent and it is plausible that the impact on wage pressure would be less (row 9) than if the expansion of jobs was evenly spread across skill categories, including those with much lower unemployment rates (Nickell and Bell 1995). Apart from the previously unemployed, the consumers of such private services (labelled 'middle earners' in the table) benefit from a fall in the price (relative to their own incomes) of such services (row 5). This redistribution, as a result of declining incomes for the low paid, is much more certain than the impact on jobs. The budgetary effect of such policies would be positive; numbers claiming benefits are reduced to the extent that extra jobs are created and benefit levels may be

The author is grateful to Wendy Carlin, Bob Rowthorn, Patrick Toche, and John Wells for helpful comments.

Table 10.1. Alternative policies for job creation

	Labour-market deregulation	Wage subsidies	Public-spending programmes	Working-time reductions	Training for unemployed	Investment incentives
1. Where jobs created	Private Services	Private Services	Public Services	General	General	General
2. Predictability of effect on jobs	Low (effect on wages and on jobs)	Low (effect on jobs)	High	Low (productivity effects etc.)	Low (effect on wages and on jobs)	Low (effect on capital spending)
3. Visibility of jobs effect	Low	High (misleadingly/displacement)	High	Moderate	High (misleadingly/displacement)	Moderate
4. Jobs bias for less qualified	Yes (main impact on low pay)	Yes (main impact on low pay)	Could be	Unlikely	Yes	No
5. Who else benefits	Buyers of cheaper services; profits up	Buyers of cheaper services; profits up	Users of public services	More leisure for workers	Long-run higher incomes	Long-run higher incomes
6. Net cost to budget	Negative (benefits, claimants down)	Positive (depends on effect on jobs)	Positive	Negative	Positive	Positive
7. Consumption of low paid	Reduced (a lot?) as unskilled wages fall	No change (costs to employers down)	No change (if pay no extra tax)	Reduces (less hours)	No change (if pay no extra tax)	No change (if pay no extra tax)
8. Consumption of middle earners	Up a lot (5 plus 6 if lower tax)	Up a bit (5 less 6 if higher tax)	Reduced (6 if higher tax)	Reduced (5)	Reduced (6)	Reduced (6)
9. Inflationary pressure (depends on 4 and 8)	Small (less qualified get jobs; middle ...)	Moderate	Large	Large	Large (but less in long run)	Large (less in long run)

reduced as well. If this budgetary gain (row 6) is passed on as lower taxation of middle earners it could moderate wage pressure further as the take-
home pay of the 'core' sectors of employees is raised (row 9). The net effect
is a marked increase in the inequality of consumption for those at work
(rows 7 and 8), though the rise in overall inequality is tempered by such
reduction in unemployment as occurs.

By contrast, increased expenditure on the public services and infrastructure (Table 10.1, column 3) creates jobs predictably and visibly (a political
benefit). Such programmes could be tailored towards employing more of the
relatively less qualified, but in any case there is no implication that their pay
is reduced. The overall effect is strongly egalitarian, as the simulations
reported in the next chapter by underline. The budgetary cost of such programmes is reduced by falling expenditure on benefit payments and by
increased tax receipts. But the net cost will not be negligible, and if it is
recouped by higher taxes on middle earners their consumption will fall (in
effect a given level of consumption is redistributed from them to those previously unemployed). This would reduce consumption inequality but would
tend to exacerbate inflationary wage pressure since those who are squeezed
have a relatively strong labour-market position. However, the wide spread
of benefits from improved public services could improve the chances of
wage moderation being negotiated (Glyn and Rowthorn 1994).

It is clear that the contrast between the distributional implications of
labour-market deregulation and higher public spending is particularly stark.
The employment effects of labour-market deregulation can be simulated in
a less distributionally unacceptable way, through wage subsidies for the
low-paid or an increase of in-work benefits aimed at increasing the supply
of low-wage labour (Table 10.1, column 2). But mitigating the distributional
impact has a net budgetary cost; if this is met by higher taxation of middle
incomes this exacerbates potential inflationary pressure. Even a policy of
investment incentives (column 6), aimed at directing job creation towards
expanding productive capacity in manufacturing, has to be paid for; if
middle earners are to foot the bill, the promise of higher real incomes in the
future may fail to ensure a sustainable pattern of wage increases. Of the various policies summarized in Table 10.1 the only ones with no budgetary cost
are deregulation and reductions in working time (column 4), policies which
in other respects are quite antithetical.

Any package for job creation with egalitarian objectives must involve a
substantial component of increased public expenditure. It would be much
easier if the net budgetary cost could be met by borrowing for then there is
the proverbial 'free lunch' as there is no need for the consumption of middle
earners to be reduced for redistribution to those finding work. Nobody has
to 'pay for' the expansion of jobs; this further implies that multiplier effects
of an initial expansion are not choked off by tax increases. Could increased

borrowing finance a major part of job expansion in the current UK context?

BORROWING

The discussion of the viability or sustainability of budget deficits is clouded with indeterminacy (see e.g. Weale 1994). One starting point is to examine the implication of deficit levels for the ratio of government debt to GDP. The long-run debt ratio b^* depends on the government's deficit as a ratio of GDP (d) and the growth rate of nominal GDP (g), according (approximately—see Bispham 1988) to the relation:

$$b^* = d/g.$$

Thus the notorious Maastricht criteria of $b^* = 0.6$ and $d = 0.03$ is consistent on the assumption that nominal growth is 5 per cent per year (for example GDP growth of 3 per cent per year and inflation of 2 per cent per year). Obviously if d/g is greater than the current debt ratio then the ratio is rising (and would converge to b^* if current values continued).

A little more mileage can be wrung out of such analysis by looking at the deficit resulting excluding interest payments—the primary deficit (pd as a ratio to GDP). Since $d = pd + ib$ (where i is the average nominal interest rate), then for long-run stability in the debt ratio:

$$b^* = (pd + ib^*)/g, \text{ which implies that}$$
$$pd = (g-i)b^*.$$

Financing expenditure by borrowing rather than taxation clearly permits lower tax in the short-run. But if the growth rate is greater than the interest rate (both defined consistently in money or in real terms) then the formula implies that the long-run primary deficit is greater the higher is the long-run debt ratio. Thus, accepting a higher ratio of debt to GDP brings lower taxation (because the primary deficit is larger for a given level of public spending) *in the long run* as well. Borrowing appears to offer an indefinite supply of free lunches.

Unfortunately, when interest rates exceed growth rates compound interest shows its vicious side; accepting a higher debt ratio in the longer-term implies a bigger primary *surplus* (pd becomes more negative) and this means higher taxation in relation to public expenditure programmes. In the 1950s and 1960s, the Golden Age of Keynesian ideas, real interest rates were comfortably below even UK growth rates (Rowthorn 1995, table 3). But even if real-interest rates in general are below the growth rate it is misleading to treat them as entirely exogenous. It is likely that beyond a certain level, a higher deficit will lead financial markets to exact a higher real-interest rate, and this is confirmed empirically (see Orr *et al.* 1995). The supply of free lunches dries up as soon as the marginal interest rate exceeds the growth rate. In any case over the past decade real interest has averaged some 2 per cent more than the growth rate. In this context a higher debt ratio clearly implies a higher long-run rate of taxation. So financing a job-creation programme with a permanently higher deficit would indeed be trading-off lower taxes now against higher taxation for the future.

This raises a fundamental question; is an expansionary deficit expected to be permanent as against a purely temporary boost to 'prime the pump' of private spending. In the latter case, where private savings at the target-output level are absorbed by private investment, then there is no need for a continuing deficit. If there really was confidence in the long-run buoyancy of private spending, then temporary budget deficits to bolster demand would be quite unproblematic. To support this outcome, the pattern of taxation could be shifted to encourage investment and reduce savings, together with lower interest rates if possible (see Hopkin and Reddaway 1994). Whilst it might be feasible to generate higher consumption, and thus bring the budget into surplus as at the end of the Lawson boom, this may be unsustainable for other reasons (balance of payments in particular). Priming the pump of private-sector accumulation, particularly in the traded-goods sector, seems essential if a sustainable expansion is to be based on the private sector. But it is impossible to have much confidence that policies to stimulate manufacturing investment will have sufficient effect, especially after the weak response of UK manufacturing to the expanded demand and rising profitability in the 1980s (Glyn 1992). Thus, whilst increasing deficits in recessions is quite justifiable, they are not necessarily self-liquidating and this limits the extent to which they can be increased without long-run consequences.

It is often suggested that in the longer-run deficits should be linked to public-sector capital spending (Maastricht's 3 per cent rule is close to European levels of public investment—Buiter *et al.* 1993). Keynes noted in 1943 that 'The very reason that capital expenditure is capable of paying for itself makes it better budgetwise and does not involve the progressive increase in budgetary difficulties which deficit budgeting for the sake of consumption may bring about or, at any rate, may be accused of bringing about' (quoted by Dimsdale 1988: 225). If public investment yields the government a commercial return, the argument is clear enough. Such investment would bring a stream of profits which would offset the interest payments and allow the capital to be repaid, implying future budget surpluses to offset the current deficit. The investment of nationalized industries, assuming it earned a real return exceeding the real-interest rate, would exactly fit this category.

Rather little of general government investment yields a direct commercial return, however. But much of it adds to the productive capacity of the economy; does investment in education (including many expenditures classified as current) similarly finance itself via increased tax revenues? Unfortunately the fact that expenditure is productive does not mean that it pays for itself in budgetary terms. In the first place only a part of the return to the economy will accrue to the government. But even if the impact on productivity is so large that the share accruing as taxation could cover the initial outlays, it will also generate other demands on the budget which would absorb most of these extra taxes. On the one hand the pay of government employees must rise in line with those in the rest of the economy if services are to be maintained; on the other hand transfer payments must rise in line with living standards if recipients are not to be excluded from general prosperity. Thus very little of the 'growth bonus' accruing to the Treasury would be available to pay interest, most of which would have to come from higher tax rates. Thus the 'golden rule', that budget deficits covering capital spending are viable, whilst those to finance current spending are not, seems to have little justification.

So what level of deficit and thus debt ratio is sustainable? The Bank for International Settlements writes that 'Sustainability refers to the ability to maintain current expenditure and revenue paths without permanently increasing government debt in relation to GDP' (1994: 33). Interpreted literally this would mean that the larger your existing debt ratio the larger the sustainable deficit (though when the interest rate exceeds the growth rate the primary surplus must be higher). However, financial markets, the ultimate arbiters of such matters, may look simply at the size of the deficit. Thus the BIS, noting the strong correlation between recent increases in bond yields and the size of the government deficit, states that 'it is difficult to persuade markets that low inflation is sustainable in the presence of large budget deficits' (1995: 88). The rational basis for this is the tendency for governments to run large deficits when faced with conflicting claims on income which they cannot resolve or contain and the temptation to allow faster inflation to erode the real burden of the resulting debt.

What does this leave the financing of a sizeable chunk of an expansionary programme by increased borrowing? The Maastricht criteria require a 2 per cent decline in the UK deficit by 1997 (OECD *Economic Outlook*, Dec. 1995, table 10), which would leave outstanding debt a little below the 60 per cent mark. These criteria have little or no objective justification (Buiter *et al.* 1993) but, short of extensive controls over the domestic financial system and its international links, confidence and the attitude of financial markets are an objective factor in the situation. Given the experience of the past twenty years it would be difficult to convince that increased deficits at the beginning of an expansionary programme would be rapidly scaled down as the private sector took up the main thrust of expansion. There seems little alternative to financing through taxation most of an expansionary programme.

TAXATION

UK Taxation Compared

International comparisons of tax burdens are always tricky at the edges (for example if state support for children is given through tax allowances then taxation will be lower than if the same support was given through child benefit). However OECD figures, reproduced in Table 10.2, give a conclusive picture of a comparatively low average tax burden in the UK. Only the USA, Japan, Australia, and Switzerland had lower shares of taxation in 1993. EC countries on average had a share of taxation one-third higher than the UK's 33 per cent.[1]

A snapshot of the structure of UK taxation compared to that in other countries can also be derived from the CSO's data. Table 10.3 shows that the UK's low ranking in overall taxation is primarily the result of lower than average direct taxes, with the UK having one of the lowest levels of income taxes on households, of employees' social security contributions and of employers' social security contributions. It is only in respect of indirect taxes (the most regressive part of the tax system) that the UK is in the top half of the ranking, with a level close to the EC average. Within the overall level of direct taxation, employees in the UK appear to pay much higher rates of tax than recipients of other incomes. In 1994 the proportion of wages and salaries payable in direct taxation was 23.7 per cent whereas the proportion payable on self-employment income and rent, dividends and interest received was only 10.6 per cent.[2] The UK tax system has also become notably less progressive than it was in 1979 (Giles and Johnson 1994; Redmond and Sutherland 1995).

Trends in Tax and Spending

Table 10.2 shows that the total tax burden in the UK appears to have fallen fractionally between 1979 and 1993. In most other countries it has either increased a lot (Southern Europe, Japan, and even the USA) or was much

[1] Updating this picture, OECD's broader series for total government revenue (*Economic Outlook*, Dec. 1995, table A59) suggests that recent tax increases worth about 1.5 per cent of GDP may perhaps have pushed the UK above Spain.

[2] If employers' contributions were included, taxes on income from employment would be 29.0 per cent. Moreover the figure for taxation of self-employment and property income must be somewhat inflated by inclusion of tax paid by life assurance and pension schemes. Neither of the tax shares deducts mortgage-interest tax relief. Source: *UK National Accounts*, 1995 edn., tables 4.9 and 9.6.

Table 10.2.   Average tax burdens 1979 and 1993

	Total taxation and social security contributions as % of GNP (market prices)	
	1979	1993
Australia	28.0	29.8 (92)
Austria	42.0	43.8
Belgium	46.1	45.4
Canada	30.5	38.6
Denmark	45.6	51.7
Finland	32.8	48.4
France	40.0	44.2
Germany	41.0	42.0
Greece	27.9	38.7
Ireland	36.0	43.0 (92)
Italy	27.9	43.1
Japan	24.6	29.8
Netherlands	45.9	48.9
New Zealand	32.9	35.7
Norway	50.5	47.8 (91)
Spain	24.4	36.4
Sweden	49.5	52.7
Switzerland	29.5	31.1
UK	**33.7**	**33.1**
USA	28.0	31.7
UK rank	9/20	16/20
EC average	37.9	44.0

Sources: 'Taxes and Social Security Contributions', *Economic Trends* (Nov. 1995 and Feb. 1992). (1979 converted to market prices using OECD *National Accounts*.) New Zealand figures are from OECD *Revenue Statistics* since the National Account data (used by the CSO) is incomplete, but it is unlikely this would affect 1993 ranking compared to UK. *UK National Accounts*, 1995 edn., tables 9.1 and 1.2, give a slightly different figure for 1993 (33.3% for 1993 and 33.4% for 1994).

higher to begin with (most of Northern Europe). Even incorporating the rise in the UK tax share since 1993, the UK still has a much smaller than average increase in taxation over the whole period since 1979. Whereas the UK was a moderately taxed country in 1979, by 1995 it was towards the bottom of the tax ranking. How was such a relatively constant revenue-share feasible in the UK given the pressures to expand spending, particularly as

Table 10.3. The structure of UK taxation, 1993

	UK % of GNP	UK ranking*	EC average % of GNP
Income taxes on households (1)	9.7	13/15	11.8
Employee social security contributions (2)	2.5	12/15	5.9
Direct tax on households (1) + (2)	12.2	13/15	18.6
Employer social security contributions (4)	3.6	12/15	9.1
Direct taxes (incl. Employer contributions) (1) + (2) + (4)	15.8	14/15	27.7
Indirect taxes	14.2	7/15	14.3
Corporation tax	2.5	8/15	2.8
Direct taxes on households, % of personal income	14.0	13/15	19.2

* UK position in ranking of countries by share of taxes/number of countries in comparison.

Sources: As Table 10.2 supplemented with OECD *National Accounts*. EC average is for nine countries with data.

a result of rising unemployment? To a minor extent this reflected an increase in the budget deficit (from 3.3 per cent of GDP in 1979 to 4.2 per cent in 1995). But the main explanation was that total government spending was hardly higher as a percentage of GDP at the end of the period. This has been accomplished only by a fierce squeeze on public spending in certain areas.

(i) Indexing benefits to prices not wages   This highly significant decision has seen the ratio of most national insurance and other benefits like Income Support declining sharply in relation to average earnings. In November 1979 the standard retirement pension for a single person represented 20.4 per cent of average earnings; by April 1995 the ratio was 14.6 per cent. Proportionately the fall represented nearly 30 per cent.[3] As a crude calculation, if benefits had kept up with earnings they would have been some £33bn. higher, or 5 per cent of GDP.[4]

This fall in the relative level of benefits has contributed to the UK's unprecedented rise in inequality; by 1990 the UK was vying with the USA for the position of the most unequal distribution of income amongst the

[3] *Social Security Statistics*, 1991, table H3.06 updated from *Social Security Statistics*, 1995, table B.1.27 and index of average weekly earnings in manufacturing.

[4] This leaves aside the large number of adjustments to the social security system which, even in the past four years, was reported in the *Financial Times*, 25 Jan. 1996, to have saved a further £4bn. A more sophisticated calculation of the impact of uprating in line with earnings would allow for taxation of benefits, the impact of higher rates of benefit on numbers eligible, etc.

OECD countries.[5] The bottom one-tenth of the income distribution have lost approximately one-quarter of their share of disposable income between 1978–80 and 1992–4[6] and most of this is due to the failure to increase benefits in line with average incomes (Redmond and Sutherland 1995).

(ii) Health and Education Spending   The growth of real spending on these services depends on the 'volume' of inputs (by and large productivity is assumed by the statisticians to be unchanging). This in turn mainly reflects the number of people employed in these very labour-intensive services, but also includes the buying-in from the private sector of such things as buildings, medicines, and schoolbooks. Bob Rowthorn (1992) used OECD data to show the relative squeeze on the expansion of these services in the 1980s. Between 1979/80 and 1988 education spending in the UK per student fell by 1.8 per cent per year, whilst rising by 1.6 per cent per year in the rest of the EC; health spending per head of the population rose 0.9 per cent per year in the UK compared to 2.4 per cent per year in the rest of the EC. Comparative data of this sort is not available for the subsequent period. Current spending on the NHS rose by 2.5 per cent per year in real terms over the period 1988–94, whilst real spending on education rose by 1.1 per cent per year,[7] in both cases around 1 per cent per year faster growth than over the previous decade, but still leaving low growth rates for the whole period.

(iii) Public-Sector Pay   Holding down public-sector pay reduces the rate of cost increases for the public services and thus the 'relative price effects' which tend persistently to push up the relative cost of public services where possibilities of productivity growth are very small. Since the comparability pay increases of 1980/1, the pay of non-manual workers in the public sector has declined relative to non-manual workers in the private sector (by some 14 per cent for men between 1981 and 1995 and 9 per cent for women).[8]

[5] Atkinson et al. (1995) show the UK in the bottom third of the ranking by 1986. Data they present for trends in individual countries, supplemented by data from the US Census of Population and from Economic Trends, 'The Effects of Taxes and Benefits on Household Income 1994/5' (Dec. 1995) for the UK, suggest that the rise in UK inequality in the later 1980s meant that it was the least equal in 1990, in terms of the Gini coefficient for the distribution of household disposable income, but that the USA probably regained bottom place by 1994 as inequality apparently fell back a little in the UK after 1990.

[6] Goodman and Webb (1994) linked to CSO, Economic Trends (Dec. 1995).

[7] UK National Accounts, table 9.3 and earlier editions. These figures are for current spending on goods and services and do not include capital spending or grants (e.g. to students).

[8] Department of Employment, New Earnings Survey, 1995 and 1981 edns.

PROSPECTS

The analysis of the previous section has shown that the average level of taxation has been prevented from rising under the Conservatives only by a squeeze on public spending which has pushed up inequality and jeopardized the welfare services. Can the public finances can be rescued by faster growth? Two senses of faster growth have to be distinguished. Faster growth in the short (or medium) term, which relies mainly on reducing unemployment (and underemployment) and which is driven by the private sector, reduces government spending on the unemployed and raises the tax base. It thus provides additional resources for public-spending programmes without the need to raise tax rates. But as suggested earlier, we do not know how to generate such a sustainable private-sector-based expansion; even pump-priming of the sort discussed above is most unlikely to be sufficient.

In the longer term, if supply-side measures succeeded in raising the underlying growth rate of productivity, could this finance an expansion of public services out of higher incomes without the need for higher taxation? This would seem a painless source of long-term finance, comparable to the short-term one of reducing unemployment. However such a 'growth dividend' is largely illusory for reasons already outlined in connection with the financing of productive public spending. If welfare benefits are indexed to real earnings (as they must be if recipients are to share in general prosperity) then this very large category of spending is automatically indexed to growth, still leaving the problem of paying for increased numbers of recipients (ageing population etc.). Faster growth cannot be diverted to restoring benefits to the ratio to earnings prevailing in the 1970s without higher taxes. Moreover, since a large proportion of the rest of public spending is devoted to paying the wages and salaries of those who provide the services, then unless their relative position is to decline continuously, their earnings (and thus the cost to the rest of society) will go up in real terms in line with the economy's average productivity.[9] Employing more teachers can no more be 'financed out of growth' than paying for more pensioners, unless it is envisaged that teachers or pensioners should not share in that growth. This leaves only the small part of public expenditure comprising those goods and services purchased from the private sector where costs would be reduced by faster productivity growth which would provide savings to be used elsewhere.

Thus achieving a faster growth rate would not prevent average levels of taxation having to be raised to fund improvements in the welfare state. It

[9] Various forms of contracting-out have reduced the share of spending paid directly to public-sector employees (for example from 60 per cent of government current expenditure in 1984 to 45 per cent in 1994) but this does not alter the broad link of these costs to average earnings.

may very well be politically easier to raise them when real earnings are otherwise growing faster (because the impact in restraining the growth of real take-home pay is less noticeable). Fiscal drag, as real incomes rise in face of a mildly progressive tax system, may even mean that tax *rates* do not have to be increased. But the average proportions of income taken by taxation must rise.

In any case, no government can be confident of pushing the private sector into a sustainable path of markedly faster expansion, which would rapidly generate more resources for the public sector without any rise in tax rates as unemployment falls and with less noticeable increases in tax in the longer run as productivity growth speeds up. The relatively slow growth, which is a common feature of all the OECD countries irrespective of the share of the government spending, represents a crisis *of* the private sector which means a funding crisis *for* the public sector. In this situation a commitment not to increase taxation implies that the funds for the many pressing claims for increased-spending programmes could only be found from economies elsewhere within the budget, as current statements by the Labour Party recognize.

The implication of this chapter is not that the share of taxation has to rise indefinitely; such long-run trends depend on underlying demand for the services and transfer incomes currently provided by the state. It is noticeable that in a number of high-tax European economies the share of taxation has grown rather little in the 1980s and early 1990s (Table 10.2), without there being a major crisis of deteriorating public services and sharply increasing inequality. But the shocking increase in poverty and perceived shortfall in current provision of public services in the UK can only be tackled through a significant increase in the share of government expenditure. It seems most implausible that increased borrowing could provide much of the resources required, most especially as the present government is bound to cut taxes at least as far as is prudently possible. We can certainly *hope* that improved economic performance would make increases in the tax share easier to absorb as productivity rises faster. But a policy for job creation and restoration of the public services cannot wait for such hopes to be realized. Restoration of greater progressivity in the tax system could mean that in the first instance much of the extra revenue could come from the best-off 10 per cent (those with incomes over £25,800 in 1993/4).[10] But in the longer run extra tax would have to come from middle incomes and there are a range of options (see for example Hills 1996). The political difficulties of gaining support for such increases in taxation may be daunting but have to be overcome by vigorous campaigning about the benefits which the spending from higher taxation would bring. If these difficulties

[10] *Inland Revenue Statistics*, 1995 edn., table 3.1.

are not confronted it is difficult to see what can be done to make serious inroads into unemployment and the appalling rise in inequality which has accompanied it.

REFERENCES

Atkinson, A., Rainwater, L., and Smeeding, T. (1995), *Income Distribution in OECD Countries* (Paris: OECD).

Bank for International Settlements (1994), *Annual Report 1993/4* (Basle: BIS).

—— (1995), *Annual Report 1994/5* (Basle: BIS).

Bispham, J. (1988), 'Rising Public-Sector Indebtedness: Some More Unpleasant Arithmetic', in M. Boskin *et al.* (eds.), *Private Saving and Public Debt* (Oxford: Blackwell).

Boltho, A. and Glyn, A. (1995), 'Macroeconomic Policies, Public Spending and Employment', *International Labour Review*, 4/5: 451–70.

Buiter, W., Corsetti, G., and Roubini, N. (1993), 'Excessive Deficits: Sense and Nonsense in the Treaty of Maastricht', *Economic Policy*, 16: 58–100.

Dimsdale, N. (1988), 'Keynes on Budgetary Policy 1914–46', in Boskin *et al.* (eds.), *Private Saving and Public Debt*.

Giles, C. and Johnson, P. (1994), 'Taxes Down, Taxes Up', *IFS Commentary*, No. 41.

Glyn, A. (1992), 'The "Productivity Miracle", Profits and Investment', in J. Michie (ed.), *The Economic Legacy 1979–92* (London: Academic Press).

—— and Rowthorn, R. (1994), 'European Employment Policies', in J. Michie and J. Grieve Smith (eds.), *Unemployment in Europe* (London: Academic Press).

Goodman, A. and Webb, S. (1994), 'For Richer, For Poorer', *IFS Commentary*, No. 42.

Hills, J. (1996), 'Tax Policies: Are There Still Choices?' in D. Halpern, S. Wood, S. White, and C. Cameron (eds.), *Options for Britain* (Aldershot: Dartmouth).

Hopkin, B. and Reddaway, B. (1994) 'The Meaning and Treatment of an "Unsustainable" Budget Deficit', *BNL Review* (Sept.) 190: 295–307.

Nickell, S. and Bell, B. (1995), 'The Collapse in Demand for the Unskilled and Unemployment Across the OECD', *Oxford Review of Economic Policy*, 11/1: 40–62.

Orr, A., Edey, M., and Kennedy, M. (1995), 'Real Long-Term Interest Rates: The Evidence from Pooled Time-Series', *OECD Economic Studies*, No. 25/2: 75–108.

Redmond, G. and Sutherland, H. (1995), 'How has Tax and Social Security Policy Changed Since 1978', Working Paper No. 9541, Department of Applied Economics, University of Cambridge.

Rowthorn, R. (1992), 'Government Spending and Taxation in the Thatcher Era', in J. Michie (ed.), *The Economic Legacy* (London: Academic Press).

—— (1995), 'Capital Formation and Unemployment', *Oxford Review of Economic Policy*, 11/1: 26–39.

Weale, M. (1994), 'Fiscal Policy and the National Debt', *National Institute Economic Review* (Feb.) 50–60.

11. 'A Price Well Worth Paying'? The Benefits of a Full-Employment Strategy

Michael Kitson, Jonathan Michie, and Holly Sutherland

According to Britain's ex-Chancellor of the Exchequer, Norman Lamont, unemployment is 'a price well worth paying' to keep down inflation. Free-market policies pursued by successive Conservative governments in Britain since 1979 have involved an additional price—as well as that of high unemployment—namely, growing inequality with a concomitant increase in poverty for many of those in work as well as out of work. In this chapter we make an attempt to calculate just how great this price has been—the price of high unemployment and increased inequality. The price involves a number of different costs, some more hidden than others. Other work has evaluated the impact of unemployment on health and crime, but the main focus of our chapter is on the fiscal costs. These costs derive from the unemployed and the working poor receiving various forms of benefit payments and at the same time paying less tax than they would were they in reasonably paid employment.

Our main purpose in making these calculations is to evaluate an alternative policy agenda involving a major public-investment-led programme involving around one million new jobs being created. Such a programme would be ambitious and expensive. The public-investment proposals outlined below would involve a gross cost of up to £17bn. a year. Against this, however, needs to be offset the savings in unemployment pay and other benefits, plus the additional tax revenues which would be received with a million more in employment; together these have generally been assumed to amount to around £9,000 per head, at least for those who were in receipt of unemployment pay. If this were the appropriate average figure for all the million individuals, then the saving to the Public Sector Borrowing Requirement of £9bn. would result in the net cost of such a programme turning out to be far lower that the gross cost of £17bn., namely just £8bn. Of course, not all the million would have been in receipt of unemployment

This chapter draws on joint work with Roger Berry and Frank Wilkinson to whom we would therefore like to express our thanks. We are also grateful for comments from Larry Elliot, Andrew Glyn, John Grieve Smith, and Carol Jones.

pay. But as detailed below, one of the findings of our research is that this intuitive belief, supported by previous research, that the savings to the Treasury would be far lower if the individuals were not drawing unemployment pay, turns out to be quite false. On the contrary, those not in receipt of unemployment pay tend to qualify for higher levels of other benefits, so the net saving to the Treasury is rather similar regardless of whether the individuals in question were receiving unemployment benefit or not. So in terms of this distinction between those who were in receipt of unemployment benefit and those who were not, it would not be inappropriate to apply the above £9,000 figure to all one million people.

But a second empirical finding of the research reported in this chapter is that the overall gain to the Treasury of someone, on average, moving from being out of work to being in work, amounts to around £10,000 per head rather than the previously believed £9,000. Thus the net cost of the £17bn. programme would amount not to £8bn. but rather to just £7bn.

Tackling the growth in inequality witnessed since 1979 by reintroducing a new top rate of income tax above £40,000 at 60 per cent—which after all was the rate which applied to the top income-tax band during almost the entire Thatcher era—would raise more than £4bn. extra income-tax revenues a year, alone therefore covering well over half the net cost of such a programme.

This suggests that maintaining high levels of unemployment and inequality involve far greater costs than has generally been realized. There is, in addition, strong evidence that unemployment increases ill-health (Burchell 1992) and crime, especially domestic burglary (Dickinson 1995; Wells 1995). Unemployment has been a major cause of the alarming growth of inequality and poverty in Britain (and indeed in many other countries); in Britain, while the richest tenth of households have become 60 per cent better off since 1979, the poorest tenth are 20 per cent worse off. Wage inequality is greater than at any time since records began in 1886. Such inequality and poverty have detrimental effects on the balance of payments constraint, with a transfer of resources to the better-off who import more (see Borooah 1988); on the real economy as consumer spending is depressed and the pressure on firms to upgrade their production processes is weakened (Michie and Wilkinson 1993); and on the government's own fiscal deficit (the Public Sector Borrowing Requirement or PSBR) (Michie and Wilkinson 1994). Rising poverty means that the cost to the state of benefits and income support increases. A growing share of the income of the working poor is met not by their employers but by the taxpayers. This not only increases both the spread and the grip of the poverty trap (whereby any increase in pay by employers is matched by an almost equivalent loss of benefits from government), it also increases the burden on public expenditure. And if total government spending is constrained—for example by the Maastricht 3 per cent formula—then this burden has to be met by public-spending cuts imposed elsewhere, cuts which may well exacerbate unemployment.

In the face of these deeply entrenched problems, many doubt the ability of governments to generate jobs and tackle inequality. We take a more optimistic view. Governments can create jobs; moreover these can be high-quality jobs that not only meet social need but also contribute to national economic prosperity. Furthermore, the cost of such a programme would be relatively modest.

This chapter is organized as follows: the following section outlines a public-investment-led strategy for the UK that would create a million jobs. We then consider the fiscal and distributional implications of such a strategy. How the net costs of such a programme would be paid for is then discussed. The simulations reported in the chapter come from running the Microsimulation Unit's tax-benefit model POLIMOD; this model is discussed, along with the specific use we have made of it in the work here reported, in a separate article available from the authors on request (Kitson, Michie, and Sutherland 1996).

A JOB-GENERATION STRATEGY

Any strategy for job generation in Britain at the present time must be based on two essential components. First, there needs to be a substantial increase in investment in the tradeable-goods sector, and in manufacturing industry in particular, in order to boost economic growth and net exports (on which see Kitson and Michie 1996a and 1996b). This is essential if we are to prevent full employment from resulting in a surge in imports that cannot be financed. It will also create orders for related service activities, as well as generating increased tax revenues to fund expanding public services. However, since manufacturing needs to achieve high levels of productivity to compete internationally, the potential for immediate job generation in this sector alone is limited. Secondly, therefore, any strategy to cut the dole queues requires increased investment, suitably targeted, in public services and infrastructure.[1]

---

[1] Glyn and Rowthorn (1994) point out that there is a third route to increased employment levels (in terms of numbers in work), namely having the total amount of paid work available in the economy shared out among more people through cuts in working time. They make the case, however, for the importance of also pursuing a programme of greater government expenditure on public services and infrastructure, and show how such a programme can increase employment in a situation where conventional Keynesian measures are inappropriate for balance of payments reasons, which they believe represent the immediate constraint in many economies such as the UK.

Moreover, it is not difficult to identify obvious areas of enormous unmet social need, where there is work to be done and where jobs can be generated quickly:[2]

- Homeless people sleep on our streets, there are record housing waiting-lists and millions of homes are in need of urgent repairs. Yet, at the same time almost 400,000 construction workers are on the dole.
- School classes are too large and investment in education and training lags behind that of our competitors, while teachers and other education workers get the sack.
- Hospital waiting-lists are at unacceptable levels, while the numbers of nurses and other health-care staff are cut.
- 'Care in the community' is little more than a fiction for many disabled and elderly people in desperate need of support. Yet the care staff necessary to provide that support are not being employed.
- Dirty streets and run-down neighbourhoods are in desperate need of attention, but little is being done.

These are just a few examples that demonstrate the need for increased spending on public services and infrastructure. We can all think of many more.

An increase in public-sector employment is therefore necessary both as an essential step towards full employment and to satisfy unmet social need. It also has other advantages. First, when private spending is sluggish an increase in public-sector demand can give a welcome boost to the economy. Secondly, targeted public spending is less import-intensive and more labour-intensive than private-sector spending; thus, a given increase in expenditure generates more jobs and has less adverse effects on the balance of payments if it comes through public spending (see Glyn and Rowthorn 1994). Thirdly, the UK lags behind the other major industrialized countries in terms of skills and capital investment—key factors in determining the future performance of the economy—and the necessary investment in education and infrastructure is only likely to come via the public sector. And fourthly, economic growth must be environmentally sustainable, but the pursuit of private profit is unlikely to ensure adequate environmental protection; improved public-sector initiatives are therefore required.

Our aim in this chapter is to identify—as a first step towards full employment—where and how one million full-time jobs could be created and the benefits these would bring. We have not sought to keep down the cost by focusing on part-time and low-paid jobs. Jobs on poverty pay are not an

---

[2] As our starting point we use the public-sector strategy outlined by Berry, Kitson, and Michie (1995, 1996) to create a million new jobs; a range of other proposals have also been suggested including those by Coutts and Rowthorn (1995) and Holtham and Mayhew (1996), and in the European context, Glyn and Rowthorn (1994).

acceptable alternative to unemployment. Clearly, however, there are people who *want* part-time work to suit their circumstances. If some of the increased employment opportunities identified below satisfy the demand for part-time jobs, then clearly the number in work will increase by more than one million.

The examples identified here are for illustrative purposes only. Clearly, other areas of public-service provision could have been included, and there are many ways of constructing a package to create one million jobs. We would not argue that this particular split is necessarily the best; more detailed work would need to be done on the costs and benefits of the alternatives. However, what we have sought to do is to demonstrate that the first million jobs on the road to full employment can be created relatively easily, that the benefits of such a programme are substantial and that the costs are modest.

Housing

The demand for council and housing association homes continues to outstrip supply. Independent studies have identified a requirement for at least 100,000 affordable new homes a year. In addition, more than three million—one in six—homes need urgent repairs costing more than £1,000. Moreover, poor housing conditions cause ill-health, currently estimated to cost the NHS £2bn. each year (Standing Conference on Public Health 1994).

The cost of creating an additional job through increased housing expenditure clearly depends upon how such expenditure is used. Building new homes for rent incurs greater non-labour costs than expenditure on renovations and repairs. However, public investment in building new homes may be reduced by drawing in private capital if allocated through housing associations. If we take estimates of the average for all housing expenditure (Ball and Wood 1994), it seems reasonable to assume a cost per job of the order of £25,000. On this basis, 150,000 jobs would therefore cost £3.75bn. This could, for example, finance the building of 60,000 more homes for rent and bring 200,000 unfit homes up to standard (Foster 1991).

Education and Training

In the latest year for which statistics are available, 1992/3, total education expenditure by local education authorities in England which could be considered staff-related amounted to £14.4bn. (CIPFA, *Education Statistics*, 1992/93 Actuals). Included here are not only the costs of wages and salaries, but also the costs of equipment and other staff-related current expenditure. Uprating for inflation gives an estimate of staff-related expenditure in current prices of £15.4bn. This financed the employment of 470,000 full-time equivalent teachers and lecturers and 360,000 full-time equivalent other staff, such as support staff, supervisory staff, cleaners, and caretakers. Three-quarters of the former were full-time, while three-quarters of the latter were part-time. Assuming that any additional staff-related expenditure was divided between teaching and other staff in the present proportions, then the average cost per job in education and training may be estimated to be £19,000.

Increasing the number of those employed in education and training by 150,000 would therefore cost £2.85bn. Any additional capital expenditure required would add to the cost. However, many schools and colleges have space that could be used if only they had the staff to do so. It is inconceivable that capital constraints would prevent substantial improvements to the quality of education and training as a result of this 18 per cent improvement in staffing.

The universal provision of nursery education for all 3- and 4-year-olds is estimated to have an annual cost of between £860m. (the National Commission on Education) and £1bn. (the Department for Education). This package would therefore permit a major start to be made to this programme with resources still left to reduce student/teacher ratios and expand the number in full-time education and training. The latter would further reduce unemployment as people took up full-time places on education and training courses, and would also help to improve the skill base of the economy.

Health

The latest year for which a breakdown of revenue expenditure is available is 1993, when £13.6bn. went on salaries and wages (CIPFA, *Health and Personal Social Services Statistics for England*, 1994). Again, however, there are additional costs of employing extra staff—such as the need for additional equipment. This brings staff-related expenditure up to £16.6bn. which in today's prices would be around £17.6bn. This financed the employment of 773,880 full-time equivalent staff. The cost per job in the health service may therefore be taken to be £23,000. An extra 150,000 jobs would therefore cost £3.45bn. It would increase NHS employment by 16 per cent.

Personal Social Services/Care in the Community

In 1993/4 local authority social-service departments in England employed 233,000 full-time equivalent staff, with a total current expenditure of £5.7bn. (CIPFA). Uprating for inflation this figure rises to £6.0bn. The cost per job is therefore £26,000. An extra 100,000 jobs would therefore cost

£2.6bn. This would increase employment in personal social services by 36 per cent.

Environmental Projects

Environmental policy can take three main forms: regulatory measures (for example, the imposition of legal standards in relation to waste disposal or pollution), 'eco-tax reform' (shifting the tax burden towards energy use and pollution), and public spending to improve the environment. A green public-expenditure programme could include environmental enhancement and clean-up activities. The cost of creating an additional job in these areas is approximately £24,000 (Jacobs 1994); 100,000 jobs could therefore be generated for £2.4bn.

Energy Conservation

Investing in a programme of energy conservation can generate rates of return that alone would justify such investment. Payback periods of less than five years are quite common. But, of course, saving energy is good for the environment and, overall, energy conservation measures create jobs. Adjusting for inflation an earlier estimate of the cost per job of £17,000 (Boardman 1991), the cost per job in this area may be assumed to be £18,000. 100,000 jobs could therefore be created for £1.8bn.

Additional Jobs

The impact of the proposals outline above, as shown in Table 11.1, would directly create 750,000 jobs. In addition, further jobs would be created due to the linkages between the above sectors and the rest of the economy. The income spent by those workers directly employed would create additional jobs throughout the rest of the economy and increased purchases would expand employment amongst suppliers. The size of these multiplier effects will depend on the way the expansionary programme is targeted and financed (as discussed below), but might lead to an additional 250,000 jobs, making around a million jobs in total.[3]

---

[3] If the multiplier turned out lower than this then a net increase of one million jobs would require a slightly larger programme, but the difference in overall cost would be small: even if the programme had to be increased by 10 per cent, the net additional cost would be well under £1bn. a year. As indicated in the text, we have at a number of stages of the analysis chosen deliberately cautious assumptions (e.g. ignoring the savings in administration costs which other estimates of the savings brought about by reducing unemployment have included), so it may well be that the net cost of a slightly larger programme would still be less than the overall figure we arrive at.

Table 11.1. A proposal to create one million jobs

Sector	Jobs generated (thousands)	Cost per job (£ thousand)	Total cost (£ million)
Housing	150	25	3,750
Education and training	150	19	2,850
Health	150	23	3,450
Care in the community	100	26	2,600
Environmental projects	100	24	2,400
Energy conservation	100	18	1,800
TOTAL DIRECT JOBS CREATED	750	22.5	16,850
Additional indirect jobs created	250	0	0
TOTAL NEW JOBS	1,000	16.85	16,850

Source: Berry, Kitson, and Michie (1995).

THE FISCAL AND DISTRIBUTIONAL IMPACTS

The cost to the Exchequer of this sort of strategy, leading to the creation of a million new jobs, would be in the order of £17bn. This would, though, be offset by savings to the Treasury from a reduced pay-out of unemployment-related benefit payments, and by increased tax revenues, leading to a far lower net cost for such a programme. To quantify these impacts we used the Microsimulation Unit's tax-benefit model POLIMOD which simulates the impact of tax and benefit regulations on the household-income distribution (see Kitson, Michie, and Sutherland 1996, Appendix; and for further details, Redmond, Sutherland, and Wilson 1995).[4] Estimates of the savings in benefits and increased revenue from income tax, employer and employee National Insurance contributions, VAT, and excise duties are provided. The results we obtain from such a modelling exercise will be influenced by the assumptions made on various sets of questions, and in particular the following:

1. First, who of those currently not working, take up the new jobs? Using the Family Expenditure Survey sample on which POLIMOD is based, we can break down the 'unemployed' into three groups: group 1 being those in current receipt of unemployment benefit (UB); group 2 being those self-reported unemployed or sick, and seeking work (not on UB); and group 3

[4] POLIMOD uses 1991 Family Expenditure Survey data which are Crown Copyright and have been made available by the Office for National Statistics (ONS) through the Data Archive and are used by permission. Neither the ONS nor the Data Archive bear any responsibility for the analysis or the interpretation of the data reported here.

being those that are 'unoccupied' (that is, not necessarily seeking work). Alternative rates of job take-up from the different groups are modelled. Throughout, we assume that the following are *not* available for work: people aged under 16 or over 59 (in the case of women) or 64 (for men); those in full-time education; people already in employment or self-employment; people on training benefits; parents of young children where there is no other non-working[5] parent (i.e. single parents and 'second earners'); and those in receipt of benefits which indicate that the person is not available for work (severe disability allowance, maternity pay, etc.).

2. Secondly, what rate of pay do they receive and how many hours do they work? The policy package referred to above, which we are here modelling, is intended to generate quality full-time jobs. We could have kept the cost down considerably by assuming that many of the new jobs would be part-time or low-paid jobs (or both). We have not done this; instead, we assume that all the new jobs are reasonably paid and full-time.[6] So, we assume that the average new job pays average national earnings, consistent with the strategy outlined above,[7] but to capture the varieties of job opportunities the earnings distribution is allocated across the middle 50 per cent of the earnings distribution (between £215 and £398 per week).[8] The earnings levels generated are allocated at random to those taking up jobs and it is assumed that they all work 38 hours a week.

[5] Where working is defined as at least 8 hours a week.

[6] In reality some would be part-time, so to this extent our estimates of the net cost of such a programme are too high—the cost would actually turn out rather lower than we suggest since the pay which the newly taken-on workers receive over and above the income they were already receiving while out of work would be likely to be less for two half-time workers combined than for one full-time worker. However, in this case the fiscal gain from increased tax revenues would also be somewhat lower, so the net difference between whether the jobs are taken as full-time or (more) part-time is likely to be small (and far less than is assumed by some when part-time jobs are presented as a relatively cheap job-creation option, since this misses the point that the additional tax revenues in such a scenario will be correspondingly lower). This is illustrated by the simulations we ran with part-time jobs reported below.

[7] The average national weekly wage is £290.50. The weighted average weekly (FTE) wage taking the largest three sectors in Table 11.1 combined—housing, education and training, and health—comes out at £312. It is not possible to calculate average wages in all sectors, nor for the additional jobs created through multiplier effects, but these latter jobs would most probably start at below the national average. Thus while the assumption of average weekly earnings may, if anything, slightly underestimate the level of wages and hence the positive revenue impact of the job-generation programme, the net effect would be marginal; even were the average wage to turn out to be much different from average earnings, which is most unlikely, additional simulations which were run with both higher and lower average earnings suggested little net effect (as reported and discussed in Kitson, Michie, and Sutherland 1996).

[8] Since there is no way of actually knowing in advance exactly what the pay will be for all the new jobs (since some of these are generated through multiplier effects and so will depend on what people happen to decide to spend their increased incomes on) and the distribution of earnings in these sectors, we did rerun our simulations with different assumptions regarding the actual pay levels for the new jobs, and found rather similar results to those reported here (see Kitson, Michie, and Sutherland 1996).

The new jobs that are generated are superior in terms of pay and hours to the jobs already being done by many of the lower paid in the sample. The simulation is based on the assumption that some of the new jobs will be taken by those currently employed, with others in turn moving into the posts being vacated; those taking up the newly vacated posts will also come not just from the unemployed and otherwise unoccupied, but also from others who, again, are already employed. This process will continue, as workers move up the earnings hierarchy, until all the net increase in employment is taken up by the previously unemployed (or otherwise unoccupied, as categorized above).[9]

Table 11.2 summarizes the results of modelling the impact on government revenue of the job-generation policies, under various assumptions. For the creation of one million jobs, four options are shown—based on different rates of job take up from different unemployed groups and alternative assumptions concerning working parents (see Table 11.2). In addition, option C shows the impact of two million jobs being created.

The first two rows of Table 11.2 show the effect of the expansion of employment on benefit payments (means-tested and non-means-tested), with the third row giving the sum of these. With a net increase of one million jobs, the expenditure saving on benefits is found to vary between £2.92bn. and £3.21bn.[10] Rows 4–5 show the impact on direct taxation (and the seventh gives the sum of these), with this revenue increasing by between £5.44bn. and £5.56bn. Row 9 gives the indirect revenue arising from indirect taxes on assumed increased spending; this ranges between £1.37bn. and £1.42bn.[11] Indirect taxes can only be computed at the household level so row 11 shows the number of households affected (that is, households including one or more person entering work) and row 12 shows the average revenue generated by these households.

The total revenue impact of a net increase in employment of one million turns out to be rather robust in the face of varying the assumptions concerning job take-up and working parents. The total revenue generated varies between £9.72bn. (assumption A_b) and £9.90bn. (assumption A_a). These totals significantly exceed 'official' estimates which put the annual cost, in terms of benefits and forgone taxes, of an unemployed claimant at £9,000.[12]

[9] Our costings therefore assume that the characteristics of the unemployed, such as family composition or housing tenure, are similar to those of the low-paid.

[10] Results are given to the nearest £10m.; this is not intended to imply that they are necessarily statistically significant to this degree of precision.

[11] We make the assumption that all the increase in income is spent on the same goods as during unemployment. The assumption that none is saved will tend to inflate the revenue estimate. On the other hand it is likely that a higher proportion of the new income will be spent on goods on which VAT is charged than was the income during unemployment.

[12] The estimate of £9,000 per claimant was given by Gillian Shephard, then Education Minister, to the House of Commons Select Committee on Employment in October 1992 and a similar figure has been estimated by Piachaud (1994). Recent figures produced by the

Table 11.2. The revenue impact of job generation under various assumptions (£bn. per annum)

	Creating 1 million jobs (alternative job take-up assumptions)				Creating 2 million jobs
	A_a	A_b	B_1	B_2	C
1. Non-means-tested benefits	0.76	0.76	1.02	0.26	1.05
2. Means-tested benefits	2.16	2.16	0.33	2.63	4.47
3. TOTAL BENEFITS	2.92	2.92	1.35	2.89	5.52
4. Income tax	2.68	2.61	1.12	2.71	5.21
5. Employee NICs	1.30	1.26	0.54	1.30	2.52
6. Employer NICs	1.58	1.54	0.65	1.58	3.07
7. TOTAL DIRECT TAX	5.56	5.41	2.31	5.59	10.80
8. TOTAL DIRECT REVENUE	8.48	8.34	3.66	8.48	16.32
9. Indirect tax	1.42	1.38	0.59	1.36	2.81
10. TOTAL REVENUE	9.90	9.72	4.25	9.84	19.12
11. Number of households (000s)	976	953	406	923	1774
12. Mean revenue per household (£000s)	10.14	10.20	10.47	10.66	10.78

Notes: Rounding errors cause some columns to not sum precisely. Total number of households: 23 million.

Assumptions for creating one million jobs:

A_a The jobs are taken by 75 per cent of the group currently in receipt of unemployment benefit plus 35 per cent of the group self-reported unemployed or sick and seeking work (but not receiving unemployment benefit), with the remainder coming from the unoccupied group. There are a number of excluded groups (see text); here it is assumed that parents with children aged under 5 and where there is no other non-working parent are excluded.

A_b As A_a except that it is assumed that parents with children aged under 11 and where there is no other non-working parent are excluded.

B_1 All the new jobs go to people in receipt of unemployment benefit. These are less than one million, namely 406,000.

B_2 As A_a except that the jobs are distributed in the same proportion to each of the unemployed groups: 20.8 per cent of all those assumed available for work.

Assumptions for creating *two* million jobs:

C The jobs are taken by 100 per cent of the group currently in receipt of unemployment benefit plus 80 per cent of the group self-reported unemployed or sick and seeking work, with the remainder coming from the unoccupied group. Parents with children aged under 5 and where there is no other non-working parent are excluded.

Source: Calculated using POLIMOD.

Our results indicate that the average cost to the Exchequer of having some-one unemployed or unoccupied is over £10,000 a year. This is significantly higher than had previously been believed. Two factors explain the differ-ence. First, a common difference from our scenario is that previous esti-mates assume that the new jobs will be lower paid than would be the case with the public-investment-led strategy outlined here. (For example, the fig-ures from the Employment Policy Institute are calculated on the assump-tion that the new jobs will only pay 80 per cent of average earnings.) Secondly, previous estimates, including those from the Treasury, do not fully account for the actual circumstances of the families of the unemployed, and the impact of the new employment on the benefits received and taxes paid. Previous estimates give even lower costs of unemployment for those not in receipt of unemployment benefit.[13] The cost of unemployment will only be lower in these cases if there is no significant entitlement to means-tested benefits and this is only likely to be the case if the unemployed per-son is the partner of someone who is in work with wages at a reasonable level. However, unemployment and employment are increasingly each becoming concentrated within households: it is likely that the partner of an unemployed person will also be without work (Gregg and Wadsworth 1995). The savings on income support and housing benefit from one or both of these people finding a well-paid job will be at least as great as the sav-ings from a person who is eligible for unemployment benefit becoming employed. Indeed, in cases where a recipient of unemployment benefit is the partner of an employed person, then the benefit savings from finding them a job will be *less* because income support will not have been payable in these circumstances. The notion that the combination of unemployment (without entitlement to unemployment benefit) and a partner in work is a relatively rare situation is borne out by our analysis using a sample of actual house-holds. The insensitivity of our revenue estimates to our assumptions about the circumstances of people available to take up jobs shows that receipt of unemployment benefit (or indeed, registration as unemployed) is not a fac-tor which determines the cost of a person not having a job. This is demon-strated by the proximity of the results for our two most extreme assumptions. If we only allow current unemployment benefit recipients to take the new jobs (B_1) the average revenue per household affected is £10,470 per year. However, if we allocate jobs proportionately to all groups assumed

Unemployment Unit (Convery 1996) estimate the revenue cost per claimant at only £7,420 in 1994/5 and £7,960 in 1995/6. Our estimates show that unemployment is a greater cost to the economy than previous work had suggested, despite the fact that some previous estimates had included savings in administration costs as unemployment falls, which we have not done; were these to be added to our estimates, the savings from a reduction in unemployment would be even greater than we have here suggested, and the corresponding net cost of a job-creation pro-gramme even lower.

[13] The Unemployment Unit estimate is as low as £4,000 in 1995/6.

to be available for work (B$_2$: only 21 per cent of each group, including those on unemployment benefit), the revenue effect is slightly *larger*: £10,660 per household. It is workless households who cost the most in terms of benefit payments: and it is increasingly people in these households who predominate among those available for work.

Table 11.2 also shows the revenue impact of creating two million jobs (assumption C). The overall revenue effect is £19.12bn. or £10,778 per job. This suggests that our results are fairly robust even over large variations in the scale of the expansion in employment.

The impact of the job-creation strategy on income distribution is shown in Table 11.3. The gains are found to be greatest for the poorest households (in both absolute and percentage terms). For instance the households in the lowest (pre-reform) decile receive an average weekly gain of £20.65 compared to an average across all households of £5.95. Additionally, a greater percentage of poorer households benefit compared to those at the richer end of the distribution.

Table 11.3. The distributional impact of creating a million jobs

Decile of household equivalized net income (pre-reform)	Average gain (£ per week)	Gain as proportion of pre-reform income (%)	% of households Benefiting
Bottom	20.65	25.9	15.0
2nd	12.20	8.5	8.3
3rd	4.79	3.3	4.0
4th	2.73	1.6	2.5
5th	4.89	1.8	3.3
6th	4.96	1.7	3.2
7th	2.93	0.8	1.6
8th	3.34	0.7	2.1
9th	0.90	0.2	0.6
Top	2.11	0.2	1.3
ALL	5.95		4.2

Note: The job take-up assumption is A$_a$ (see Table 11.2).

Source: Calculated using POLIMOD.

To demonstrate the robust nature of these results in face of the full-time/part-time split of jobs, instead of one million 38-hour jobs, we re-ran the model on the assumption of 700,000 such jobs plus 600,000 19-hour jobs. It is assumed that each person selected for employment is equally likely to work full-time or part-time. If part-time, they work 19 hours for half the weekly pay they would have received on a full-time basis. People with children under 5 who were previously excluded from the new jobs are now available for the part-time jobs. Run D thus builds on run A_a with two alternative assumptions: Assumption (i) keeps the same numbers drawn from the unemployed groups 1–2 as in run A_a (although some may end up in part-time jobs) and assigns the remainder of the jobs to group 3 and group 4 (the new group of parents) in the same proportion as each other, although only people who are not carer-parents of under-5s can get full-time jobs. Assumption (ii) concentrates more of the jobs (both full- and part-time) in the groups most likely to be seeking work, allocating the residual as before. Table 11.4 shows the revenue effect of these schemes in relation to A_a. Table 11.5 shows the distributional effect of D(i).

Creating more jobs at a lower average weekly wage produces higher savings on benefits but reduced gains in tax revenue. The overall revenue effect is much the same. More households benefit by a smaller average amount. Allowing the carer-parent of under-5s to have new part-time jobs has the effect of spreading the benefit (somewhat) higher up the household-income distribution (the people in the new jobs are more likely to have working partners).

Table 11.4. The revenue impact of increased part-time/full-time employment under various assumptions (£bn. per annum)

	A_a	D(i)	D(ii)
1. Non-means-tested benefits	0.76	0.84	0.87
2. Means-tested benefits	2.16	2.52	2.62
3. TOTAL BENEFITS	2.92	3.36	3.49
4. Income tax	2.68	2.44	2.41
5. Employee NICs	1.30	1.24	1.23
6. Employer NICs	1.58	1.40	1.39
7. TOTAL DIRECT TAX	5.56	5.08	5.03
8. TOTAL DIRECT REVENUE	8.48	8.43	8.52
9. Indirect tax	1.42	1.44	1.41
10. TOTAL REVENUE	9.90	9.88	9.93
11. Number of households (000s)	976	1207	1195
12. Mean revenue per household (£000s)	10.14	8.18	8.31

Note: Rounding errors cause some columns to not sum precisely.

Source: Calculated using POLIMOD.

Table 11.5. Distributional effect of D(i), with increased part-time employment

Decile of household equivalized net income (pre-reform)	Average gain (£ per week)	Gain as proportion of pre-reform income (%)	% of households benefiting
Bottom	20.39	26.3	17.6
2nd	8.29	6.0	8.0
3rd	5.10	2.7	4.9
4th	4.50	2.2	4.2
5th	5.84	2.0	4.6
6th	3.84	1.3	3.2
7th	2.02	0.5	1.8
8th	4.09	0.9	3.4
9th	2.01	0.4	1.3
Top	3.46	0.4	2.6
ALL	5.96		5.2

Source: Calculated using POLIMOD.

HOW TO PAY FOR ONE MILLION JOBS

The creation of the one million jobs described above would involve a net cost to the Exchequer of around £7bn. This would allow public spending to be increased by a total of £17bn., offset by savings in unemployment-related benefit payments and higher tax receipts which together would pay for £10bn. of the increased public spending. The obvious question that remains, though, is how is the net increase of £7bn. to be financed?

Since our primary aim here is to identify a short-term programme to create a million jobs, we will not consider longer-term measures to finance full employment, such as reducing the level of military expenditure to that of our EU partners. However, at present an estimated £6bn. from the sale of council homes is set aside for debt repayment, and £3bn. of these capital receipts might reasonably be used to fund the housing programme. The remaining £4bn. could be funded by a combination of public-sector borrowing and increased taxation. £2bn. increased borrowing is well within the annual margin of error of estimation of the Public Sector Borrowing Requirement. The orthodox view that increased borrowing—even on such a modest scale—would lead to an increase in interest rates and thus 'crowd-out' private investment has little basis in theory or practice. In a world in which capital markets are highly integrated, one would not expect UK government borrowing to exert significant pressure on interest rates, since the UK is a relatively small economy. For example, long-term rates in the UK were higher in the late 1980s than today, despite the PSBR being in surplus. And again when the PSBR for 1993–4 turned out to be £5bn. less than anticipated, interest rates did not come tumbling down. There need not therefore be undue concern that £2bn. of extra borrowing would increase interest rates.

£2bn. in additional taxation can easily be found even without plugging tax loopholes, which, although essential, will take some time to implement. For example, £2bn. could be raised by increasing corporation tax from 33 per cent to 36 per cent, which would still leave it significantly below the European average of 40 per cent. Rates of inheritance tax and capital-gains tax and tax reliefs could also be changed to mobilize such modest resources. Alternatively, a new 60 per cent band on taxable income in excess of £40,000 would raise over £4bn. a year. This is still a small amount compared to the £15bn. in tax cuts received by the top 10 per cent of income-earners under the Tories, but it would allow the whole of the remaining net cost of the programme to be paid for with no additional borrowing whatsoever.

If, however, some increased borrowing was actually thought to be desirable in the first instance, then some of this increased tax-take from the highest paid could be redistributed through the income tax system by raising tax allowances, thus helping to partially overcome the increased inequality in after-tax incomes engineered by successive Conservative governments since 1979. We therefore modelled the effects of combining a new 60 per cent rate on incomes of £40,000 with an increase in the tax threshold, increasing the personal allowance by £1,000 per year.[14]

This increase in allowances has a direct cost of £5.385bn., with some knock-on effects on means-tested benefits and indirect taxes. The distributional effects of this new 60 per cent top-rate of tax on incomes over £40,000 with an increase in allowances were then combined with the programme to increase employment along with the introduction of a minimum wage of £4.15 per hour.[15] The results are shown in Table 11.6.

The effect of increasing tax thresholds is to distribute more to the middle and upper end of the income distribution. Nearly all of these households are net beneficiaries, whereas the households at the bottom of the pre-reform distribution contain a lower proportion of taxpayers (even after the extra jobs and minimum wage). The most effective way of tackling inequality and poverty is thus found to be through direct job-creation measures, along with the establishment of a national minimum wage. The best use of

[14] No change is made to the additional married allowances, but single age allowance is also increased by £1,000. The thresholds to the standard and higher rates are *reduced* by £1,000 so that they cut into incomes at the same point as currently. We are simply increasing the band of income on which no tax is paid, at the expense of the 20 per cent band. The change has the same cash value to each taxpayer (£200 per year), except where taxpayers already pay less tax than this.

[15] The impact of such a minimum wage is discussed in Kitson, Michie, and Sutherland (1996).

Table 11.6. Distributional effect of increased employment, a minimum wage, and a new top-rate tax plus increased allowances

Decile of household equivalized net income (pre-reform)	Average gain (£ per week)	Gain as proportion of pre-reform income (%)	% of households benefiting %	losing %
Bottom	24.99	31.4	33.4	0.0
2nd	16.28	11.6	35.7	0.0
3rd	9.87	6.4	52.0	0.0
4th	8.62	4.7	63.1	0.0
5th	13.41	5.2	85.5	0.0
6th	13.55	4.6	93.1	0.0
7th	12.15	3.5	96.7	0.0
8th	11.76	2.8	97.5	1.2
9th	6.71	1.6	95.4	4.3
Top	−20.13	−2.5	74.4	25.3
ALL	9.72		72.7	3.1

Source: Calculated using POLIMOD.

tax revenues from the highly paid is not, therefore, to fund tax cuts for the rest, but rather to fund the sort of programme outlined in this chapter.

CONCLUSION

The gross cost of creating a million new jobs through a public-sector-led strategy, involving an expansion of good-quality jobs in the public services, would be nearly £17bn. However, our modelling of the impact which this would have on tax receipts from, and benefit payments to, households indicates that the net benefit to the Treasury of this increase in revenues and reduction in expenditure would amount to more than £10bn., leaving a net annual cost for the programme of less than £7bn. This could easily be financed—it is less than 2.5 per cent of current tax revenues—with various options set out above; the introduction of a new 60 per cent income tax band at £40,000 would alone cover more than half the net cost (raising £4.2bn. a year).

An increase in public-sector employment, in addition to helping to counter high and persistent unemployment, would provide other economic and social benefits. First, it would help to reverse the massive shift in income towards the rich that took place in Britain throughout the 1980s and 1990s; reversing this by increasing employment and achieving a more equitable distribution of income would relieve pressure on public finances as people are raised out of state dependency and as the costs of administering the tax/benefit system fall. And secondly, particularly in the area of education and training, it would improve the stock of human capital and help to raise the long-term growth rate (as emphasized in much of the new growth-theory literature). Thus, while our modelling results would suggest that the initial costs of a public-sector-jobs strategy would in any case be rather modest, over the medium- to longer-term even these costs would fall, as higher economic growth would raise tax revenues still further. Indeed, the public-investment-led programme would lead to additional public revenues directly by way of rental income from the houses built, and so on. Also, by providing enhanced public services the sort of favourable political conditions would be created in which the case for increased taxes, should these prove necessary, could best be made.

Unemployment today is thus not the result of the working of immutable economic laws. There is no substance to the claim that if the worst-off in society accept a cut in their living standards, long-term prospects would be restored; the opposite is more likely the case. Nor is unemployment the result of there being too little work needing to be done to employ all those who seek employment. Both private need and public squalor are on the increase.

Of course, governments are continually under pressure from business, the 'City', and elsewhere to cut back on public employment and public intervention in the economy. This needs, though, to be met by even greater pressure for progressive economic policies. In practical terms this means forcing government to expand public employment on improving the welfare state and environmental programmes, as well as taking measures to increase the level of industrial investment and upgrade the productive infrastructure. Only in this way can we create the conditions for sustainable economic growth.

REFERENCES

Atkinson, Anthony B. and Micklewright, John (1991), 'Unemployment Compensation and Labor Market Transitions: A Critical Review', *Journal of Economic Literature*, 29/4 (Dec.), 1644–727.

Ball, M. and Wood, A. (1994), *How Many Jobs Does Construction Expenditure Generate?*, Discussion Paper in Economics 2/94 (London: Birkbeck College).

Beale, N. and Nethercott, S. (1988), 'Job-Loss and Family Morbidity: A Study of Factory Closure', *Journal of the Royal College of General Practitioners*, 35: 510–14.

Berry, R., Kitson, M., and Michie, J. (1995), *Towards Full Employment: The First Million Jobs* (London: Full Employment Forum).

Berry, R., Kitson, M., and Michie, J. (1996), 'Creating Jobs Fast', *New Economy*, 3/3 (Autumn), 133–7.

Boardman, B. (1991), *Fuel Poverty: From Cold Homes to Affordable Warmth* (London: Belhaven Press).

Borooah, V. (1988), 'Income Distribution, Consumption Patterns and Economic Outcomes in the United Kingdom', *Contributions to Political Economy*, 7: 49–63.

Burchell, B. (1992), 'Changes in the Labour Market and the Psychological Health of the Nation' in J. Michie (ed.), *The Economic Legacy: 1979–1992* (London: Academic Press).

Convery, P. (1996), 'The Real Cost of Unemployment', *Working Brief*, Unemployment Unit (Dec. 1995–Jan. 1996), 16–17.

Coutts, K. and Rowthorn, R. (1995), 'Employment in the United Kingdom: Trends and Prospects', ESRC Centre for Business Research, Cambridge, Working Paper No. 3 (Feb.).

Deakin, S., Michie, J., and Wilkinson, F. (1992), *Inflation, Employment, Wage-Bargaining and the Law* (London: Institute of Employment Rights).

Department of Employment (1991), Research Paper No. 87.

—— (1993a), *New Earnings Survey* (London: HMSO).

—— (1993b), *Employment Gazette*, Oct. (London: HMSO).

—— (1994), *Employment Gazette*, Feb. (London: HMSO).

Dickinson, D. (1995), 'Crime and Unemployment', *New Economy*, 2: 115–20.

The Economist (1994), 'A Bad Case of Arthritis', 26 Feb., 92–3.

Foster, S. with Burrows, L. (1991), *Urgent Need for Homes* (London: Shelter).

Glyn, A. (1997), 'Paying for Job Creation', this volume.

—— and Rowthorn, B. (1994), 'European Employment Policies', in J. Michie and J. Grieve Smith (eds.), *Unemployment in Europe* (London: Academic Press).

Gregg, P. and Wadsworth, J. (1995), 'Making Work Pay', *New Economy*, 2/4 (Winter), 210–13.

Harvey, M. (1995), *Towards the Insecurity Society: The Growth of Mass Self-Employment and the Construction Industry* (London: Institute of Employment Rights).

HMSO (1993), *Households Below Average Income; A Statistical Analysis 1979–1900/1* (London: HMSO).

Holtham, G. and Mayhew, K. (1996), *Tackling Long-Term Unemployment* (London: IPPR).

Jacobs, M. (1994), 'Green Jobs? The Employment Implications of Environmental Policy', Report for the WWF.

Kitson, M. and Michie, J. (1993), *Co-ordinated Deflation: The Tale of Two Recessions* (London: Full Employment Forum).

—— —— (1996a), 'Britain's Industrial Performance Since 1960: Underinvestment and Relative Decline', *Economic Journal*, 16/434 (Jan.), 196–212.

—— —— (1996b), 'Manufacturing Capacity, Investment and Employment', in J. Michie and J. Grieve Smith (eds.), *Creating Industrial Capacity: Towards Full Employment* (Oxford: Oxford University Press).

—— —— and Sutherland, H. (1996), 'The Fiscal and Distributional Implications of Job Generation', ESRC Centre for Business Research Working Paper No. 37

(Sept.), Cambridge and forthcoming, *Cambridge Journal of Economics* (1997), 21/1 (Jan.).

Layard, R., Nickell, S., and Jackman, R. (1991), *Unemployment: Macroeconomic Performance and the Labour Market* (Oxford: Oxford University Press).

Michie, J. and Wilkinson, F. (1992), 'Inflation Policy and the Restructuring of Labour Markets', in J. Michie (ed.), *The Economic Legacy: 1979–1992* (London: Academic Press).

—— —— (1993), *Unemployment and Workers' Rights* (London: Institute of Employment Rights).

—— —— (1994), 'The Growth of Unemployment in the 1980s', ch. 1 of J. Michie and J. Grieve Smith (eds.), *Unemployment in Europe* (London: Academic Press).

Philpott, J. (1994), 'Unemployment, Inequality and Inefficiency', in A. Glyn and D. Milliband (eds.), *Paying for Inequality* (London: IPPR/River Oram Press).

Piachaud, D. (1994), 'A Price Worth Paying? The Cost of Mass Unemployment', *Economic Report*, Employment Policy Institute, 8/6 (Sept.).

Redmond, G. and Sutherland, H. (1995), 'How has Tax and Social Security Policy Changed Since 1978?: A Distributional Analysis', Microsimulation Unit Discussion Paper, No. 9508, DAE, University of Cambridge.

—— —— and Wilson, M. (1995), 'POLIMOD: An Outline', Microsimulation Research Note, No. 5, DAE, University of Cambridge.

Rowthorn, R. (1977), 'Conflict, Inflation and Money', *Cambridge Journal of Economics* (Sept.), 215–39.

Sawyer, M. (1995), 'Obstacles to Full Employment in Capitalist Economies', in P. Arestis and M. Marshall (eds.), *The Political Economy of Full Employment: Conservatism, Corporatism and Institutional Change* (Aldershot: Edward Elgar).

Standing Committee on Public Health (1994), *Housing, Homelessness and Health* (London: Nuffield Provincial Hospital Trust).

Sutherland, H. (1995), 'Minimum Wage Benefits', *New Economy*, 2/4 (Winter), 214–19.

Ullah, P. (1990), 'The Association Between Income, Financial Strain and Psychological Well-Being Among Unemployed Youths', *Journal of Occupational Psychology*, 63: 317–30.

Wells, J. (1994), 'Unemployment in the UK: The Missing Million', *European Labour Forum*, No. 13.

—— (1995), 'Crime and Unemployment', *Employment Policy Institute Economic Report*, 9/1 (Feb.) (London: Employment Policy Institute).

Wilkinson, F. (1992), *Why Britain Needs a Minimum Wage* (London: Institute for Public Policy Research).

INDEX

256 INDEX

debt (*cont.*):
  monetizing 58–9
  ratio of to GDP 224
  repayment 6
  see also deficits
Deery, S. 155
deficits: 119, 224
  expansionary 225–6
  fiscal 1,7
  spending 61–3
  see also fiscal policy, Public Sector
    Borrowing Requirement
demand xiv, 3, 26–7, 30, 59, 77–9, 81–5,
    186, 192, 199
Depression, 1930s 19, 41
deprivation, social 119
deregulation 162, 164
  see also labour market
devaluation 108
development debate 12–13
Dickinson, D. 235
Dimsdale, N. 225
disinflation 179, 186, 188–9
  see also fiscal policy
disputes, industrial 215
distribution 223
  see also fiscal policy, income, inequality,
    job creation, labour market, poverty,
    wages
dividends 216
dollar, depreciation 63–4
Dréze, J. 77
Driffell, J. 132

earnings 177–81
  see also wages
East Asia, industrializing countries 155
Eatwell, J. 2, 23, 76–94
Eckstein, O. 41
economic:
  growth *see* growth
  policy 1, 120–1, 194–203
    see also fiscal, industrial, monetary,
      labour market, policy
  prosperity 8
    see also growth
Economic Policy Council 210
Economist 24
economists 185–6, 191
economy:
  capitalist 194
  dual 79
  flexible 5
  global 2, 11–12
  liberal 14, 17, 21, 116
  monetary production 199
    see also employment, growth, policy

open 12
effective demand *see* demand
Eichner, A. S. 201
Emerson, M. 161
Emerson, R. 207
employers' contributions 161
employment:
  adjustment costs 136–7
  creation 12, 68, 160
    see also job creation
  determination of 133
  fixed-term 161
  growth of 25
  law 132
  legislation 98
  levels of xiii, 4
  low productivity 3
  protection 160
  public sector 132, 237, 250
  relationships 137–41
    see also full employment
Employment Policy Institute 245
Employment Protection Act 167
equalization, factor-price 25
European Union (EU):
  employment scenarios 146
  growth scenarios 146
  law 4
  public investment 225
  social security contributions 160–2
  taxation share 227
  transnational collective bargaining 153
  unemployment 76
  White Paper 145–6, 159
Ewing, K. D. 4, 153–74
exchange controls 14
exchange rate:
  depreciation 63–5
  equilibrium 201
  flexible 14
  floating 200
  nominal 16
  overvalued 12
  real 16
    see also devaluation
expansion: 23, 50–2, 54–7, 60, 67
  aggregate 59
  expansionary programme 61, 64, 69,
    221–33
  financing of 57–8
  monetary 58–9, 63
  public-sector-led 7
    see also fiscal policy, growth
expenditure:
  capital 225–6
  government, on health and education 230
    see also fiscal policy